the

ADULT
CHILDREN
of
DIVORCE
WORKBOOK

This *Inner Workbook* is
part of a series that explores
psyche and spirit through writing,
visualization, ritual, and
imagination.

Other books in this series include:

At a Journal Workshop
BY IRA PROGOFF, PH.D.

Following Your Path
BY ALEXANDRA COLLINS DICKERMAN

The Inner Child Workbook
BY CATHERYN L. TAYLOR, M.A., M.F.C.C.

A Journey Through Your Childhood
BY CHRISTOPHER BIFFLE

The Path of the Everyday Hero
BY LORNA CATFORD, PH.D., AND MICHAEL RAY, PH.D.

Personal Mythology
BY DAVID FEINSTEIN, PH.D., AND STANLEY KRIPPNER, PH.D.

The Possible Human
BY JEAN HOUSTON

The Search for The Beloved
BY JEAN HOUSTON

Smart Love
BY JODY HAYES

Your Mythic Journey
BY SAM KEEN AND ANNE VALLEY-FOX

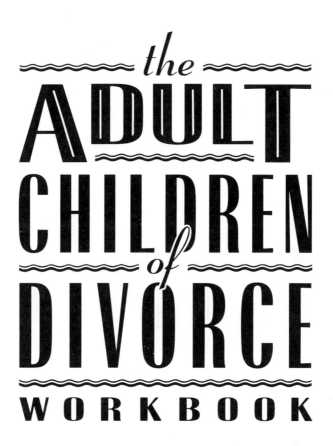

the ADULT CHILDREN of DIVORCE

WORKBOOK

A COMPASSIONATE PROGRAM FOR HEALING FROM YOUR PARENTS' DIVORCE

Mary Hirschfeld, J.D., Ph.D.

JEREMY P. TARCHER, INC.
Los Angeles

I dedicate this book to my ACDs:
Marla and David Hirschfeld

Jeremy P. Tarcher, Inc.
5858 Wilshire Blvd., Suite 200
Los Angeles, CA   90036

Distributed by St. Martin's Press, New York

Design by Lee Fukui

Manufactured in the United States of America
10   9   8   7   6   5   4   3   2   1
First Edition

CONTENTS

ACKNOWLEDGMENTS

This book has been through many readings, accompanied by continual trimming and tweaking. More paragraphs and pages of the text hit the wastebasket than found their way into print. Along this paper trail, I had the professional help of many people whose efforts are gratefully acknowledged.

For showing the way and providing many helpful hints at the outset, I would like to thank Dr. Leonard Felder. During the early morning phone calls my agent and good friend Merle Horwitz helped lighten trying moments. For finding multitudes of research studies no matter how painstaking the effort and wending her way through the Los Angeles traffic on her motorcycle to rush them to me, I am grateful to UCLA graduate student Diana Brief.

This book has benefited from the editorial recommendations of Beverly Berwald. Colleen Todd was always available to move the project along; her untiring efforts are appreciated. I also want to thank Aiden Kelly and Christen Hohenadel for their assistance.

Last, but by no means least, I would like to thank my family and friends who helped me get through the doubts, jitters, and the burnout times.

A Personal Note

I t was September 1969, and my husband and I had just returned from a Labor Day celebration with friends. I was excited because the next day would mark my first day as a lawyer. I chatted away about the two court appearances I was about to make for my new employer, my gray flannel suit and shiny new briefcase laid out for an early start.

Later that evening, long after the children had gone to bed, it became clear that my husband had something on his mind. I had been so caught up in my excitement that I didn't realize this until he cleared his throat and finally spoke.

"Honey, I'm leaving."

"Oh?" I asked casually. "Another business trip?"

"No," he replied calmly. "I'm leaving."

I stopped dead in my tracks. I looked at him with disbelief. He couldn't mean what I thought he meant. In the enveloping daze, the meaning of his words slowly filtered through. Was it possible that he was leaving me and our two children, never to return? Could he be ending our marriage? It appeared so.

His announcement was turned into action later that week, shattering the family foundation. I had never lived as an unmarried woman; my wedding had taken place one week after I graduated from college.

I felt lost. I didn't know how to live outside a family, though people found that hard to believe. "It's easy for you," said divorced women acquaintances, "you're an attorney!" As if a law degree made me immune to the pain of a fractured personal life. In truth, the confidence I gained in law school was of great help later, but immediately after the breakup that confidence disappeared.

The first stage I went through was shock. How could this happen at a time when our lives were so rich and held such promise? And how could it happen with no warning, no danger signs at all? I would later discover that the warning signs had been there, but I had not understood them.

I had learned the value of family from my parents. As a child survivor of the Holocaust, I had seen firsthand the wisdom of keeping families strong: the survival rate of members of strong families was definitely higher during the war.

I thought I had married a man who felt the same way, since his mother died when he was ten years old and his father remarried women who were emotionally unavailable. I didn't know that adult children of broken parental bonds are likely to repeat their parents' patterns, unless they have consciously cleared away the wreckage of the past and freed themselves from its dictates.

As a young child, I had learned to appreciate family, and had accepted its typical squabbles. That there was life before I entered the world was a strange notion, but it became real as I learned family history. Many snowbound evenings were spent by a crackling fire, listening to my mother's stories: how she and my father met, what she did as a young girl, what my aunts and uncles were like, whom my sister and I resembled.

A glimpse into my parents' happy years revealed them as proud young marrieds, touched by the history of their time, shaped by their financial struggles throughout the depression and by how they overcame the economic turmoil. I learned about family loyalty, about money, about the value of education. As my sense of self took shape, I was provided with a firm sense of belonging and continuity. I was also taught independent thinking. All of this, along with a great deal of good fortune, added up to an ability to survive disastrous times.

Still, the most difficult times were those I was yet to face. It's one thing when strangers treat you badly, because you know that the embrace of those who love you will ease the hurt. It's another thing entirely when people whom you love abandon you. You lose hope when the hurt comes from inside—inside your family, inside your heart. It is a hurt that has no equal.

My husband and I knew people who had divorced, but they suffered extreme circumstances, such as physical violence and overt displays of unfaithfulness. None of this applied to our marriage, so I never considered us a target.

I went back to school in 1965 after our second child started nursery school. I decided on law school because I had always been intrigued by the concepts of justice. My decision was embraced by my whole family, although they were as surprised as I was when I enrolled. To lessen the impact of my new involvement, I tried to have my books put away when the children or my husband were at home. Although the fear of failure drove me to overpreparation, I was stunned when my first examination paper was held up to the class as a model for identifying legal issues. By the time the course was over, I had accepted the fact that I had a natural bent for the law, and I was deeply pleased with my valedictorian award.

While I was in school the world was changing. The shedding of a spouse was becoming a more accepted life event, although its new acceptability did nothing to lessen its impact. Marriages that had looked as solid as bedrock were crumbling. Yet when my marriage ended, I felt responsible for what I perceived as my failure. So it happened that in September 1969 my first day on the job as a lawyer became a nightmare, and I soon lapsed into a clinical depression.

I needed help, but at that time there were few mental-health professionals especially trained to treat the divorcing family. I consulted a highly recommended psychiatrist, who diagnosed the cause of my problem as unresolved Oedipal issues with my long-deceased father. My plea for guidance with preadolescent children went unanswered. Instead, the doctor interpreted such requests as avoidance and resistance. Eventually he became so frustrated with me that he terminated my therapy.

Despite this unfortunate first encounter with psychotherapy, I recovered, but I resolved one day to become a psychotherapist myself and to help others through the trauma of divorce.

In the 1970s, as the divorce rate escalated, people began to seek out women lawyers. Men sought out women lawyers because they felt a woman would have a better chance of communicating with their angry spouses. Women turned to women lawyers because they hoped to be better represented. One client told me that she switched to a woman lawyer because the legal establishment seemed to her a men's club: "During our first appearance in court, my attorney, the opposing attorney, my husband, the bailiff, and the clerk were all men. I questioned whether any of them could understand what my children and I needed."

At that time the legal practice of divorce was not held in the highest esteem; with some important exceptions, the best minds did not practice matrimonial law. In fact, most lawyers ran from dealing with the emotionality of clients, and many attorneys handled divorces only as a favor to clients or when they were desperate for work.

But a new style of divorce professional was beginning to emerge. Some lawyers and psychotherapists who had been through divorces, and who had been deeply and surprisingly affected by them, began to bring new understanding and thoughtfulness to the divorce process. They helped to shape the field into a recognized specialty, with special training and certification.

I was worried that the trauma of divorce would leave lifelong scars in the hearts of children. It was clear to me that if we were to help the next generation, we would have to keep legal wrangling to a minimum and help couples divorce in less damaging ways. I thus became convinced of the value of a nonadversary resolution to divorce problems.

I began to assist couples who wanted to escape the escalation of hostilities. They would come to me saying, "We don't want two attorneys. Can't you represent us both?" Bound by the code of legal ethics, I could not represent both sides of an adversary conflict, but I could represent one and allow the other to represent himself or herself. In this way, I could help hammer out agreements without rancor. However, to make sure that the legal rights of both parties were adequately protected, I insisted that an advisory attorney be employed to review the agreement prior to the actual signing of it. This eventually led to the pioneering practice of divorce mediation.

I followed the dictates of my conscience, and when my children were old enough to stand on their own feet, I eased out of law and into psychology. I took a leave of absence from my legal practice to return to school. As finances were at stake, and because I was driven by solid goal-directed dedication, I galloped through the two-year program in a year and a half. I had always studied psychology on my own because it interested me, so I was able to consume the material with great ease.

Professionally, I have been very fortunate. The media discovered my work, and, through interviews on radio and television and in magazines and newspapers, I was able to promote the idea that nonadversary divorce was possible.

In the last few years my practice has seen a profound influx of grown-up children of divorce. My observations about these clients, their problems and struggles, along with the experiences of my own children, moved me to write this book.

More recently, I returned to the role of student once again, this time to obtain my Ph.D. This gave me the opportunity to focus my attention on the topic of this book: adult children of divorce.

In 1982 I remarried. My husband, Ray H. Daley, is a loving, kind, funny, and wonderful man. He gracefully copes with our two-name family with humor and dignity.

So this book, which was really begun in September 1969, now becomes a reality, thanks to the faith and guidance of my publisher, Jeremy Tarcher, and his wonderful organization, as well as to my children and my patient husband, who have gone through its growing pains with me.

But most of all, adult children of divorce, this book is a gift from your counterparts to you. I hope it will help create a better future for you and for your children.

INTRODUCTION:
HEALING FROM
YOUR PARENTS'
DIVORCE

T his is a book of healing and reconciliation. Its purpose is to help you understand how divorce affected you as a child, and what impact it has on your life today.

Whether your parents shielded you during the difficult times or whether they drew you into the conflict, whether your story has harrowing twists and turns or whether your life was, on the surface, simple, your parents' divorce had long-term effects that may still be plaguing you today. The breakup of a family is a terribly complex life event, leaving in its wake many feelings that children have a hard time understanding.

If you are an adult child of divorce, you may have a difficult time with your feelings about divorce, even though as an adult you are expected to understand your feelings and have greater emotional resources with which to heal yourself. But, given the willingness to seek the truth, you can free yourself from the dictates of the past. To paraphrase the American philosopher George Santayana, those who learn to understand their history are no longer doomed to repeat it. Concealment of the past keeps old wounds open and festering, but truth brings freedom.

The miracle of healing starts when we admit the existence of the wounds by describing them honestly, allowing the wounded past to emerge from the haze of pain and confusion. Reality frees our hearts, and the truth frees our minds. Truth allows us to reconcile disparate voices in our heads, and it helps us heal the breach in our hearts. Acceptance of the past allows us to untangle hidden loyalties to a parent whom we rejected or who we feel rejected us, and forgiveness allows us to repair our ability to love.

Michelangelo, it is said, was once asked how he carved his magnificent statue of David out of a piece of marble that was considered unusable. Apparently he had been unaffected by what others saw as a flaw in the stone, for he replied, "I just cut away the parts that were not David." Healing is similar, in a way, to shedding the unwanted parts that prevent you from expressing your true self. As you read this book and do the exercises, you will gently be guided through your inner world. You will discover aspects of yourself that are unwanted—the remnants of old wounds—and will distinguish aspects of yourself that are desirable, unique traits—*your genuine self*. Recognition starts the healing; releasing fosters it; establishing new behaviors completes it. There are myriad tiny steps along the way. Some of these will emerge as recollections, revelations, old feelings, new learning, and new ways of looking at your life. The final steps come when you blend your new awareness into fresh patterns for your life.

Healing is not a race. It takes exactly as long as it needs to take. Do not concern yourself with time. You may need time to incubate a revelation or you may not. You may want to pass by some material, to return to it another day. Sometimes results are immediately visible, but sometimes they take a long time to appear. Each topic area will have its own weight in your life, and probably no two areas will merit the same amount of attention. Friends and family members may read this book, and they will move at their own speed. Do not let that concern you. Your process of healing and growth is unique. Respect it!

Changes typically happen in one of two ways. Life may change unexpectedly, demanding that you adjust. Such adjustment often creates growth. Or change may be triggered by something as simple as a desire to understand yourself better. It may arise from dissatisfaction with life or with a relationship, or from a need to eliminate recurring emotional distress. These are some of the reasons people have come to see me with the determination to change. Whatever your reason may be, this book offers the blueprint for such growth.

You may contend: "I don't want to change. I like myself just as I am." The word *change* used in this context is misleading, because change through growth brings out the person you were intended to be. *Change* in this sense simply means shedding limiting thoughts, emotions, and behaviors, thereby revealing the authentic you.

When you read the stories of adults who, like you, are children of divorce, perhaps you will find parallels to your own life. Even if the details are not the same, the personal patterns and the problems with romantic relationships may be. After the initial surprise, the pleasure of revelation may emerge. You may discover that the troublesome traits you had thought uniquely yours are, in fact, common to many adult children of divorce.

ABOUT ADULT CHILDREN OF DIVORCE

If you are a child of divorce or if you have such a person in your life, you have much company. There are approximately 20 million adults in the United States whose parents divorced while they were children. Although there has always been divorce in the United States, its numbers exploded in the 1960s and 1970s.

Since 1972, more than 1 million children under eighteen years of age have been involved in a divorce every year. Since divorce has been on a steady upswing for over a century, and as adult children of divorce, or ACDs, are more likely to divorce than others, I am concerned that future numbers may exceed any that we've seen before as divorce passes down from generation to generation.

That this trend will continue is supported by predictions from the United States Bureau of the Census: of every one hundred children born in 1983, forty will live in a family where there is at least one divorce, and five will experience a prolonged parental separation; and 60 percent of all children will spend some time in a single-parent household before reaching eighteen years of age. Since most parents remarry, some of these children will also spend some of their growing-up years in one or two blended families or stepfamilies.

These and other reasons dictate that we have special concern for the children of divorce. Divorce creates a family crisis. The proper raising of children takes time, energy, and stability, both financial and emotional, and despite the best of intentions, divorcing parents operate with reduced efficiency. The custodial parent is usually overwrought with responsibilities, while energy and patience are at a premium.

Fathers (or mothers) on furlough from the family have to contend with being a part-time parent, which causes interruptions in their flow of information about the children and in their own growth as parents. Both mother and father are beginning a new life cycle, marked by sudden shifts of values and priorities.

Children who live in an intact family are more likely to represent the highest priorities for the adults in the home. They are central to the parents' happiness, because they are extensions of the union and a reminder of the love that created them. This situation changes in divorce and in remarriage: children become also-rans in the demands for parental attention as the parents move on to the awesome task of building new lives for themselves.

I intend to challenge the almost universally held assumption that children are better off out of a dysfunctional or unhappy home than in it. Children may be better off if one dysfunctional home is replaced by two functional homes, particularly if abuse, incest, or violence has marred the original home. However, although divorce may cause day-to-day stress to abate, it often simply creates two dysfunctional homes out of one, and the children's needs are not met in either. Furthermore, many homes that appeared to be just fine for the children before the divorce become torn asunder and racked by conflict for long periods of time.

The children are central in such conflict and feel split within themselves as the two people who created them and on whom they depend become increasingly distant from one another. There are many homes in which the parents are not as happy or fulfilled as they would like to be, yet the children do not feel or see this unhappiness. On the contrary, the children may receive much attention and affection as the parents try to compensate for their own unhappiness. On the other hand, there are divorced homes in which the parents find happiness with new partners or fulfillment in new endeavors, while the children continue to bear the brunt of unhappiness and conflict. We need to remember that, from a child's point of view, a dysfunctional parent is a parent who fails to meet the *child's* needs.

In some instances, the dysfunction that existed before the divorce may have caused some of the ACDs' pain. It is almost impossible to separate the effects of predivorce dysfunction from postdivorce dysfunction. Still, ACDs most clearly remember the troubled times during and for long periods after the divorce as the most trying times. Similar results are cited by Judith Wallerstein in her landmark fifteen-year study of sixty middle-class families who divorced "under the best of circumstances." In her book, *Second Chances,* Dr. Wallerstein describes the families as "still in crisis, with their wounds wide open," a year to eighteen months later.

A crisis-stricken family is a dysfunctional family. For children to whom a day seems to stretch forever, twelve to eighteen months of crisis seems like an eternity!

In all fairness, parents' new, happier marriages can yield benefits to the children, and many ACDs have spoken of strong, loving relationships with stepparents. But keeping children receptive to getting a new stepmommy or stepdaddy usually requires an artful touch and much psychological work for everyone. As we will see in chapter 3, blending families is, at best, a monumental task requiring a tremendous amount of skill and goodwill.

THE INTERVIEWS

At the time I started this book, the literature yielded little data on adult children of divorce, so I decided to gather such information by means of interviews. I am pleased to see that since then, additional information has been published.

While writing this book, I spoke with hundreds of ACDs, and formally interviewed two hundred of them. My sample included persons from all walks of life. The subjects had to be under sixteen years of age at the time their parents split up, and had to be at least twenty-three at the time of the interview. Although most ages were represented, the bulk of the sample was aged twenty-six to forty, which roughly coincided with the ages of baby boomers. I interviewed each person who wanted to be interviewed. Some ACDs had very clear memories: others' pasts were shrouded in stubborn fog. Some were incredibly insightful; others had trouble making sense of their past.

The Subjects

There is no simple way to find a group of adult children of divorce. To secure a broad sample, I reached out through newspaper advertisements and notices posted in community centers, as well as by the word-of-mouth network of friends and supporters. Fortunately, Los Angeles, where I work, is the largest melting pot in the nation, and yielded a sample that included thirty-two states and two foreign countries. The income levels ranged from below average to the very rich, and educational levels from the high-school dropout to the highly educated. This book is thus based on a fair sample, though not one random enough for statistical analysis.

Many ACDs became very emotional: unexpected tears often flowed. A fiftyish truck driver's hard crust went through a gradual meltdown as we talked, and he turned into a sad five-year-old boy right before my eyes as he remembered his father driving away. "I haven't cried since that day," he mused as he recovered from his memories.

The Nature of the Interviews

I conducted most of the interviews face-to-face. I inquired into the pre- and postdivorce home. I wanted to know about the changes that took place; the effects of the divorce on the adults and on the children; the symptoms of emotional distress among family members and how such distress was handled; preexisting family dysfunction; whether physical, psychological, sexual, or substance abuse intensified or abated after divorce; the changes in circumstances following the divorce; the family culture; the texture of the family relationships; and the ACD's adult romantic history.

What the Interviews Revealed

The interviews left no doubt: *divorce and its aftermath wounded adult children of divorce*. These wounds often still showed up in self-defeating ways. The legacy of divorce showed up in recurring problems:

1. ACDs have difficulty forming appropriate emotional bonds with romantic partners. The love bonds tend to be immature, pseudomature, or rigid.

2. ACDs have problems with self-esteem.

3. ACDs have problems valuing their masculinity or femininity.

4. ACDs have problems with identity. Both men and women rely on external sources to shore up their identity.

5. Some ACDs have little sense of emotional entitlement in their romantic relationships. They feel undeserving of love, dignified treatment, or respect.

6. ACDs have problems with delayed maturity, particularly in the romantic arena.

7. ACDs have problems with self-control, which show up as substance abuse or other types of obsessive-compulsive patterns.

8. ACDs have problems with commitments, again predominantly in the realm of emotional attachments.

9. ACDs have problems with changes, unless they themselves create or control those changes.

10. ACDs share a pervasive sense that no one will ever satisfy their needs.

THE GOALS OF THIS BOOK

The goals of this book are threefold. The first is to provide information about a child's divorce experience, as seen through the eyes of that child as an adult. The second is to promote healing and reconciliation among the family members of ACDs.

The third, and most important, goal is to help adult children of divorce become free from the legacy of the past, heal within, and move on to create fulfilling love relationships.

This book does not presume to judge people who are divorced, nor does it judge divorce itself. It does not point a finger or assign blame. There is an Indian saying that you cannot know another person's path until you walk in their moccasins. In human relationships no one can know another's pain completely, nor should one person judge another's personal decisions. Divorce, like marriage, is a very personal decision, one that each individual must make for himself or herself. This book is not about divorce; it is about the long-term effects of divorce on children. When the parents of ACDs divorced, the popular wisdom was that it was not going to hurt the children. The parents did not intend to harm their children. Even today, when we know a great deal more about the effects of divorce, there are circumstances in which I feel divorce is still the best option. This book is not an indictment of that option, any more than it is an indictment of the parents of ACDs who chose that option.

However, we have come into an era in which we value marriage more than we did in the last few decades. We also have some excellent professional help available for ailing marriages. Given this, if we can become convinced that an intact home is better for raising children than a split home, and if that conviction can help families stay together until the children become adults, so much the better. This may sound idealistic, but what is wrong with having ideals?

If you are a child of divorce and you still either blame your parents for the way you were treated during and after the divorce or blame yourself for not being more successful in life or in your love relationships, this book will help you. If you are angry or resentful with absent parents, with neglectful parents, or with parents who turned their attention to new families, attention that you feel justly belonged to you, doing the work in this book may free you.

In order to heal from a hurt you must name it, claim it, relive it, and finally exhaust it. By following the path laid out in this book you can resolve the residue of unfinished grief.

But all the suggestions this book offers, all the retrospective glances it provides, are only guides. You will need to filter its guidance through your own special blend of sensibilities, accept what is right for you, and pass over what is not.

As a human being you are fortunate: you are programmed to heal. Otherwise you would still wear every black-and-blue mark that came your way, physical and emotional. The adage *time heals* discounts our power to heal ourselves. It is not time that heals us, though healing does take time. Our bodies, our minds, and our hearts heal us. They heal the injuries to our bodies, and they heal the injuries to our hearts.

TO THE READER WHO IS NOT AN ACD

I expect that many people who are not ACDs will read this book, perhaps out of a desire to better understand a loved one who is an ACD. Although the searchlight is trained on the ACD's clusters of issues, each of us may take away something from the principles outlined in this book.

HOW TO USE THIS BOOK

You are about to embark on an intensely personal experience and a fruitful journey. The itinerary for this journey—from your family life prior to its disruption, through the divorce and its aftermath, into the present time—is laid out to provide optimum guidance. Each chapter covers an area of importance, and the work in each chapter will build on the results of other chapters.

Each chapter except chapter 1 presents three types of material. First, there are case histories and interpretations of those histories. Second, there is in-depth psychological information about a variety of personal attributes. Third, there are materials to foster healing. These include a variety of questions and exercises for you to contemplate and answer in writing. I strongly suggest that you start a *healing journal* to keep track of your progress. (More about that later.)

Chapter 1 is devoted to a brief walking tour of the changing family. I touch on the psychological and legal aspects of divorce, its stages, and how couples get trapped into conflict. In this chapter we also start the journey toward healing.

Chapters 2 through 10 tackle one main topic each. In chapter 2 we see how divorce affects children at various ages. In chapter 3 we look into the lives of ACDs during their family breakup. The healing exercises in the first three chapters guide you through your childhood memories.

In chapter 4 we examine sibling relationships and children stepping into adult roles. The healing exercises help to understand and make peace with sibling relationships. Chapter 5 approaches the problems of addictions and obsessive/compulsive behaviors. The exercises here help you with self-forgiveness and avoiding relapses. Chapter 6 looks at how we become who we are and how the parental rift impedes the growth of identity. The exercises help you clarify and strengthen your sense of self.

Chapters 7 through 10 address the issues of love and delve into the nature of the love bond, courtship, and marriage, because for healing to be completed, not only do you need to heal your heart, you also need to heal the ability to build relationships you can trust. These chapters will show you, step-by-step, how to repair your love bond and create and enhance your love partnerships.

Chapter 7 addresses the issues of the love bond and its injuries. Chapter 8 looks at courtship and how to capture love. Chapter 9 explores specific problems that plague some ACD marriages. And in chapter 10 we look at how ACD marriages succeed. The exercises are designed to assist communication and to strengthen marriages and other love partnerships. Finally, in the Epilogue, you will find a few thoughts about parenting.

You can read and work with this book whether or not you have been in therapy. If you are in therapy, or if you are working a twelve-step program, this book will be a valuable adjunct to your other work. If you are not in therapy, and your emerging feelings signal that you may want additional help, please consider contacting a psychotherapist. I recommend that you interview therapists carefully to find someone who is trained in issues of divorce recovery.

You may choose to do the exercises as you come to them, or you may choose to read the entire book first, and then return to do the exercises. You will also gain from the personal stories shared by ACDs, which seem to operate somewhat as cosmic group therapy.

STARTING A HEALING JOURNAL

The most efficient way to keep track of your healing is by keeping a log, which I call a *healing journal*. This journal is a very special book: it is the book *of* your life and *for* your life. The journal will contain your record of this guided tour through the labyrinth of the mind, the nooks and crannies of the heart. In it you will visit those moments during which pain, and even joy, were born.

Although preparing for the pain is important, healing discoveries do not merely arrive on the coattails of high drama. Sometimes a healing moment arrives like a whisper, and awareness breaks through as if a soap bubble were breaking, dissipating confusion. Then the burden of long-held feelings will slowly give way to clarity and understanding.

You may ask, "Why can't I just think about the exercises? Why do I need to keep a journal?" There are several reasons that I recommend keeping a written log of your thoughts:

- Adult children of divorce often have a lot of trouble remembering important times. You will find that when you write, memories that would not otherwise occur to you will drift into consciousness. Merely thinking about them does not accomplish as much.
- When you write about your life, you are paying valuable healing attention to yourself.
- The very process of writing about a problem rather than thinking about it gives one a focus and momentum that mental processes not fully articulated on paper rarely have.
- As a therapist, I ask clients to write down important new insights they gain during a session. Likewise, when you are re-

viewing and evaluating your life, new awarenesses float to the surface of your mind. When they emerge, they seem as clear as a bell and as real as your dining-room table. A day later, however, they may have disappeared like yesterday's clouds from the sky. Without a written record, these milestones of growth may be difficult to appreciate, because tangle-free awareness feels so natural that you may think you never felt any other way.

- The written record will serve as a snapshot of these rich moments, and you will be able to visit them again and again.
- The journal will contain reminders of your progress. It is similar to the door frame or measuring stick with which your parents measured your height. Do you remember the pride you felt when you went to that door frame and found you had surpassed the last mark by an inch or two? The growth of understanding and the expansion of the heart are more readily measured by the mental door frame of your journal.

Consider using a school-type notebook or a blank-page journal. Make it special. Make it look like you. Perhaps you want to paste your baby picture on the cover, next to a current picture. Perhaps you want to draw or paint the cover. Would a family tree be your choice for the first page? Whatever you decide on, make sure all the materials are in a safe place. If you jot down little notes to yourself throughout the day, put them in your journal as soon as you can.

The journal does not have to be perfect; it doesn't even have to be beautiful or good. And it definitely need not be judged, by you or by anyone else. It simply needs to be.

It is joyful to keep a journal. Have fun with it. The writing soon becomes second nature—as will that act of respect and intimacy with yourself. You are important enough to write a book about!

When you commune with your journal, write out the questions and exercises as they are posed in the book. This will allow you to make the contents of the exercises fully your own.

Later, I will talk about ways to handle emerging feelings, and I will help you see your coping techniques and your defense mechanisms. Overall, however, consult your own inner wisdom; it will still be the best judge of what is appropriate for you. If you listen closely, you will hear your wise inner voice. That's the one you refer to when you say, "I knew this all along" or "Why didn't I listen to myself?" It's not the noisy chatter-chatter of the mind. It is the quiet voice you can hear when you slip into your own stillness. If you listen to that voice, you will know what is most appropriate. You may go as quickly or as deeply as you wish, or as slowly and as carefully; either way is perfectly fine.

Healing involves your thoughts as much as it involves your emotions. These twin processes travel on parallel rails, although they are not necessarily at the same place at the same time. Sometimes our feelings get ahead of our understanding; at other times our understanding gets ahead of our feelings. If you are someone who responds readily with good reasons and keeps your emotions under control, you need to work more on unlocking your feelings. If you readily bathe in a flood of tears, you may need to work more on understanding these feelings.

We feel most right with ourselves when our thoughts and feelings progress at approximately the same pace. Ultimately, a mark of health is that thoughts, feelings, and actions are in harmony with one another.

You will find three main types of exercises. The first will encourage you to record your thoughts and recollections, make lists, write letters, and conduct dialogues. Among these first exercises, I offer a group in which you're asked to complete sentences. Sentence completion allows you to reach deeply into your mind's recesses and retrieve dusty associations that you may not have known were there. Forcing yourself to repeat the root sentence also produces a momentum that takes you deeper into the psyche and therefore generates more rewarding answers. The bounty of your mind may yield up long-forgotten words, ideas, and concepts. By revealing to yourself how these associations are formed, you may mirror the inner workings of your soul.

There is a trick to working these exercises. You need to do them quickly and automatically. It is not your reasoning or logic that interests us here. It is the association chains that have formed in your mind over the years and still make up the basis of some of your thought patterns.

Secondly, there will be *guided fantasies*. These exercises, done with your eyes closed, will guide you to imagine certain events or conjure up certain images. A tape recorder will allow you to record the guiding words in your own voice, but it is not imperative that you use one.

Third, you may want to have some crayons with which to draw

pictures, as well as highlighters for emphasis. We sometimes deal with impressions for which we can't find words. Drawing with crayons will help you express those nonverbal responses. Keep all your materials together so they will be immediately available for you when you need them.

Many ACDs say that while they were in the intense phase of their journey of self-discovery and internal change, on the outside their lives seemed very quiet. Although the benefits of this work will eventually improve your life, don't look for such evidence right away. Your journal will be a chronicle of your changes, and you will be able to look back at some of the early exercises and realize just how far you have come. It may take some time, but be patient with yourself.

When you reach the end of this journey, your notebook will probably look like a collage. Keep it in a safe place, because, if you wish, the exercises in this book can remain your personal secret; no one has to know about them. *You need not share them with anyone except as you choose to do so.*

Whether it is specifically stated, as it sometimes is, or not, as you move from chapter to chapter, go back and review your journal writing for patterns and lessons. With each moment of understanding, one more piece is added to the jigsaw puzzle of who you are. So make a mental note that every time you complete a chapter you will review your earlier writings before proceeding onward.

The fact that you are willing to spend time with this book shows that you are on the right road. Keep in mind that in dealing with memories you are dealing with things long past. No matter how intense, unpleasant, or hurtful they are, they can be handled. Now is the time to acknowledge them and to move forward. Out with the old; make room for the new! The rewards of healing are ahead.

As you start on the healing journey, I would like to convey my personal hope for you: that this book will help unblock your road to the happiness you dream about, and to the love relationships you deserve.

1

The Birth of a Wounded Generation

The first wisdom of sociology is this: things are not what they seem. Social reality turns out to have many layers of meaning. The discovery of each new layer changes the perception of the whole.
PETER L. BERGER

It is no secret that a widespread breakdown swept through the traditional American family in the 1960s and 1970s. In this chapter we look at the influences that led to divorce becoming more acceptable and more prevalent than it had ever been.

To make peace with the breakdown of your family, it helps to see your parents apart from their roles as mother and father. If you are the child of divorce, a walking tour of marriage and divorce will give you some new insights into divorce. A sampling of your parents' contemporary history, social pressures, and moral trends will provide you with a useful backdrop to your family's destiny.

THE FAMILY: A CHANGING INSTITUTION

At one time, the word *family* referred to a fairly large group of people: parents, children, grandparents, and sometimes aunts and uncles, living in close proximity to one another. This *extended family* was an institution that was respected and supported by its members.

In the last two centuries ever more rapidly changing social and economic forces severely tested the status of the family. Changes started with the industrial revolution of the late eighteenth century and exerted tremendous pressure on the family. This set the wheels in motion for a drastic reorganization. People migrated to the cities, away from the farms, where they had lived with their extended families. This migration gave birth to the trimmer *nuclear family,* consisting of father, mother, and unmarried children. By the time the twentieth century rolled around, most American households were nuclear families, and by the time World War II ended, extended families were a rarity.

Divorce in the Old Days

Before 1969, when the first no-fault divorce law was enacted in California, divorce was difficult to obtain and carried a social stigma. People undertook the commitment of marriage for life, and the popular notion was that in order for a marriage to fail, one person had to be either *mad* or *bad*—at fault or insane. Although divorce became a civil matter in America as early as the establishment of the American colonies, it was deeply influenced by the Judeo-Christian ethic, which deeply disapproved of the breaking up of families. In the Christian view, divorce was morally wrong, and in the Jewish religion, though divorce had always been allowed officially (albeit only the husband could obtain it), it was strongly discouraged.

Thus even in the early twentieth century a divorce was still difficult to get, and socially it was the cause of much disapproval. The 1940s experienced a significant upturn in divorce, due in part to World War II, but also due to widening prosperity. The 1950s witnessed a return to traditional family values, accompanied by a predictable decline in the divorce rate.

Before the no-fault family law statute was passed, the trial court obligingly asked, "Whose fault is it?" The proper answer was to name the offending spouse and the legal wrong he or she had committed; among these wrongs were mental cruelty, adultery, and abandonment. Evidence of insanity was also a proper cause for divorce. The accused party could defend against these accusations, and if the defense was victorious, the divorce was denied, thus sentencing the unhappy spouses to additional years of marriage.

If the aggrieved plaintiff won, he or she was given alimony, some portion of the family's property, and, depending on the prevailing philosophy pertaining to children, perhaps the custody of the children. The words describing the legal rights were borrowed from criminal law, which is why the children are granted in the *custody of*, and parents are allowed *visitation*.

The Changing View of Reasons for Divorce

Once, not so long ago, people tried to cite a single reason for divorce: alcoholism, drug abuse, infidelity, abandonment, physical or mental cruelty, and so on. Still, one factor alone is rarely the cause of a divorce. Many hidden influences contribute to the breakup of a home, among them:

- the prevailing morality of the times
- social pressures and influences
- personal beliefs
- contemporary romantic notions
- prior sexual experiences
- the opportunity, particularly women's,
  for financial independence

As the soil for mid-twentieth-century social upheaval—the women's movement and the sexual revolution—was being prepared, the divorce rate became a telling benchmark of its advent. Measuring this phenomenon, demographers tell us that the divorce rate more than doubled between 1960 and 1975 and the number of children involved in divorce rose from 333,000 in 1953 to nearly 1 million in 1974. Although the divorce rate has declined from its peak in 1979, more than 1 million children still experience the breakup of their families every year. Children were once a deterrent to divorce, but by 1973 more than 60 percent of divorcing couples had children.

No trend in American family life since World War II has received more attention than the rising rate of divorce. We have become all too familiar with the precipitous upward spiraling of numbers that indicate the breakdown of the traditional home. More significant than these numbers, though, is the shocking speed with which the prevailing attitudes were swept away.

A less than happy marriage was no longer to be tolerated. Although the previously prevailing morality dictated that the marriage stay together for the sake of the children, a new school of thought was emerging that said, "It's better for the children to grow up in a broken home than a breaking one." The first wave of outward-bound spouses consisted mostly of husbands, but wives were not far behind. Women who in prior generations had been the core of the family as the matriarchal heads, and who would go to any lengths to preserve even a failing marriage, were also touting separation and ultimately divorce as their road to happiness. The middle class, which had always been relatively immune to divorce, was, if not ready to embrace it with open arms, at least considering it.

The "Me" Generation Is Born

About 1960, the attitudes of what Tom Wolfe tagged the "Me Generation" started to become evident. People began to question the paths they had taken in life: "What [or whom] am I giving up for this marriage?" "Is this career depriving me of personal happiness?" "Why did I have these children?" "What do I really owe my children?"

Daniel Yankelovich, an analyst of social trends and public attitudes, capsulized the radical change in this way: "Americans searching for self-fulfillment became a grass-roots movement involving as many as perhaps 80 percent of all Americans. It was as if tens of millions of people had decided simultaneously to conduct experiments with living, using the only materials that lay at hand—their own lives."

As the Woodstock generation led society into an era where no man had boldly gone before, public opinion and the pressure of the community, which had kept families together, weakened significantly. Divorced men treated their married buddies to tales of their sexual conquests and marijuana highs. "You haven't done it until you've done it high on grass!" they openly bragged. To men who married young, whose early years were marked by a scarcity of available sexual partners, the tales were often irresistible.

As one by one the seemingly solid marriages crumbled, people shuddered in horror as they wondered who in their circle of friends would be next. It was like watching an epidemic. When it finally happened to close friends, it brought disbelief and unease. Some couples clung to each other as if in a lifeboat, yet secretly questioned whether they were being naive. If both spouses could not anchor themselves to something stronger than the trends of society, such as a deep belief in the family, they were at great risk of being swept away.

It was no longer possible to stem the tide by making divorce difficult to obtain. And it was no longer politically savvy to thwart the wishes of the voters, especially since some of those divorcing voters were upstanding citizens. As divorce started to lose its stigma in the 1960s, its numbers exploded.

Since the law usually follows social trends, as opposed to setting them, legal realities echoed the changing social realities. Thus by 1970 the first no-fault legislation had been enacted in California. It paved the way to speedy freedom for divorcing couples. If no property or custody issues were in conflict, all one spouse had to do was file for divorce and testify that "irreconcilable differences have caused an irremediable breakdown of the marriage." The divorce was then granted so rapidly that sometimes the client was unaware that the proceedings were over. One's day in court, in which grievances could be heard, became an abbreviated, surgical procedure, ending the marriage swiftly and efficiently. The change was staggering.

The "me" attitude had arrived in full force, and some leaders in the expanding domain of psychology reflected a new stream of psychological thinking and preached the importance of feeling good. The philosophy was blatantly pitched by such number-one best-sellers as *Pulling Your Own Strings* and *Looking Out for Number One*. At the root of the cultural revolution of swelling self-importance were the most basic changes in the way society viewed the American family and its dissolution.

THE TROUBLE WITH DIVORCE

Theoretically, for a broken or unhealthy marriage, divorce is a useful remedy. If the couple parts, and the court oversees the division of assets and liabilities, the scheduling of support payments, and the maintenance of the children's welfare, everyone is ready to go on to a better, more satisfying future. Unfortunately, a peaceful transition is difficult to orchestrate in real life. For the spouses, divorce unleashes a psychological and practical earthquake that rearranges all the pieces of their lives. It is surprisingly difficult for even the most well-intentioned couples to avoid the numerous pitfalls and create a peaceful transition.

In one way, divorce is akin to a death in the family. Grieving for the loss of the marriage is similar to grieving for a deceased spouse, with the stages in the grieving process being denial, depression, anger, ambivalence, and, finally, acceptance. Whereas the death of a spouse is finite—there is no turning back from it—and whereas the deceased spouse is generally fondly remembered, the death of the intact family through divorce is a choice that appears to be reversible and is surrounded by feelings of failure. But whose failure?

Because all divorces involve both legal and psychological processes, divorcing couples find themselves involved in two kinds of strife: one that includes the legal issues, and one that involves the psychological ones. The psychological stages color and distort the legal process, and vice versa. It is very hard to segregate these two aspects of divorce, to think clearly of division of assets while feeling angry or betrayed.

As people traverse the various psychological stages of divorce, they find that some stages recur, while others seem never to end. For example, they may become stuck forever in ambivalence, unable to move into acceptance. And yet they need to move through each stage before the doors to the future appear to open again. Unfortunately, this is easier said than done.

Why Do Divorcing Couples Fight?

The biggest factor contributing to the unfolding divorce scenario is escalating mistrust. In spite of marital hurts, the overwhelming majority of divorce cases do not start out with either of the partners on the warpath. Though the potential for war is ever present, most couples have very good intentions about dissolving the union amicably. It is only after attorneys are consulted, after the papers are prepared and served, after the dollars and cents and other intimate details of the marriage are in writing, that stark reality sets in: the marriage is over.

The emotional side of divorce usually begins with one spouse distancing himself or herself, while the other spouse may or may not be aware that a significant change is taking place in the marriage. The legal side of divorce typically begins when a spouse consults a lawyer. The preparation of the documents and their filing often coincides with a separation, although sometimes a couple separates long before any papers are prepared. This separation can last anywhere from a few weeks to a few months, while the couple decides whether to seek out a means for reconciliation or a means for severing the marriage permanently. While this stage is being played out, both parties may be flipping through a card deck of memories.

When and if separation gives way to the first stages of the legal divorce process, both parties may find unresolved feelings rising to the surface, feelings surrounding the perceived and actual injustices committed by both partners. Because you cannot legislate the consciences of people, the blaming for the failure of the marriage ricochets from "It's his fault" to "It's her fault" to "Oh, God, maybe it's *my* fault." The pressures continue to heat up the boiling pot of emotions, demands begin, and curve balls are thrown. The spouses (on the counsel of their attorneys) each push for much more than the other spouse knows is needed or feels is just. The custodial spouse, usually the wife, feels betrayed by the paltry sum offered for the support of the children, and while the other spouse, usually the husband, pushes for more visitation, the custodial spouse strikes back by requesting limitations. It becomes a struggle for power fueled by a sense of betrayal shared by both parties.

This emotional nightmare continues as a disturbing irony plays itself out: no matter how long a couple may have been married, or how many confidences they might have shared, their attorneys now caution them against talking to each other.

As the injured parties move into the next legal and psychological stages, suspicion and anger escalate. The intimacies the couple once shared are now so many dangerous weapons to be used against each other. Everyone's loyalties come into question: the attorney does not return calls. Has he or she been bought off? Relatives may even seem to side with the soon-to-be ex-spouse. Even one's own children may be subjected to second glances and questions about their loyalties.

As the suspicions grow, each spouse begins to feel completely alone, and the paranoid thoughts begin to take on a life of their own. Will anyone ever be trustworthy again?

The Agony Continues

The time during the actual legal divorce is very stressful, because besides experiencing emotional pressures, people try to look into the uncertain future. Also, there is much to do: one spouse must move out; visitation days need to be set up; banking and financial matters must be handled. Hearings in court are scheduled and must be attended, meetings with attorneys take place, worries about whether the strain will affect the job crop up. Children's usual needs must be tended to, in addition to their needs for solace and comfort during this unsettling period. Unfortunately, the parents do not have much time or energy left over for their children—or for themselves, for that matter. Perhaps there will be time later.

Once a couple shares children, the relationship with the ex-spouse never ends; it just moves into another venue. Judges today often award the children in joint legal custody, which makes it mandatory for the parents to decide cooperatively on important issues like education, health, and religion. But if they are smarting from having truly irreconcilable differences, it becomes difficult for them to cooperate with each other on sensitive issues. And so the agony often continues for years, through the issues presented by the raising of the children.

We are all influenced by the times in which we live, and many factors contribute to the downfall of a marriage. What may have been an issue in the '60s may not be important in the '90s, and so an understanding of the influences of the time when the divorce took place may expand the ACD's view of his or her personal history. That expanded view may include the myths that were and are still prevalent regarding children and marriage.

Myths About the Children of Divorce

Myth. Children are better off out of an unhappy home than in it.

Reality. Children are often unaware of the unhappiness of their parents, or if they are aware of conflict at home, they accept it as a matter of course.

Myth. Children are better off out of a dysfunctional home than in it.

Reality. A dysfunctional family may be dysfunctional for the parents, but it is not necessarily so for the children. Divorce does not necessarily cure dysfunctions, and the family situation may become more dysfunctional for the children after divorce.

Myth. We need to protect the children from the bad parent.

Reality. What may appear to be a bad husband or wife may be a good father or mother. Also, only in extreme cases will the court divest a parent of his or her visitation rights. In all others, the children must cope with the bad parent and his or her influence during visitations without the good parent's protective presence.

Myth. After a period of adjustment, the children get over their parents' divorce.

Reality. Children recover from the active grief, but they may never get over their parents' divorce, with the possible exception of very young children. Because children tend to bury their injuries, they seem to make a better adjustment than they actually do. The effects may lessen with time, and with appropriate contact with both parents, but their lives will never again be the same outside of the intact home.

Myth. The children will feel burdened by the sacrifice of the parents' staying together for their sake.

Reality. Unless specifically informed, the children often have no knowledge of the parents' sacrifice or feel that the parents' sacrifices are their due.

Myth. Fighting for custody will make the child feel loved and wanted.

Reality. Fighting for custody makes the child feel torn and deeply conflicted. Children commonly feel, "If my parents loved me they would not do this to me."

In some unhappy marriages, as the parents turn their focus away from each other, the children may experience a benefit as the parents seek pleasure by turning their attention toward nurturing the children. Drifting marriages are often held together by the shared love of the children.

The parents, in avoiding the trauma of a splitting home, are providing a gift to the children, who otherwise might become battered by the process of divorce and its aftermath. A family that splits lacks the chance to cycle through the unhappy phases and into a better time, which often happens when the children are grown and the most stressful years are left behind. Research shows that for couples who stay together, marital satisfaction increases at that time. People who stick it out for better or worse often feel they have achieved something of incomparable value: a history shared with each other, with children, and with a community of friends. In spite of intramural family squabbles, staying together can be very instructive to the child growing up as far as learning the values and integrity of the family group.

This is not to say that families ought to be kept together at all costs. There are families that are ravaged by physical or sexual abuse, by one highly dysfunctional spouse, or by a substance-abuser spouse whose presence implies day-to-day indignities to his or her victims. Nothing said here about the value of family is intended to imply that placing lives in physical or emotional peril ought to be condoned. Still, whether to divorce or not is a painfully difficult decision, even with the freedom that the no-fault divorce and societal permission bring. Especially when we consider what has occurred over the last two or three decades.

Today, more than 25 million children are living with one parent, usually the mother. Unfortunately, most of these women are barely surviving at an income many times below the poverty level. No-fault has spawned a new generation of single-parent poverty. Though women are more savvy today about their expectations, and acquire more training to prepare for a lifetime of work, there are still many conflicts that one-parent families have to face. Even two-parent, two-paycheck families have to juggle, but single parents can survive only by straining to their limits.

Families Are Forever

More than two decades after the family was placed on the endangered-species list, marriage rates are still robust and the traditional family—father working, mother at home with the children—does still exist. Ten to 15 percent of all U.S. families are such traditional nuclear families. There is a scattering of extended families as well.

There is a groundswell of yearning for stability, as well as the recognition that there are no strict rules in matters of marriage and divorce. Perhaps as a society we are realizing that there is no school, class, or book that can teach a child about endurance, loyalty, the many dimensions of love in relationships, and the day-to-dayness of a marriage in the way a family can. True, there are unhappy families in which the child learns the negative side of human relationships as well. Still, except for a relatively few extreme cases, the ACDs that I interviewed, in looking back, would have preferred the intact home to the divorced home.

If the divorce is inevitable, the goal of divorcing couples should be to reach, if not a happy medium, at least a medium that leaves the fewest scars and leaves intact those virtues—like compassion, caring, and honesty—that a good family can foster. If that can be done, the child will at least survive the divorce process knowing that the intangibles of life—support, understanding, and comfort—can always be found in the bosom of the family unit, whatever form that may take.

As we now take the first steps on the journey of healing, pause to ask yourself what aspects of your life you recognized in the discussion about divorce. The following exercises will help you re-create some of your past as you start to move along the road to personal reconciliation.

HEALING JOURNAL EXERCISE: ACD THEMES

The following is a partial list of themes in the lives of ACDs. Place a checkmark next to the items that apply to you. Add any themes important to you that may not have been listed. Then select your combination of themes for the healing journey. In contemplating these themes you will see where you've been and where you are now. In moving through them you may be alerted to parts of your life that you need to improve or to new choices you may want to make.

I may have had problems with the following items in the past or have problems with them in the present:

Past		Present
_____	obsessive/compulsive behaviors	_____
_____	substance abuse	_____
_____	fear of abandonment	_____
_____	fear of love	_____
_____	fear of marriage	_____
_____	feelings of alienation	_____
_____	setting appropriate limits	_____
_____	knowing who I am—identity	_____
_____	feeling unlovable	_____
_____	low self-esteem	_____
_____	forming or retaining romantic relationships	_____
_____	satisfaction eluding me	_____
_____	attachments or commitments	_____
_____	ability to trust	_____
_____	frequent feelings of resentment	_____
_____	feelings of disappointment with myself	_____
_____	feelings of disappointment with others	_____
_____	disappointment with life	_____
_____	having to control	_____
_____	recurring depressions	_____
_____	recurring anxiety	_____
_____	feelings of emptiness	_____

Once you have selected your themes, the journey through your childhood may help you recognize the origin of these issues. As you begin to sort through the past, healing will occur.

Many ACDs are great at denying their emotions. These were habits born of necessity long before now, and often resulted in a partially numbed heart. As you go back into the past, you will start to let some of those feelings of long ago emerge. Your feeling muscles may be a little weak; they need some exercise to strengthen them.

How to Handle Emotions

The key to a lighter life is to feel what you are feeling when you are feeling it. The heaviness we feel is often the weight of suppressed emotions. Some people become confused between emotions and thoughts or between emotions and actions. They may ask, "If I feel angry, don't I have to do something about that anger?" Or they may query, "If I feel affection for someone, shouldn't I decide what that means to me?" Although you will probably want to act or evaluate, you don't have to do either one. Because of such common misconceptions, people often push emotions away, putting them in jail.

Your emotions are not enemies to be jailed. You were born with a full spectrum of them, and the potential to feel them all is still there. You may be more familiar with some than with others, but regardless, when released they are allies to be trusted. *Feelings are the confirmation of your reality*. Emotions that have been locked away for a long time often appear with great force. While you are reading this book, you may find such powerful feelings evoked, sometimes more forcefully than you expected them to be, and you may feel like they will overwhelm you. If you are not ready for them, you may choose to return to them another day. There may be flashes of memory; there may be fleeting images. That's okay too. The ultimate goal is to get through the tunnel of clogged feelings so that you can arrive at those feelings that are appropriate today.

HEALING JOURNAL EXERCISE: SETTING YOUR GOALS

To gain the most from the healing process that lies ahead, you need to decide what goals you wish to attain, what aspects of your life you would like to improve, what conflicts you would like to resolve, and what changes you wish to make.

Some people are reluctant to set goals because they fear failure. Yet goals are merely directions. Setting goals will simply shepherd more of your energies in the direction of healing and recovery.

Referring to the list in the preceding exercise, decide what changes you wish to make in your life by completing the following sentences. State each goal as specifically as possible. For example, *One of my goals is to improve my self-esteem* or *One of my goals is to have a better relationship with my husband.*

One of my goals in writing my healing journal is _____.
Another goal is _____.

Now write down how your life will change when you reach that goal. For example, *When my self-esteem improves I will get a better job, a better relationship, or I will feel better about myself.* Again, be as specific as you can be.

Once you have set your goals, rank them. *And remember, there are no right or wrong answers here.* No one is judging what you write in your journal.

HEALING JOURNAL EXERCISE: JOURNEY THROUGH CHILDHOOD

Now it's time to visit your family of origin. You can't effectively forge a new life without looking into the window of your childhood home. Looking back helps you move forward.

Each of us is a generational link in the chain of our families. Our bodies and our psychological propensities are shaped by the genes and chromosomes of generations that went before us, while our habits are influenced by family culture. During divorce, this continuity gets lost. The legacy of that loss is a sense of alienation from our roots and from our world. *Do not let your family's divorce rob you of your family inheritance.*

In preparation for this memory walk, you may wish to consult a wonderful book titled *A Journey Through Your Childhood*, by Christopher Biffle. It offers additional guidance to those who have forgotten their childhoods.

Next, gather as many of the following materials as you can.

Memorabilia. These items may include report cards, a toy from long ago, or anything that evokes memories. If you have family photographs, study them and describe them in your healing journal, writing down what you see.

Who is standing next to whom?
What do the expressions on their faces say?

Who looks happy? Who looks sad?
Whom do you resemble?
Write a short story about each picture.

Music. This is a quick way to reconnect with the past. Pick up an album of music from your childhood, and listen to its songs.

Aromas. These may also trigger special images. Consider getting out your mother's old cookbook and cooking something that evokes a pleasant childhood memory.

Locations. These are also memory ticklers. If possible, visit your old house, your schoolyard, the home of your best friend from second grade.

Family members. They are good sources of information. Ask everyone, even family members whom you have not seen for a long time, about your childhood.

Also, start tracking your dreams. In the darkness of the nighttime, dreams may reveal the stores of your unconscious that are not visible in the light of day.

You may ask, "What will this do for me? I know what happened in the past!" You may know some of what happened in the past, but just knowing does not complete the business of the past. To let go of the injuries of yesteryear, we have to make accessible as much of the stored hurts, confusion, sense of betrayal, and shame as possible. On the other hand, you may also hit upon good times and fun events that you may not have thought about for many years. That also is valuable.

Now that we have laid the groundwork for your healing journal by a first look at your childhood, your emotions, and your goals, we will focus on your family before the divorce took place.

HEALING JOURNAL EXERCISE: REMEMBERING THE PREDIVORCE FAMILY

Describe your mother, father, and siblings before the divorce, starting with your earliest memory. Describe your relationship with each of them, and their relationships with each other. During divorce the good times and the caring aspects of family relationships may become disparaged, lost, or just forgotten. Recall them now. Think back to holiday gatherings or Sunday outings.

List your grandparents, aunts, uncles, and cousins. Describe their personalities, their histories, what you may know of them. Describe where they lived in relationship to your house, and recall family get-togethers.

As you take this mental walk through your childhood, keep in mind that when you invite memories, the bad memories may surface first, pushing away good memories. Don't despair! You will see that eventually bad memories give way to good memories. The results gleaned from the journey through your childhood will not only create room for the good that got lost, but provide you with greater understanding of the present.

You may begin to see that the effects of your childhood divorce were long lasting—that despite denial, they have helped shape you. As you complete these first steps you may realize that you can move your life to higher ground.

In the next chapter, we will explore how children of different ages react to the splitting family. You will start to think about your life before the divorce, and what you were like when divorce visited your home.

2

THE WOUNDING OF INNOCENCE

His best companions, innocence and health;
And his best riches, ignorance of wealth.
OLIVER GOLDSMITH

Divorce is very different for a five-year-old, for a twelve-year-old, and for a teenager, but grieving for the loss is universal. As we explore how children interpret divorce at different stages and how early childhood decisions and behavior are affected, we will see how they express grief.

THE WOUND THAT KEEPS ON WOUNDING

What is the wound that keeps on wounding adult children of divorce? How has this hurt endured through decades of growth? Why are adult children of divorce still fighting the ghosts of their parents' divorces?

There is nothing that hurts more than the wound that is meted out by the most important people in our childhood, our mother and father, because it violates the promise, implicit to life itself, to provide continuous safety and care. I believe most human beings unconsciously believe that a mother and father, when they create a life, enter into a tacit agreement to continue the family as a unit and to be present to guide the children until they can claim the world as adults. When parents do this, they create the illusion for their children that the world is a safe place; it nourishes trust and allows the children to build a healthy foundation for all of life's tasks. While infants glow with innocent trust, they quickly voice their needs and expect their caretakers to fulfill them.

The Love Bond

In its most primitive form, love is symbiotic. The mother's breasts swell with milk, and she needs the infant to draw that milk from her; each is served. In concert with physical symbiosis is its twin, psychological symbiosis: our hearts swell with love for our newborns, and we feel a primal attachment to them. Hence the foundation for all human relationships is laid as the love bond is formed.

HEALING JOURNAL EXERCISE: FIRST MEMORIES OF MOTHER AND FATHER

At the very core of all relationships are the relationships you had with your mother and father as an infant. You are invited to return to your first memory of your parents, to reexperience the feelings that may still wield power over you. As you move through this exercise, jot down quick thoughts, images, or emotions that dance into your consciousness. Use the memory ticklers you gathered for the childhood-journey exercise in chapter 1. First read the instructions through once; then go back and follow them.

Wherever your mind takes you will be a good starting place. One ACD I spoke to insisted that his first memory of his mother was from the time when he was eighteen. As he then started to ask himself, "Where was my mother during holiday dinners, or just any dinner?" shreds of the past started to emerge. As ACDs often barricade their hearts during divorce, so they also place large fences around memories. Even if you are dissatisfied with your responses to this segment, just reading the exercise will start you thinking.

Recall your earliest memory of your mother. Give your mind the opportunity to slide backward in time. Bring her to mind as clearly and as fully as you can. Notice everything. Set the scene down on paper, as if you were giving instructions for actors in a play, and describe it down to the finest detail. If it's a very early memory, you may *sense* her more than remember her. Don't try to decide yet what any of these memories or sensations mean. Simply allow them to return to you. Additional details will occur to you if you keep asking yourself questions.

- What do you think, sense, or feel about your mother?
- Where were you?

- Where was your mother?
- What was your mother doing?

Capture details of the scene in your journal. If words don't describe what you sense or feel, draw your impressions. When you are finished, stop and allow the sensations and memories to sink in. Try to revive your past as if you were seeing it for the first time. Don't judge your memories or evaluate them, because judging and evaluating only get in the way of progress. Your healing self will make the connections you need to make.

Your first memories may explain much. Tapping into the fundamental ways you related to your mother and father will allow you to recognize patterns you had forgotten a long time ago. Rediscovering these patterns may reward you with an increasing sense of awareness: "So *that's* why I think that" or "So *that's* when I started to do that." Those associations in turn will lead you to a greater understanding of the choices you make.

When you are ready, repeat this exercise with memories of your father.

One of the benefits of mobilizing your early memories or feelings is that you may start to question some things you hadn't thought of before, such as:

- "Is that feeling familiar today?"
- "In what way am I still like I was as a small child?"
- "When did I change?"

For adults whose childhood was marked by divorce, conflicts often overrode the sweet memories of early years. That first vignette, whatever age you selected, may be a metaphor for your place in the family and your relationship with your mother and father. It may demonstrate to you the reasons you had to employ the tactics you did to get along or to get your needs met.

The Perfect Scenario: Preparation for Separation

From the first cry of an infant's life, he or she will be engaged in myriad steps of growth and thus in a continuing scheme of preparation for separation. As parents impart skills for living to their children over the years, preparing them for independence, the love bond gradually thins and loosens. When the child grows into adulthood, the bond dwindles, only to spring forth anew when love calls in its sexual, adult form.

Since few parents have perfect insights into their child's abilities, they cannot precisely judge when to loosen the reins, but the emollient effects of love overcome many errors of judgment. Ultimately, the patterns encoded in that first love bond between child and parents set the patterns for future love relationships.

While the parents guide their child toward independence, the child also signals to the parent when he or she is ready for more independence. When a parent leaves the child prematurely, the effects of the child's broken or tattered bond are felt through all affectional relationships. That parent's departure is not the only loss, however, as divorce is replete with many other losses.

HEALING JOURNAL EXERCISE: TYPICAL EVENTS AND ACDs' RESPONSES

The splitting of a family creates many losses for both the child and the adult. The losses from the child's perspective are listed in Table 2.1. When you read through this exercise you may experience feelings left over from that time. When you were a child you probably did not share or even recognize these feelings during times of crisis. Now is the time to process them. As you look over the list, check the items that apply to you. Recall your age at the time the particular event happened, and write your age next to that event.

Your family may have been one in which the tension had escalated so much that your reaction to the changes was one of relief or elation, perhaps accompanied by sadness. You may feel guilty, as other ACDs do, about having felt relief or elation. It's important to note your reaction, and how you felt about your reaction as well.

Regardless of the form that the upheaval of divorce took, regardless of whether you were rescued from an untenable situation, you probably still had more than your share of reasons to grieve. You may feel disloyal to either your mother or your father because you are admitting that the divorce hurt you. We will come back to those feelings in chapter 4, in which we delve into conflicting family loyalties.

Review each item that you checked and decide for yourself how you expressed yourself in your home. Children's distress is often overlooked. Was yours? No one wants to see his or her child hurt; thus parents often wish away those hurts. Hurts cannot be wished away, so you may still be carrying around those unacknowledged hurts. Call on

TABLE 2.1. CHILDREN'S LOSSES FROM DIVORCE

Divorce Events	Your Age	Typical Loss to Child
Father or mother leaves the home	_____	Sense of being lovable
Parents busy rebuilding their own lives	_____	Parental attention
Parents changing lifestyle or residence	_____	Familiar relationship with resident and nonresident parents
Custodial parent goes to work	_____	Status
Lower income, moving to lesser home	_____	Status
Moving away, sometimes many times	_____	Comfort and familiarity of surroundings
Loss of friends; extended family entering and leaving the family through remarriage	_____	Stability
Parents fatigued from own crisis	_____	Security
Combination of all factors	_____	Security, status, comfort, attention, and self-esteem

your emotional resources to accept events of the past. It is the acceptance that will rid you of the echoes of the past. Acceptance is not approval, by the way. Acceptance simply means acknowledging what really happened.

For each item, you may ask yourself: "Have I fully let go of this?" If you have not, let go now, and in the letting go the emotions will surface. One way you can tell whether you have let go is to ask yourself if you still wish it hadn't happened or if you are still angry about it. If you still blame someone, you haven't let go.

Work through the first layer of emotions that arise now. Although you may not be able to resolve all the emotions at this juncture, you can revisit them from time to time as you continue through this book.

CRITICAL AGES FOR THE CHILD OF DIVORCE

Every stage of a child's life is critical to his or her development; there is no free zone into which a divorce can fall with impunity. However, children's reactions to divorce differ, depending on their age, emotional maturity, and mental capacity.

Even a baby growing inside the mother experiences the trauma of divorce. Rage, fear, and anxiety rush through a pregnant woman who has just separated from her husband; her intense feelings automatically trigger a series of chemical changes in her body that directly affect the fetus. The intense, continued stress and tension set off her adrenal glands. Tremors of stress may become waves of hyperactivity in the unborn; rare as that may be, if they are kept up, the baby may force its way into the birth canal prematurely. The full-term baby may be born with a lower birth weight, indigestion, and a heightened need for reassurance.

The six-month-old baby, whose unblinking gaze signals a serious study of the people around him or her, will respond to divorce as a loss of stimulus or input. By one year of age, the baby's memory and awareness have gradually expanded. Strange people and places may engender fear. As the attachment to parents becomes stronger, the separation of the mother or father from the baby's life creates a sudden vacuum of trust.

The Defenseless Age: Eighteen Months to Three Years

Toddlers aged from eighteen months to three years struggle to bring order into a world that is both exciting and terrifying as they demonstrate power and new-found strength. They feed themselves now and speak in two- and three-word sentences, mimicking the big people in their lives. The presence of mother and father consistently reassures them that it's all right to explore the world.

During family disruption daily routine is shattered. This disruption is reflected in the child's nervous, out-of-control behavior. With the child's imagination far outstripping experience, reality begins to merge with fantasy. The child becomes fearful that the other parent will leave, too; and though the child cannot articulate the tempest of his or her emotions, symptoms of anxiety such as difficulty in sleeping, bed-wetting, whining, trouble with eating, and clinging occur. These symptoms are the same signals children give at an earlier age to elicit care and attention from their parents. If these signals do not bring the desired attention, despair may follow.

A Conscience Is Born: Ages Three to Five

One of the most difficult stages for children whose parents' divorce occurs between ages three and five. It is during this period that a person's emotional blueprint is laid out for the rest of his or her life. The individual's outlook on life and his or her attitudes are determined by how well he or she completes the tasks at this level of development.

Children prepare to take the tentative concept of self, shaped mostly by their parents, into a more competitive and less friendly arena: school. With a leap of faith that mommy and daddy will be at their sides when needed, these little ones trudge off into the big world. It is important for them to feel the protection of two caring parents.

Also during this stage, the first stirrings of innocent sexuality fuel rivalry and competition to capture the ideal mate—the opposite-sex parent. Children must learn that they cannot have mommy or daddy as husband or wife, that instead they must eventually move into the world to search for a mate.

Two other major events unfold during these years: children's egos give rise to the belief that they stand at the center of everyone's world; coincidentally, their consciences are born. These shadowy, though strict, taskmasters boycott the "bad" through a knowingness that haunts. The "good" and moral become known by the absence of guilt. When things go wrong between themselves and their parents, children's consciences gang up on them. Children of this age often accept the blame for mommy or daddy leaving and then drag the burden of guilt around like a heavy stone. They react to divorce by denial, by lowered self-esteem, by a cloying need for approval. Witness the story of Bonnie.

BONNIE: TOO GOOD FOR HER OWN GOOD

Bonnie's case focuses on guilt, something once referred to as "the Mafia of the mind." Her history highlights a sensitive and deeply feeling child, who took upon herself an abiding sense of unworthiness, expressing itself in a sacrificial stance in life. This stance marked her relationships from age five, when she lost her mother. Bonnie's example eloquently shows how these formidable emotions sabotaged her romantic relationships.

The first time Bonnie came to see me she was determined to have a quick fix for her romantic problems. She said, "I don't want to spend a lot of time or money on the past. I just want to find out why I always end up with bums for boyfriends." She was adamant about not wanting to examine her home, which had broken up when she was five.

Bonnie had a harrowing romantic history. She was twenty when she fell in love with Richard, a man she saw as a victim of alcohol. The alcohol made him fly into rages. She tried to help him, but her good deeds met with only a barrage of bruises and blackened eyes. Finally she left the relationship.

Bonnie's second boyfriend offered a short respite. He differed greatly from her past boyfriend; he was a widely respected lawyer in the community, was well liked, and had no alcohol-abuse problems. Soon, though, his game of cruel perfectionism emerged. He called it constructive criticism, but Bonnie eventually saw it for what it was: verbal abuse. The litany of Bonnie's shortcomings was masterfully presented as a case for the prosecution: "Bonnie, you are so dumb. Do you have to be so awkward? Why are you so thin? You call this dinner?"

After Bonnie escaped from her second abusive relationship, she rebounded with a third boyfriend—too soon, and by far the worst. After Bonnie became dependent on him, he raped her. More than once. In fact, regularly. Bonnie's self-esteem nosedived, as did her trust in men.

"Are all men cruel?" she asked me.

"No, Bonnie," I assured her.

"Then why do I keep getting punished with these cruel ones? What is the matter with me?"

After some work, Bonnie allowed me to glance into her childhood. As she started to understand the significance of her history, the question she posed took on greater meaning.

With a catch in her throat, Bonnie introduced me to memories of her alcoholic mother, banished from her home by her father. After a period in which she and her two siblings bounced from parent to parent, custody was awarded to her father, and Bonnie never saw her mother again.

As suddenly as her mother left, she was replaced. "My father had courted my stepmother, Sally, in a neighboring town. We didn't know her until the day she moved in with her own three children." Hungering for a mother, Bonnie quickly accepted the ready replacement and set out to win her love and approval. It was not easy because, though she was once the oldest of three, Bonnie was now the middle child of six—just a face in the crowd.

Bonnie recalls feeling lost and insignificant. She carried around a batch of guilt, feeling that no matter what she did she was doing something wrong. To compensate for her feelings she became a model child. She scrubbed, diapered, and helped cook meals at the tender age of five.

Bonnie's untiring efforts extended to school as well. She became very popular in high school, partly because of her ceaseless devotion to her friends' needs. She starved herself and worked too hard. Well into adulthood, she was still sacrificing herself on the altar of guilt.

In therapy, Bonnie visited many stations of feelings. She slowly traced her guilt to the disappearance of her mother from her life. Then she stopped at the station of grief for a while until she found the station called anger. How could her parents be so unfeeling? How could they wrest her mother from her? Bonnie's emotional purging reached a high point the night she went home with my instructions to write—but not to mail—a letter to her mother. The letter was born of the trauma of emotional rebirth. She wrote for five hours, during which time she traversed a lifetime of denial of her secret yearning for her real mother, and the great loneliness in her heart. Once she tapped into this reservoir of pain, she was on the mend.

The Dawn of the Age of Reason: Six to Ten

Known as the early latency period, ages six to ten are a quiet period in a child's development. The tensions of earlier conflicts have subsided, and children are now free to develop, to accelerate their independence from family.

Children at this age strongly identify with their parents as sex-role models, as well as ideals of behavior. Their pride in their mothers and fathers borders on worship; they absorb these models and make them their own. Since children now view their parents as cohesive, the departure of one signals the imminent loss of the other. The collapse of the family saps the strength of the children. They become fearful and insecure. Helpless to stave off the disruption, the children feel betrayed and at a loss as their sense of security shrivels.

MORRY: THE CURSE OF IMPORTANCE

It is conceivable that, at one time or another, all children wish they could become the most important person in a parent's life—more important than the other siblings (Mom's favorite), more important even than the other parent. Morry's case demonstrates that when this wish comes true, that importance becomes a curse.

Morry is a man in his late thirties, who came to me through a newspaper advertisement. He bore the evidence of a divorce suffered at age eight.

> Morry's cryptic answers about his role in the armed forces and his references to high-level secret duty told me not to pursue that line of questioning. Morry implied that it would be better for me if I did not know what he did with army intelligence.
>
> Morry's parents couldn't live with each other, but they couldn't live without each other, either. Even before Morry was born, his parents established a precedent by divorcing and remarrying. They separated again when Morry was seven, and reconciled two more times before finally accepting the fact that they were not meant to be together.
>
> Emotional volatility was a constant in his life, and Morry soon found out that he was in a power position. As a go-between in the family, "I could get anything I wanted," Morry bragged. "New clothes, a new bike, whatever. It was fun." Using his power and volunteering for the role of arbitrator, Morry listened to unending complaints.
>
> "For a long time I tried to decide who was right and wrong. Mother would talk against Father and I would be on her side and mad at my dad. Then I would have a good time with my dad and did not want to be mad at him." Realizing that his was a false power and that, in fact, he could not help his parents, thirteen-year-old Morry retired to the sanctity of his room, shutting down his feelings, with books as best friends for the duration of his adolescence. This decision came after his mother claimed that his father had given her a black eye, which Morry didn't believe, thinking that she had blackened her own eye to win Morry's loyalty.
>
> Morry's power had come with a grim price tag. Its cost was the loss of respect for his parents, the loss of trust, and the loss of a firm footing in life. He stayed in the house, regardless of who ended up in possession of it in the cyclic separation. He isolated himself from the battlefield, at the same time isolating himself from friends.

It took a Vietnam battlefield to resuscitate Morry's emotions and bring him out of his shell. The peril of that war provided him with what he described as the "perfect line of work" as a jungle fighter. His emotional liability in civilian life, that of not trusting anyone, became an asset in the war zone. He liked his work: "I felt good on the battlefield. I felt like I finally had a family, because the danger made us pull together."

Morry was unsuccessful in his one attempt at marriage. "My buddies all got married so I thought I would try it," he said. He referred to his marriage as one might speak of a routine task. It held no special place in his life. He was incapable of giving of himself, though he was financially generous: "I gave her all my paychecks, but I was never there." His wife finally got tired of waiting for him and left. "I was glad," he said, adding in a tone of understatement, "I don't think marriage and family are for me."

Morry had accepted his anger and had become accustomed to emotional isolation as a way of life. I was puzzled as to why he had called me. He told me that he had never told his story to anyone. He said that he wanted to talk about it and—was there a catch in his voice that belied the military precision? Perhaps. And perhaps this interview shined a little light into a soul that had endured pain in dark silence for too many years.

The Age of Black-and-White Morality: Nine to Twelve

Children between the ages of nine and twelve have exacting, rigid codes of ethics. Their black-and-white morality knows few shades of gray. When parents step out-of-bounds, when they break the rules they've set up for their children, the children feel angry and betrayed. When family discord strikes, one parent becomes the bad parent and the other the good. Children at this age feel indignation at the betrayal of the good parent and anger for the bad one. Their ethics seek punishment to correct the imbalance.

Though nine-year-olds' achievements outside the family are important sources of identity and esteem, they also gather self-esteem via the parents' accomplishments. They rely on them for clear projections of morality and ethics.

When parents break the rules, the child responds with limitless anger. He or she directs the hostility toward the "bad" one, because the child feels righteous indignation: the child and the "good" parent have been betrayed. The child's clear-cut ethics seek punishment to right the moral imbalance. Fortunately, children of this age have enough distance from their parents not to blame themselves for the divorce. But a feeling lingers in many of them that if their parents really loved them, they would never have divorced. This was true for Debbie, whose story follows. Many confess to daydreams and fantasies of their parents coming back together again. Debbie's case also demonstrates the profound effects of a sudden, traumatic change in the family's life.

Debbie: When the World Turned Upside Down

When her mother and eight-year-old brother, Mark, picked her up from school that day, Debbie knew that something was wrong. There was an urgency and preoccupation to her mother's directives. "Don't dawdle," she said sharply as Debbie was swept rather unceremoniously into the car. An unexplained feeling of nausea began to rise inside Debbie as her mother stepped on the accelerator. Debbie and Mark's usual sense of comfort at seeing mom after school and accompanying her on errands was gone, as fear skittered through them. In another split second, they went careening across a major boulevard at breakneck speed. "I didn't know this woman," Debbie recalled, remembering only that her "milk-and-cookies and Brownie-leader mother" suddenly vanished, only to be replaced by an enraged person on a chase "just like in the movies."

The two children had been abruptly plunged into family problems the night before. "Mark and I had heard Mom and Dad argue. I got scared when I saw Mom start to cut Dad's pants in the closet with a pair of scissors. He grabbed the scissors from her and raised them as if he were going to stab her. I screamed, 'Stop, Daddy.' He slowly put down the scissors and walked out."

The shock that this turn of events caused put Debbie into an emotional tailspin. Hers had been a family that had swept all problems under the rug, and it wasn't until her father's affair surfaced that family members gave way to buried passions. There were serious effects in Debbie's life for about eighteen months. Her grades plummeted. Fearful of falling asleep, she stayed up nights and started to have learning problems.

As an adult, Debbie was still feeling the disruptive effects of that initial upheaval. To this day Debbie struggles with a grave dislike of changes, and a need to control her environment and make it as predictable as possible. When control slips from her hands, she easily retreats into confusion, though she is very intelligent. Her need for control has suffocated potential intimate relationships.

Fortunately, not all children witness such a dramatic introduction to their parents' impending divorce, but the apparent suddenness of the family's breakup is usually shocking to them. Children seem to have radar for this event, with many ACDs recalling a premonition several hours before the announcement was made, though they might have had no reason to suspect anything.

The father might have suddenly appeared at an unexpected time of day. Then, even if the father was not usually given to talks with the children, he would call them together. After gathering the children on his lap the father would say something like: "Your mother and I don't love each other anymore; so I'm leaving now." Or he might just say, "Your mother has asked me to leave." This announcement, which one ACD tagged the Divorce Announcement Ritual, often comes with neither preamble nor postscript. Then, swiftly, sometimes immediately, the deed is carried out, and the father is gone. Many grown-up boys and girls still think of that as one of the worst, most tearful memories of their lives. "I worried so much about my dad and how sad he was for a long time, and I prayed for him every night for years," said Bob, whose father took off for the opposite coast to nurse his own sadness.

In the midst of divorce, it is not uncommon for parents to act more immaturely than their children. This break in authority is a clear signal that no one is in control. Like a fine tapestry, an intact family draws its beauty and strength from its members, each of whom has a role and a place woven into the fabric as a whole. It is the job of the parents to set the limits, and it is the job of the child to test the borders of his increasing autonomy. When parents allow the slow expansion of limits, the child gradually internalizes appropriate boundaries, secure in the knowledge that he will be guided to where he can set the size of his own world.

When a youngster becomes a teenager, he is much more competent than his younger brothers and sisters. Does this increased competence mean that a teenager can go through a family breakup and be less affected by it?

"Pushing the Envelope" in the Teen Years

As the early astronauts searched for the limits of space, so do youngsters during the stormiest period in their development—their teen years—search for their personal limits. These years are marked by the advent of sex hormones coursing through our bodies, causing a transformation from child to adult, a process marked by mercurial mood changes, personality changes, a budding sense of adult identity, and seesawing self-confidence. One moment we're all-powerful; the next we are beset with insecurity. The transition from gawky kid with ill-fitting physical and psychic pieces to a man or woman is what some psychologists call a rebirth of identity. As our perceptions of the adult world change—we may now criticize our parents for the same qualities that we admired them for just a short time before—we also push the envelope, testing authority, hoping that the envelope will withstand our experiment. Teenagers exhibit all stages of their development in rapid succession. One moment parents are certain they are talking to adults; then before their eyes their offspring turn into six-year-old children, belying their deep voices or curvaceous bodies.

Teenagers must reinvent the world for themselves. They must rebel. The family structure is a much-needed safety net. Although the teenager may not know or admit this, if a parent leaves, the absence is felt as a personal abandonment.

A father makes an important contribution to his family by providing a sense of control and accountability. His presence also establishes a sexual balance to the family; he is immensely significant to the teenager's development of a sexual role identity. Sigmund Freud's influence on psychological literature is reflected in the studies of early childhood development as well as mother-child relationships. Only recently has the research community in psychology inquired into the father's effects on the identity formation of children. Based on their own studies and those of others, Dr. Henry B. Biller at the University of Rhode Island and Lloyd J. Borstelmann at Duke University have concluded that "it is the father who is the primary influence regarding sex roles for both boys and girls." It is the father who provides a deep validation of a boy's masculinity and a girl's femininity. His absence sharply affects this development.

Stephanie's case shows the importance of a resident father during the teen years and how a teenager reaches for the comfort of substitutes. When her father left the home Stephanie was thirteen, a pivotal age in the sociosexual budding of a girl.

STEPHANIE: GAINING VALIDATION FROM BOYS

Stephanie's neighbors knew her family to be upstanding, church-going, solid, old-fashioned people who valued hard work and education. Yet a closer look revealed an undemonstrative father and a mother hungry for affection and understanding. She lavished her pent-up affection on Barry, her son, but her frustration on Stephanie. Stephanie was smarter and more able than her brother. She also strongly resembled her father, whereas Barry's face mirrored their mother's looks.

Stephanie remembers her mother's blame game and its absurdity: "If you didn't do so well in school, Barry wouldn't have so much pressure." Stephanie's confidence was bolstered by her staunch ally, her father. Though he praised her only indirectly by applauding her homework, she felt loved and appreciated. She cherished the time she spent with him, especially when he took her to the office on Saturdays to help him. Stephanie knew that she was the lightning rod in their family, and even had perverse satisfaction in absorbing her mother's displaced wrath. She sensed that somehow she helped the family to survive.

After the family split and her father moved out, Stephanie lost her usefulness in the family and her time with her father. Her belief in her attractiveness plunged to an all-time low. Even the time she spent with her father wasn't satisfying anymore, because the visitation always included Barry. So instead of Saturday visits to their father's office ("Barry was too young to go"), they went with him to movies or stayed at home watching TV. Eventually some women joined them, and their times together became so uncomfortable and meaningless that Stephanie stopped visiting her father.

Stephanie did what gave her the most pleasure; she plunged into school and work. She also yielded to sexual enticements. She became sexually active; Stephanie always had to have a man. At first her experimentations were with teens close to her own age, until she found that older men were more satisfying to her. She also started to drink. After years of tussle between her bouts of alcohol, her healthy side, the side that revered hard work, won out. Today, after earning an MBA and living though many tumultuous relationships, she is married and has an excellent position and a bright future with a computer company. Though she is married, she still fights those old feelings of being unattractive and unfeminine. She still looks to men for reassurance, which she seeks in the form of extramarital affairs.

Perhaps it is too simplistic to say that divorce at five will cause an excessive sense of guilt, a divorce at eight a propensity for sadness and responsibility, a divorce at eleven problems in peer relationships, a divorce at thirteen sexual self-doubts, and a divorce at any age self-esteem issues. So much depends on what happens in the aftermath of divorce, and how the relationships with the parents are maintained.

The rest of the exercises in this chapter will help you identify where you were developmentally when your family disruption took place. They will also help to continue your stream of awareness by putting more of the pieces into place. By revisiting those times and understanding the influence they had, you may start to dissolve some deeply held but false beliefs about yourself. You may also learn to understand the bases of some psychological problems—such as recurring depression, unexplained anxiety, and unwelcome dependency—that may still plague you today.

HEALING JOURNAL EXERCISE: HOW OLD WERE YOU WHEN

Answer the following questions.
How old were you when

you suspected that your parents had marital problems?
you suspected they were going to divorce?
you were informed about the impending divorce?
your parent moved away?

Return to each of your answers and recall what you were learning at that time. If you were not yet in school, recall the toys with which you played, and how you felt; remember what each of your parents meant to you. Make the answers as complete as possible.

If, instead of a specific memory, you get a body sensation, hear a song, or have any other reaction, describe those reactions in detail. If they are from an age before you were forming words, you may draw, instead of write, an answer. Your reactions will eventually all join in helping you to understand yourself better and will allow you to progress more quickly.

For example, you may write, "When I ask myself what my parents said to me about getting a divorce, I do not remember, but I get this confusion in my head." Then describe what that confusion feels like. What you are experiencing is your special response to the events. If you were young, you did not understand the concept of divorce and, of course, you would have been confused. If you were older and understood divorce, the confusion may have been a defense against painful feelings. You may ask yourself how long it has been since you felt that confusion. If it is still with you in difficult moments, you may still be using it to make yourself feel less bad. It is worthwhile for you to pay attention to your style of defense and make it your friend. Don't fight it; allow it to be there. It is your protector, and when you feel safer it will lift its veil. You might want to dialogue with it in writing. This may feel silly at first, but the dialogue may reveal deeply buried inner truths. The dialogue might run as follows:

You: "Hello, confusion."

Confusion answers: "Hello back."

You: "I've always known you were there."

Confusion: "Yes, I am your friend and occasional visitor."

You: "How can you be a friend when you make things hard to understand?"

Confusion: "I have a message for you that you don't want to hear."

And so on.

Continue with the dialogue so long as it seems appropriate. That may mean three lines, or it may mean a couple of pages. One of my clients dialogued with a pressure in her head over her right temple through several episodes until she found out that the pressure meant a midnight visitor when she was six years old. Prior to the dialogue, she did not recall that her mother had visited her in the middle of the night after the divorce because her mother was frightened and felt insecure. Her mother's fears terrified my client. Dialoguing with the pressure in her head cleared up a long-standing mystery once my client understood how that symptom had absorbed her terror.

Developmental stages. Continue the prior exercise by identifying your developmental stage at the time your family split up.

- What grade were you in?
- What were you learning?
- What were you playing?
- Who were your friends?
- What was the most important task you were learning in school?
- What was the most important task you were learning socially?

Don't evaluate anything you've written, and move on to the next exercise.

HEALING JOURNAL EXERCISE: THE EFFECT OF THE FAMILY SPLIT

To overcome the residual effects of the family split, it is important for you to accord it appropriate significance and set it into the proper frame. Your mother or father moving away from you marked an important period in your life. It's valuable to write in your healing journal about the feelings it triggers until the feelings abate. Do not be frightened of the distress you feel; you can release it once it is fully felt.

Now recall when you first learned that your parents were separating. Allow these questions to be a guide into your memories.

- What do you remember about the family splitting up?
- Recall how it was handled.
- Who told you about it and what did he or she say?
- Which of your parents left?
- To what extent did you experience it as a crisis?
- What have you told yourself about the divorce?
- Whose interpretation of the events did you adopt?
- Who comforted you?
- How did you comfort yourself?

Dr. Bruno Bettelheim, the famous child psychiatrist, writes in his book *A Good Enough Parent* that "children often question the soundness of the parent's demands. But the child may follow his parent's orders only with great inner reservations, since he has no power to refuse. Being forced to act in opposition to one's beliefs is a very distressing, debilitating experience, even should the outcome of one's actions be favorable." Although Dr. Bettelheim was not referring to a splitting family, his words were never more applicable.

- Do these words remind you of something that you had to do because you had no power to refuse?
- Was it about your parents' divorce?

Many ACDs have told me that they feel somewhat responsible for the breakup of their parents' marriage. As unrealistic as that belief may be, many ACDs carry a suspicion in their heart that if only they had been better children, their families would not have split up. Or that if only they had not done something, their father or mother would not have left.

In order to get to the source of those feelings, complete these sentences.

- If only I had _____ [fill in something you feel you should have done], my family would not have split up.

Furnish as many alternative completions to that sentence as you can. Don't judge or evaluate your answers. Just notice what is stored in your mind. Then complete the following sentence.

- If only I had not _____ [fill in something you feel you should not have done], my father/mother would not have left.

It is also possible that, instead of feeling that something you did or did not do caused your parents to break up, you feel that the cause was some flaw that you had no control over: "If only I had been prettier/handsomer/smarter/more lovable, my father/mother would not have left me."

For now, simply take a look at the contents of your mind. Just the act of writing down the words of self-blame will draw off some of the poison of these thoughts so that you can view them for what they are.

The truth is:

No matter how good you might have been, if your parents wanted to split up they would not have stayed together.

No matter how bad you might have been, if your parents wanted to stay together you would not have been able to split them up.

Your parent's leaving was solely his or her decision, made for his or her own reasons, to satisfy his or her own needs.

If you are carrying around these heavy bricks of blame for something over which you had no control, you may lay them down now.

HEALING JOURNAL EXERCISE: THE TRAUMA OF DIVORCE AND YOUR REACTIONS TO IT

Divorce is often experienced as a trauma by the children of divorce, and as a crisis by the family. There is a condition call Post-Traumatic Stress Disorder (PTSD), which is brought about by the distress of a trauma. The trauma shakes our notions of safety and invulnerability and refutes the feeling that life makes sense. The effects of the trauma interfere with our positive view of ourselves. The trauma gets inside us and stays, sometimes for a few days and sometimes for many years. Its wounds need to be cleansed and its manifestations understood. In children many post-traumatic symptoms are explained as the behavior of a bad child. In truth they may simply be evidence of PTSD.

Now ask yourself:

- What new behaviors did I adopt?
- What symptoms of distress did I show? (Typical examples: bed-

wetting, pervasive sadness, lying, stealing, starting or increasing alcohol or drug use, problems in school, heightened dependency, frequent tantrums or other expressions of anger.)

• How did my view of myself change?
• Did I feel vulnerable?

Recall your childhood expectations regarding your family.

• Do you remember feeling shocked when your family split up?

Recall specific promises that were made.

• Which promises were kept?
• Which promises were not kept?

Recall your expectations and fantasies of how life would be as an older child or as a grown-up.

If the answers are not flowing as you would like them to, once again pay some attention to your resistance to digging deeper into your soul. Complete these sentences:

• One reason I am reluctant to answer this question is

   _____.

• Another reason I am reluctant to answer this question is

   _____.

Provide as many different answers as you can. The reasons you have given for not wanting to answer these questions may be familiar to you from other areas of your life. These reasons harden into walls that block your path in life. It is worthwhile to take down these walls. Your effort will be richly rewarded by the ease with which you will be able to move on with your life.

3

LIVING IN A
DIVORCED FAMILY

*When the family is in order, all the social relationships of mankind
will be in order.*

THE BOOK OF CHANGES

Although throughout this book we gather the impressions of
ACDs living within the divorced family, in this chapter we will
focus on ACDs' most universal postdivorce issues. First, we will look
at ACDs' struggle with changes in day-to-day life; then we will examine the transition to the remarried stepfamily; and finally we will see
how new rules, relationships, and invisible loyalties are handled.

We hear from Jim how his childhood fell into ruins due to a continuing custody fight; Jerri tells of coping with sudden changes while
beset with money problems and rapidly changing stepfamilies; we
cheer for Lauren, who broke away from a dysfunctional mother to enjoy her father's good care; we ache for Joyce, an emotionally isolated
child who turned to prostitution in her search for love.

Not all situations are equally difficult. Extended family goes a
long way in providing support and continuity in a child's life, and there
were some supermoms and superdads fondly remembered. Still, the
death of the original family, despite the parents' best intentions, produced chaos for some part of the childhood or adolescence of ACDs.

THE STRUGGLE FOR SURVIVAL AND SELF-PRESERVATION

The overriding impression of those growing up in a divorced home is
that after the divorce their lives suddenly turned *formidable*. It was as

if a big security blanket had been wrenched off the home, exposing the occupants within to an inclement world. The carefree days of childhood vanished, to be replaced by an intense, enduring anxiety. *Children often felt alone after the family split up, because no one understood their side.*

The Shadow of Divorce

A great many aspects of life may be threatened in the postdivorce home. The following is a listing of some of those areas.

- relationships with mother, father, siblings, and extended family
- sense of intimacy with mother or father
- continuity of life as the children knew it
- values the children knew and lived by
- the rung on the ladder of intellectual and emotional development
- notions of morality
- role in the family
- sense of security

The lackluster days were replete with dark faces, financial worries, explosive anger, fear, and discontent. Wherever ACDs lived, the one constant in life was change, with quantum leaps toward the negative. The scenarios portrayed could put TV soaps to shame. The disappointed spouses seem to have fallen victim to their worst instincts: collusions, lying, cheating, abandonment, even violence.

From ACDs' recollections, it was evident that few parents had any idea how difficult their children's lives had become. Many ACDs complain that their parents still do not know, and would not accept it if they were told. And even if the parents did know the difficulties their children were dealing with, most had to turn a blind eye to them. As time moved forward, certain obligations had to be met, and most parents became busy with financial and personal worries.

The children intuitively knew that their parents could not handle more, and as a result they often kept their problems to themselves, and so endured a certain loss of intimacy. For many ACDs, one of the many casualties of divorce was their sense that "Mom knows me" or "Dad knows me."

Children and adults often went without adequate help for their emotional problems, reducing everyone's ability to cope. Despite that, children were faced with challenges such as moving to unfamiliar surroundings, while still grappling with the emotional impact of the divorce.

Day-to-Day Life in the Divorced Home

The postdivorce home is rife with feelings of abandonment. ACDs often are left alone while the resident parent goes to work—sometimes for the first time. In some instances the children are very young, though four-year-old Suzanna was younger than most. "Mom went to work many nights, and I was alone, because Mom could not afford a baby-sitter," she recalled. "I wasn't allowed to go out, or answer the door if someone came knocking. I invented my real daddy to feel less terrified, though I didn't remember him, because he left when I was six months old."

Clearly, not all situations share the same degree of difficulty, but most ACDs describe the postdivorce years as being intensely unhappy. Predictably, those children who fared the best were the ones whose parents either set aside personal rancor or kept it under wraps. The winning strategy was free, uncomplicated access to both parents. And money helped. Those whose families did not have severe financial problems, and whose lives remained stable and reliable, came through in the best shape.

Children are not typically grateful for good parenting, because they can't tell the difference until they become adults. But ACDs knew when a parent performed well, and they were grateful. They dubbed the parents who were able to rise to the task without overplaying or underplaying the parental hand *supermoms* and *superdads*.

One factor that served as a major contributor to some children's well-being was the presence of extended family: grandparents, and sometimes aunts and uncles. The more the merrier. When grandmother, grandfather, aunt, and uncle step in to take up the slack, they may serve as emotional stabilizers. "We went to live upstairs from my grandparents," said Darryl, "and I got to know them well. My granddad and I played ball and took walks. My grandmom spoiled me with my favorite foods. They were great!"

The importance of a family to a child's well-being is also underscored by how some youngsters adopted their friends' families. Said one ACD, "I practically lived at Bobby's house and became their third son. His mom and dad were terrific. To this day I call Bobby's father Dad and he calls me Son."

The "Happy Again" Parent's Home

What happened when parents eventually reestablished their lives and enjoyed happier circumstances? Didn't this improvement overcome the trauma of the divorce? It certainly helped, especially when the bridge from the old life to the new one was carefully maintained with a consistent, dependable set of rules. Still, there were problems. Most of the children had felt central to the lives of their parents in the predivorce family; they no longer felt that way in the split family, especially when their parents' lives involved new romantic partners. By the time the new life began to take hold, the children's trust in a happy home had been seriously eroded. They were cautious about becoming attached to the new romantic partner. "I saw so many boyfriends and girlfriends come and go that I wasn't convinced the last one wouldn't go also," said Brad of his father's new wife. Said another, "I liked Mark, my mom's first boyfriend. Since she broke up with him, I don't really care who she is with."

Although the creation of a stepfamily does not provide an instant cure to the problems of divorce, it can, and in many cases does, provide a return to happiness for the parent, happiness that can add to the child's sense of well-being and security. Some ACDs also told me that they were relieved when one of their parents remarried, because they didn't have to worry about that parent's welfare.

A stepfamily can offer many benefits to the child of divorce. To blend all the interests, however, takes caring, supportive parents who are willing to walk slowly, feeling the way, ever mindful of the concerns and worries of the child. A few sessions of family counseling at the outset can avoid complications later on, and are strongly recommended.

Children of Relief

Did those children whose homes had been dysfunctional fare better after divorce? What about those who grew up in homes of abuse?

The most relieved children were those whose parents had been each other's targets of physical or emotional abuse. Children who had been targets of abuse themselves had more complicated feelings.

Allen, who was an abused child, recalls being deeply relieved when his father—whom he dubbed the "six-foot hand"—left the home, so that Allen no longer had to worry about the next unexpected assault. Still, he missed his father and yearned to be with him. "I should have disliked the guy," he muttered, "but I didn't. He used to beat me with a belt, and leave it draped on the door handle as a reminder. Some days I could not open or shut my door, there were so many belts draped across it."

Paradoxically, part of the loss for abused children such as Allen was that they had fantasized that one day they would either be able to finally please their parents or become big enough to successfully stand up to them. Allen said, "I always thought about how I would tell my dad to knock it off, and if he didn't, I was planning how I would hit him back."

Abused children need professional psychological help to sort out the confusing feelings surrounding separation from the abusive parent. When they don't receive such help, they often continue the patterns of abuse, either by becoming abusive to themselves or to others, or by seeking out other abusive people. They need to learn that they are blameless, and that physical abuse is wrong and is inexcusable.

The themes covered in this chapter thus far have probably brought back some memories for you. Capture those memories in the following exercises.

HEALING JOURNAL EXERCISE: CHANGES

This segment deals with additional parts of the past. Even for those of you who have worked on your relationship with your parents in therapy, looking at those relationships through the special focus of these questions will bring new awareness. The answers may transform blank spaces in your memory into integrated pieces of information, thereby providing a greater foundation for healing. If journaling brings up sadness or anger, these feelings need to be released. As you release these unpleasant feelings, you will soon be rewarded with a lightness that letting go brings. In any event, a deeper understanding of yourself will emerge.

We are going to catalogue major dates of your life from the divorce to the time when you left home. If you don't know exact dates and a little research doesn't yield results, guessing will suffice. The catalogue may look like this:

My parents split up when I was in second grade so I must have been seven, and that makes it 1965.

Mom and us kids moved to another house when I was in third

grade, so I moved when I was eight. I also moved to a new house when I was ten.

I was sent to live with my aunt from the time I was eleven years old until I was thirteen.

Now list in your journal all important events in your life.

- When did you move, and where were the places you lived?
- What schools did you attend?
- Who were your friends in each school or neighborhood?
- Where did you spend summers?

Keeping in mind the summary of threatened losses of ACDs you read about on page 34, ask yourself which items on that list apply to you. You may conjure up a typical family scene from your life after the family split up. Take a look at the people in that scene and then complete these sentences:

- After my family split up there were problems with the following relationships: _____.
- After my family split up, there were problems with the following aspects of my life: _____.
- One thing I was afraid of losing was _____.
- Another thing I was afraid of losing was _____.

If memories continue to flow, keep writing. If you feel like going further, elaborate on what you just uncovered. Continue to note your feelings as you do this.

Although in this chapter you are mainly dealing with unfinished losses, if you recall positive aspects of relationships during these times, make a note of them also.

In your journal, write about the changes in your relationships with your parents. You may start like this:

- What happened in my relationship with Dad was _____.
- What happened in my relationship with Mom was _____.

While you do these exercises, you may be dealing with denial—minimizing the effects of the childhood divorce. You may see beyond the denial by remembering the wishes and fantasies you had. Complete the following sentences:

- I wish Mom had/hadn't _____.
- I wish Dad had/hadn't _____.

Did you express these wishes at the time you had them? Express them in your journal now. Address your mother and father directly by writing:

"Dear Dad [or Mom]: One thing I wish you had done after the divorce was _____."

"Dear Dad [or Mom]: One thing I wish you hadn't done after the divorce was _____."

Get a sense of where your resentments live:

- "Why couldn't you have _____?"

The letter to your parents can be continued during the reading of this book.

Now catalogue the changes in your life after the divorce by making two columns in your healing journal. In the first column list those people who were in your life before the divorce. In the second column list the people in your life after the divorce. Ask yourself the following:

- How are these lists different?
- Who is missing?
- What does each missing person mean to me?
- Who has been added?
- What does each new person mean to me?

Now focus on changes you observed in your parents and in other family members. Complete the following sentences.

Some of the ways that my mother changed after the family split were _____.

Some of the ways that my father changed after the family split were _____.

What the changes in my mother meant to me was _____.

What the changes in my father meant to me was _____.

The information regarding the changes in your parents may become useful to you when you look into certain insecurities or fears you may have had.

Allow the memory walk through your childhood to continue. Then, when you feel ready, read on.

IF IT'S TUESDAY IT MUST BE DAD'S HOUSE

Most ACDs hungered to see the absent parent, and visiting was a cherished time. It had its problems, too, however. Jerri said, "We got pretty crazy after three days at Mom's, four days at Dad's except on alternate weekends, etc." Debbie, who was shuttled back and forth with clockwork regularity, related: "I never knew where my things were." Most children did not spend enough time with the visited parent to establish a normal life.

The most difficult issue for ACDs was being drawn into the center of their parents' criticism of one another as, in their presence, their parents impugned each other's motives and attacked each other's actions. From the mother, typical accusations were: "If your father loved you, he would pay child support." Also: "When your father pays what he is supposed to, you can go see him." Sandy was told, "Your father doesn't care about you! He only wants you to live with him to get back at me." Fathers most often accused mothers of being crazy. Their onslaughts sounded like this: "Your mother's whole family is crazy" or "Your mother doesn't know what she's doing with you kids."

Return to your journal now and continue your recollections.

HEALING JOURNAL EXERCISE: LEGACY OF VISITATION

Were you one of those ACDs who felt conflicting feelings when visiting the parent you didn't live with all the time? Perhaps in walking through these exercises you can clarify these feelings.

- Recall the first time you visited the absent parent.
- What was your visit like? Describe the feelings you had when you were leaving your resident parent.
- Describe the feelings you had toward the parent whom you were visiting. If you can't recall feelings, describe how you behaved when you were there.
- What was it like when you saw the parent in his or her new home?
- Could you confide in either of your parents? Which one? Complete these sentences:
- One thing I could never talk about with mom was _____.
- One thing I could never talk about with dad was _____.

Were you drawn into conflicts? If so, describe them.

After identifying some of the feelings, notice whether you still feel those feelings and under what circumstances they emerge.

The answers to the preceding questions may provide clues to the feelings of ambivalence and the emotional conflicts that find their way into your relationships. Your answers to the questions in this segment may help you understand the origins of the problems that may plague your love relationships.

Whom Do You Want to Live With?

In staying with the theme of postdivorce issues, one of the most wrenching questions children can be asked is: "Whom do you want to live with, me or your mom?"

What the children respond to is different. They either hear, "Whom do you love more?" or they ask themselves, "Which of my parents needs me more?"

From biblical times to the present, Solomonic wisdom has held that the true love of a parent will prevent the child from being cut in half. Yet in divorce, either the parents or the judges not only divide the children, but sometimes ask them to lay out the parameters for the subdivisions of their hearts. Asking the children to make such a decision carries far-reaching practical and psychological implications. How can a child leave either parent when the child loves and needs them both? The boy needs the nurturing of his mother but knows he needs to become like his father. The girl needs her mother's affection, yet she yearns, especially as a teenager, for the assurance of her femininity, something that only her father can provide.

JIM: A CHILDHOOD FROM HELL

Jim's case offers us insights into the destructive force of a protracted child-custody fight, letting us see that in long family wars the winners are also losers. It is a story that he tells with unwavering conviction. Jim's swarthy face still reflects distress when he recalls being caught between two parents, both demanding their parental and financial rights at any cost.

> "It all started innocently enough when Father loaded some of his possessions along with me and my brother into his truck, and we headed toward the river to go fishing. What we didn't know was

that he wasn't planning to go fishing, but was taking us to our uncle's house in another state. We also didn't know that Mother, who was tired of his violent outbursts and his controlling ways, had asked him for a divorce.

"We were introduced to those facts on that trip, and before we could recover from the shock, my father asked, 'Who do you want to live with, your mom or me?'"

Paralyzed with indecision, Jim could not answer his father. He loved both of his parents.

For weeks Jim could not talk to his father about his worries, and about the depression and anxiety he felt, because his father would react by sobbing uncontrollably, agonizing over his son's concerns. He couldn't talk to his mother either, because that was not allowed. Their father and uncle were trying to convince the boys that their mother had gone crazy.

"Life with my aunt and uncle was the summer in hell. They never cared for the way my mother raised us. They called us the barbarians and said they were going to fix us."

Pretty soon, Jim started to eat enormous amounts, began to space out, and escaped into a science-fiction fantasy world. Jim's worries about his mother were relieved at the custody hearing: "She was just the same. She was not crazy."

Though custody was awarded to their mother, the battle continued. They were blackmailed: "If you don't want to live with me, you don't love me," their father told the boys. "If you don't come live with me, I will never talk to you again and I will disown you." There was the call for insurrection. "Hit her back if she tries to discipline you," the father enjoined Jim. The father wasn't alone in his war. Mom had her own arsenal. She taunted the father, trying to get him to lose his temper, so that she could claim in court that he physically abused her.

Jim's escapes into other worlds became more frequent. He pretended to be taking trips on a spaceship: "My starship from *Star Trek* had a phaser that actually worked—I tried to convince people. I told them I could actually burn paper with it, and I got real mad if they didn't believe me." Jim was moving toward the edge of reality. Then he discovered a safe way to fill the yearning for safe, affectionate human contact—homosexual experimentation. The boys he was with really liked him. "I could not be with a girl, because I wasn't strong enough to test whether in heterosexual relationships people always destroy each other," he recalled.

The "craziness," which started for Jim at age eight, finally ended when he turned eighteen. "Even World War II only lasted six years," Jim mused. "Ours lasted ten." His father won—and lost. He won because he forced the sale of their home. He lost because he created deep ravines in his son's affection for him.

Jim is on the mend today from a host of emotional problems: painful shyness with women; intense fear of rejection; frequent depression; and a recurring sense of futility. He doesn't binge very often now when he is depressed, and in fact he recently lost sixty pounds. He is talented and highly articulate, yet his work-related achievements are, at best, modest because he has difficulty making a commitment. He feels that, had he grown up under "normal circumstances," he would have been a high achiever.

Jim's testimony corroborates other evidence showing that protracted divorce wars always produce severe psychological problems in the children over whom those wars are fought. These family wars take their place next to child abuse, alcoholism, and incest in creating severe emotional problems.

Why are such wars fought? Custody wars seem to be fought for avowed legitimate reasons:

- to protect the parents' or child's rights to one another's presence
- to provide the more stable home
- to protect the children from an inadequate or dangerous parent

But a closer look often reveals the true hidden agenda—parents fighting to:

- exonerate themselves
- punish each other for the presumed failure
- try to break a seemingly indestructible emotional bond

The Fight Over Money

Fighting over money—a recurring theme in ACDs' histories—is a painful thorn in the sides of ACDs. Stretching sparse resources is not unlike pulling on a blanket to cover a family. When the family draws apart, the blanket gets shredded, with the children drawn into the struggle. As pawns in this tug-of-war, they were told: "Ask your dad to buy you shoes," "Ask your dad to buy you a party dress."

Divorce is expensive financially as well as emotionally. While the expenses of running two households now have to be covered, the earnings of the parents tend to go down. The split family often finds itself suddenly poor, sliding down a steep economic incline. "The income of single-parent families created by divorce or separation falls by 37 percent within four months of the breakup," a recent study conducted by Andrew J. Cherlin, a Johns Hopkins University sociologist, found. "It's a national scandal," he states. Custodial mothers especially are beset with economic problems because of their lower earning capacity and the fact that only 44 percent of mothers of children of divorce receive child support from the absent father. Mothers still tend to the care and feeding of the children, but with much less money than before. It's no wonder that many single mothers today live well below the poverty level and must seek welfare. "Welfare dependency doubled" after divorce, the study concluded.

In the next case history we meet Jerri, whose mother, as part of the 56 percent who get no support, was beset with financial problems.

JERRI: THE SUDDENLY POOR

Jerri and her family were among the suddenly poor. Their money problems created additional points of trauma in the home, which was headed by a mother who had been a minister's wife and never had to work for wages. Now the children not only had to learn to live without one parent—the powerful guiding light in their lives—they also had to learn to live differently, without some basic necessities.

> Jerri's nostalgia is evident when she recalls her early days. She remembers the respect they received as a minister's family. Then her father became the permanent chaplain at a major hospital in Texas, and Jerri, her mother, and her four siblings were uprooted. On top of that, no sooner was the moving van unloaded than Jerri's father moved out of the family home and moved in with a girl who had also made the trek to Texas.
>
> The minister's actions stunned his family. Honesty, morality, tradition—all of which had been drummed into Jerri—flew out the window. Lacking financial resources, the family was forced into subsidized housing: "Not only was it a comedown, but we were on top of each other, with no privacy. I remember often being hungry after mother went to work at two jobs to put food on the table. You could cut the tension in the house. My brothers and I took it out on each other; there were terrible fights."
>
> Jerri's father claimed he could not afford to pay the fifty dollars per child that he was ordered to pay. Bitterness and disbelief color Jerri's memories: "I always saw my father and his wives in nice

homes while I walked around in a tattered bra and shoes that were worn out." She tried to stave off the feuding. "When I was with Mom I had to defend Dad, and when I was with Dad I had to defend Mom. But how could a kid win against two adults? They know all the arguments."

Jerri tried hard to maintain her relationship with her father, but it was difficult. His circumstances kept changing. "Father's first girlfriend didn't stay around long, but my father found three others to marry over the following twelve years. With the four stepmothers came nine stepbrothers and -sisters. Each time my father married, he told us, 'We are all one family now.' Then, bingo! We had a new family again." Jerri and her siblings scrambled to find their place within the new families. It was difficult, because the power kept shifting as new favorites emerged. Jerri didn't feel that she was a favorite: "I always had to sleep with the kid who peed in his bed, and, being older than most, I got stuck baby-sitting and doing dishes. My father always seemed nicer to my stepbrothers and stepsisters than he was to us." According to Jerri, money problems got in the way of filial love: "It makes it much harder to keep loving your parents when you resent them for playing money games and not providing well for you."

Discontinuity is difficult to adjust to, because continuity and consistency are important components of a child's life. Not only is it reassuring to know that life, as much as possible, will be the same; that knowledge also builds a reliable internal scaffolding of reality.

THE CHICKEN AND THE EGG

There is no question that divorce creates emotional problems for adults, but their preexisting emotional problems also contribute to divorce. Likewise, children who have emotional problems may find their problems magnified. Children who are prone to acting out do so even more, and are given to extremes of behavior.

Living with a Dysfunctional Mother

Some families break up because the healthier spouse can no longer tolerate the highly dysfunctional spouse. After divorce, dysfunctional parents become highly dependent on their children, whom they need for their own emotional purposes. Such children sometimes become more tightly bonded to the needy parent and, as we will see in chapter 4, become the needy parent's caretakers.

If the children are fortunate, the dysfunctional spouse is the absent spouse. Where the child has to live with the dysfunctional parent, life may become nearly intolerable. Raising children single-handedly taxes even the strongest person, and it becomes a nearly insurmountable task for a person weakened by emotional problems.

When situations become intolerable, some adolescents run away. There are over 1 million runaways each year. Youths are far more likely to run away from divorced, single-parent, or blended families than from intact families.

Children of divorce also drop out of high school twice as often as children from families that stay together. But there are other ways of leaving home. One study on young suicides in Los Angeles County found that:

- 72 percent had one or both natural parents absent from home.
- 84 percent of those with stepparents wanted the stepparent to leave.
- 58 percent had a parent who was married more than once.

A teenager may use the threat of living with the other parent to elicit care, as a tool to gain control over a parent, or to assess his or her importance. Sometimes the custodial parent hopes to gain control over a recalcitrant adolescent by employing the same tactic: "I am going to send you to live with your father!"

In Lauren's situation, we see a mother whose irrational behavior drove her daughter to try to leave home: "I knew I had to leave home because mother got crazier and crazier and I felt increasingly unsafe."

LAUREN: LIFE IN THE CRAZY LANE

Lauren's mother was always somewhat volatile, but her explosive nature took a quantum leap after the divorce. Her emotional problems, which seemed under control during the marriage, shot to the surface during and after divorce, and grew intolerable to Lauren.

> Lauren compares her life with her mother to walking across a field littered with explosives waiting to be detonated. The mother would come bursting into any room unannounced, screaming. "In my home," Lauren recalled, "offering a friend a Pepsi resulted in my mother throwing the six-pack down the stairs.

"Mom tried to erase Dad and nearly succeeded. I was five years old when Father left. He tried to stay in touch, but whenever he called, my mother got even crazier, so he stopped calling. His gifts were never given to me. Years later I found some unwrapped dresses in the attic."

No longer able to tolerate her mother's tantrums, Lauren left when she was sixteen. She talked to a friend of her older brother, an attorney, who helped arrange a hearing with a social worker. "Mom threw a fit at the hearing. The social worker became convinced that a foster home was well in order for me." To Lauren's astonishment, instead of allowing that, her mother sent Lauren to her father. It had been eleven years since Lauren had seen him.

When Lauren went to San Diego to reunite with her father, she was eager for a fresh start. The modern-day Cinderella story unfolded, complete with an elegant mansion and a kind, understanding stepmother. The night-and-day differences, such as calmness, reasonableness, and consistency, surprised Lauren and left her awestruck. The couple's willingness to explain things and to discuss difficult issues was nothing short of miraculous.

Though Lauren was allowed to smoke cigarettes, albeit outside, her father asked that she not smoke marijuana: "He said to me, 'Frankly, I can't say anything morally about your smoking pot, because I drink, and I don't know that pot is much worse. But pot is illegal. So I don't want you to smoke it in this house.'" Lauren never smoked pot again in the house.

Still, she bore a deep imprint of the past. Everything felt odd. Lauren's anxiety intensified. Though her father was genuinely concerned about her welfare, Lauren felt uncomfortable and inappropriate in his home. She had been drinking since the age of twelve and had felt comfortable with like-minded peers as friends; she felt ashamed that she didn't fit in with the "good" kids. She felt like a member of the lower caste, a ward—someone who needed retraining "like a puppy dog."

She did not feel valued for who she was, but for the potential of who she could become: "I knew I was not okay in the eyes of my dad and stepmom. Although I appreciated that they were teaching me manners, I also resented them for it. I wanted them to accept me as I was." Still, living with her father and stepmother gave her hope that maybe there were human relationships that work.

My interview with Lauren revealed two sides of her: the side she brought with her from her mother's house; and the side that was slowly developing under her father's care. After years of therapy and an increasingly "normal" life, Lauren has forgiven her mother, and excuses her for being "nuts," but she has not yet exonerated her father for abandoning her. "He should have done something," she insisted, in the face of evidence that her mother created the impossible situation. Lauren recognizes that she has a long way to go to get over her feelings of abandonment and her fear of trusting men.

Every home has its own unique family culture. As in Lauren's case, the change from one culture to another can be shocking. Each home has a distinct notion of what is important. The differences pertain not only to things that money can buy, but also to discipline, nurturance, manners, habits, dress, meals, religion, ways of celebrating holidays, and so on. If the ways of the other home are not what a child is used to, the change interferes with a stable sense of reality, identity, and self-worth. To a child, even more than to an adult, he or she is what he or she does. Children express themselves more by what they do than by what they say. In being required to do things differently they may feel they are not themselves, that they are not a part of the family.

Being rescued from a dysfunctional parent's abuse does not serve as an instant cure, because the family culture is already imprinted on the child's core personality. As Lauren's case illustrates, though a child or an adolescent who has lived in a volatile atmosphere too long may on one hand be relieved, on the other hand he or she expects, seeks, and is ready for impending explosions. When the nervous system is used to explosions, comfort is suspect; peace is jarring.

Children who experience major childhood disruptions are particularly apt to hold on to their past ferociously. ACDs are no exception.

WHEN CHILDREN OF DIVORCE ACT OUT

One way some children react to the stresses of family life is by acting out. They do this to regain attention and to test boundaries. They demand that their distress be noticed. When children fight, steal, lie, resist authority, and use foul language, the hidden message may be:

- "I want to be loved."
- "I need to be held."

- "I wish to be a part of your life."
- "I am in deep emotional distress."
- "I need help controlling myself."

Hard to read as these signals are, the parents usually compound the confusion by responding:

- "So you want to be bad?"
- "You want to make trouble for me?"
- "You want to drive me away?"

The deeper the child's emotional distress, the more extreme the acting-out behavior becomes. Unfortunately, the more extreme behaviors are met with a parent's desire to distance himself or herself from the child. Acting-out behavior may become violent, crazy, and sadistic, and may have no bounds. Sadly, the failure of the acting-out behavior to yield the hoped-for effect can result in an adolescent running afoul of the law, or in a lethal act of self-destruction. An acting-out child needs strictly enforced controls, consistency, and a great deal of reassurance.

JOYCE: THE ABANDONED GIRL

Just as a parent's emotional problems may become magnified via the divorce process, so, too, can a child's. For Joyce, a disturbed, unhappy child prior to the divorce, her separated family served only to intensify her problems.

"I felt thrown away by my mother after she moved us away from the rest of our family," Joyce stated in her direct style.

"How were you discarded?" I asked.

Joyce responded: "She would go away for long periods of time. After I became fourteen I was left completely alone for three months at a time. She paid the rent, but I felt ashamed, and so I didn't tell anyone but my best friend." Her companions were a family of stuffed tigers—her favorite was the daddy tiger—and her real dog.

Joyce painted a vivid portrait of escalating emotional problems in a young girl who went from daydreaming and doing badly in school to tantrums, and from tantrums to bed-wetting (into adolescence), to setting small fires, and to drugs. All these behaviors helped fulfill her mother's prophecy that she was a troublemaker and a brat. Expectation is a powerful force that drives a child's behavior.

The breaking point was reached when her girlfriend ran away, leaving a note saying that she was going to commit suicide. "She was my very best friend in the world. I believed it was my destiny that everyone leaves me; so I struck back at something I loved. I hung the family dog," she said, in a voice surprisingly monotonous considering the contents of her words.

Joyce's behavior spoke of a desperately sick person's cry for help. Whatever her punishment for hanging her dog would have been, at least someone would pay attention to her pain. And, in fact, someone did. She was sent to live with her father, but that didn't work out and she returned to her mother.

She then found a way to be valued—through men, particularly when they gave her money: "I didn't care about the money, but I cared that men thought enough about me to give me money." Men and money together became prostitution. "I finally felt valued and useful. I really enjoyed it."

Eventually, as she was sinking further into street life, Joyce was recruited by an organization that offered child prostitutes an alternative. "They really cared," she said, still amazed. Joyce responded well, and started her long trip back to a life in which she can feel valued for who she is.

Joyce defended against her deep sadness and intense anger by externalizing her feelings—somehow putting them out into the world. Other defenses are more common, as you will see in the following exercise.

HEALING JOURNAL EXERCISE: DEFENDING AGAINST PAIN

To defend ourselves against pain, we have to postpone our feelings, cut them into small pieces, and then take them in small, digestible bites. The mind is very clever in protecting us; it has many ways to delay the unwelcome effects of difficult events. Sigmund Freud named the processes of postponement *defense mechanisms*. Of these, some of the most familiar are:

denial: disbelief; deferring belief in a changed reality ("This isn't really happening to me"; "This isn't a problem!").

dissociation: splitting one's thinking into compartments, creating independent psychological processes. "I am not really here," the mind might say, wandering off, while the body has to stay.

intellectualization: dissecting a problem solely in intellectual terms to avoid feeling. When we ask "Why did I do that?" or other such *why* questions, chances are this defense mechanism is at work.

projection: seeing one's own feeling or traits in someone else. An example would be pushing off responsibility for some of our bad traits by saying, "She brings out the worst in me."

repression: pushing unwanted impulses or feelings out of consciousness. "I don't remember" is a familiar phrase in the language of repression.

In order to identify your own style of defense, recall one or two events that were hurtful to you. Then notice what your mind or body did to defend you against these assaults. Did you externalize by acting out your feelings, or did you internalize and hold your emotions inside? Perhaps you have done both at different times.

Look at the list of defense mechanisms above and identify those that are familiar to you. These are the most common ones, but there are many more. In your journal describe the special style that provided you with emotional escape.

Now look at what you have just written and see whether these ways of avoiding discomfort are still with you. Are they your friends today, or are they now hindering you? If they are hindering you today more than helping you, make a note of them and add them to the list of goals that you compiled at the end of chapter 1.

While falling in love and becoming parents often bring out the best in people, divorce seems inevitably to bring out the worst. Children often see their parents' worst faces during divorce, as they live with a mixture of betrayal, abandonment, manipulation, confusion, sudden shifts in values, poverty, and insecurity. ACDs say that a deep ravine of insecurity coursed through their lives when they could no longer take for granted that their parents would continue to love them. The world may not see the worst faces of divorcing families, but the children of divorce do.

Where the children went through the creation of a stepfamily, an entirely new set of adjustments had to be made. In the next section we will see how these changes are dealt with.

THE STEPFAMILY

The stepfamily is a mixed bag of happy expectations and frequent confrontations. Even without a history of major problems, it is difficult to create a new family out of two adults who are in love and one or more children who are not. Characteristically, everyone who enters the blended family or stepfamily has fantasies and expectations, while carrying a bag full of the unresolved past. Injuries from the ending of a previous family must be healed in the new situation.

The parents are excited about their brand-new start and look to the future with great anticipation. The children—from prior marriages, and for whom the new family presents a complex emotional development—usually look at the present warily, with questions like:

- "What does this mean to me?"
- "Will I be taken care of?"
- "Does my new stepmom or stepdad care about me?"
- "What if I don't like them? Will something be taken away from me?"
- "What if I like them? Will I hurt my real mom or dad?"
- "Will I get to like my stepparent, and then will he/she leave me, too?"

The children may be jealous of this new love interest who is occupying their parent's time and affections, which they feel rightfully belong to them. Also, the fantasy that mom and dad will get back together has to be tucked away forever.

By now, memories of custody battles, money problems, or stepfamily events may have been triggered. Let's return to *your* story.

HEALING JOURNAL EXERCISE: DRAWING ON YOUR MEMORY

Using crayons, draw a picture to depict a memory, a feeling, an attitude, or anything else from the time you became part of a stepfamily. The picture does not have to be accurate or true to life. It can consist of random lines, dots, dashes, or anything else that you transfer onto paper from your mind or from your heart. It can be a portrait of the family, or a drawing of the house in which you lived.

Then go back further in your history and recall the first time you were presented with either your mother's or your father's potential new mate. Were you aware of the importance of that moment?

Freeze that moment in your mind and describe it in your healing journal. Then tell whether the first impressions you had of your potential stepparent were accurate. Then describe your stepsiblings. What were your impressions of each one?

WHO IS KIN AND WHO IS NOT?

To the children, the differences between blood kin and kin by marriage, invisible in the family of origin, now become critical. Family feelings that were once taken for granted now become questions of choice. "Do I want to accept this person as a family member?" is the pending question. Feelings of kinship take time, and parents' wishes that the children like everyone cannot be legislated.

Following are some of the roadblocks that prevent the child of divorce from blending in with a new family.

- The child feels left out in choosing the new family.
- The child does not like the stepparent or the stepparent does not like the child.
- The child resents the stepparent's authority.
- The child feels cheated because he or she is losing his or her rank order in the family.
- The child does not like the stepsiblings.
- The living arrangements become difficult and lacking in privacy.
- The family styles and rules are different.
- Sexual issues abound in the stepfamily, because the children are aware of the greater physical affection between the parents, to one of whom the incest taboo does not apply.
- The stepparent is aware of the budding teenager's sexuality.
- The children are sexually aware of the stepparent.
- There are cases of attempted and actual incest.

The kinship issue was documented in a study that explored family feelings. In the study, members of families were asked to list people whom they considered family. This is what the study revealed:

- Only 1 percent of the parents failed to mention their biological children.
- 31 percent of the children or adolescents did not list their residential stepmother or stepfather.

- 41 percent of the children did not list their residential step-siblings.

The passage of time alone is no indicator of whether stepkin will acknowledge each other and form a family. Only sensitivity to the issues, in addition to proper effort, will help redraw the map of a functioning, blended family.

While the whole family is considered a system, any two members sharing common interests, attitudes, or values and having positive feelings toward one another is a subsystem. In divorced-remarried families, the boundaries are ambiguous because, as we have just seen, the perceptions of individual family members can vary widely as to who is in or out of the family, and who is performing which roles and tasks within the family system.

Loyalty: The Shadow of the Invisible Parent

Loyalties create paradoxes. Without even realizing it, a youngster may be more loyal to the parent who is absent than to the one who is present. Loyalty conflicts may be conscious or to a great extent unconscious. Such conflicts may show up in the formerly good child's hard-to-understand conduct, like repaying a stepmother's or stepfather's kindness with rudeness or rejection, or sudden moodiness, antagonism, or misdirected violence. Even more puzzling to everyone is the child who takes on the habits and ways of the absent parent, even if the child wants nothing to do with that parent.

Showing affection or appreciation for a stepparent may feel like a betrayal of the absent parent. Children beset with such loyalty conflicts are unable to express why they behave badly, and in truth they often feel like monsters, not understanding themselves.

There is a broad range of attitudes among ACDs toward their stepparents. To some, a stepparent is no more important than a fly on the wall; others embrace the stepmother or stepfather fully as their own parent. Some are cautious about their feelings even decades later, and still others clearly harbor very strong negative feelings for years. "I hated my first stepmother. She had a lock on the refrigerator at my dad's house. We had to ask permission to eat," recalled an outraged Frannie, still sounding personally violated. She gleefully revealed that in her complaints to her father he took her side, and soon he parted from that wife. However, most ACDs whom I interviewed displayed no passion about their stepparent; the prevailing attitude was a shrug of the shoulders.

HEALING JOURNAL EXERCISE: VISIBLE AND INVISIBLE LOYALTIES

This exercise deals with loyalties and relationships within your stepfamily. If your mother and father are both remarried, deal with each one's new family separately. Do this exercise even if their marriages ended.

First, make a list of the members of your mother's stepfamily, and then of your father's. Then do the following separately for each stepfamily.

Draw a very large circle, the size of a page of this book, and write your name in the middle of the circle. Then write in the name of every member of your blood family and stepfamily, writing the names of people to whom you feel or felt the most loyalty closer to the center of the page.

Then, to make your relationships clearer, draw a red line between yourself and each person with whom you felt a shared loyalty bond.

What about the others? You may share an invisible loyalty bond with those toward whom you had no feelings of loyalty. Such invisible loyalty may be expressed through actions, such as providing care, or continuing a relationship despite the fact that you claim not to want to do so. Try to see how invisible loyalty bonds expressed themselves in your life.

Then draw a blue line between your name and the names of those toward whom you have exhibited such loyalty through action, though you don't actually feel the loyalty bond. Are there names connected to yours with blue lines that surprise you? Can you explain your actions in a way other than that you harbor feelings of loyalty that you are not aware of?

Look back over the preceding exercises and reflect on what you have learned about yourself and about the loyalty bond. Some important information may be emerging about your family relationships.

Do they form a pattern?
How do these patterns play themselves out
in today's relationships?

Summarize in one sentence the most important new awareness you have obtained.

Childhood always ends, even a childhood beset with custody battles, stepkin, or culture shock. Unfortunately, childhood is prematurely curtailed for some ACDs, who assume adult responsibilities too soon.

The next chapter devotes itself to a full discussion of the creation of child parents. We will visit some of these premature adults and explore their sibling relationships.

4

THE PERILS OF PARENTING TOO YOUNG

"My brother always protected me and accepted punishment for the problems I created. It gave me hope that I would become strong like him."

APPY, ACD

One child's kindness toward another child often raises a knot in the throat of the onlooker. Such was the legendary case of a young boy named Howard Loomis, whose mother, in an act of surrender to poverty during the Great Depression, had taken him to Father Flanagan's Boys Town, a home for abandoned boys, in Omaha, Nebraska. Father Flanagan welcomed the shy six-year-old and instructed him to go upstairs to the sleeping quarters. The boy did not move. He couldn't move: his legs were crippled. Another youngster, himself not much bigger than the boy, noticed Howard's withered leg and, knowing that crippled children were not allowed at Father Flanagan's, quickly stepped up and said, "I'll carry him up, Father."

Father Flanagan objected: "No, son. He is too heavy for you."

The older boy unhesitatingly spoke the words that became the maxim for Boys Town and perhaps for children caring about children everywhere: "He ain't heavy, Father, he's my brother."

Siblings are sometimes the unsung heroes or heroines in divorce. In this chapter we will see the important roles brothers and sisters play in splintering families. We will meet Bill, who became the consummate parent at nine years of age; Jennie, who at age four helped her sister with an emotional crisis; and Fawn, who, though only a child, was the most responsible member of her family. But there is a price to pay for wearing those big shoes, and we will explore the perils of parenting too young.

SIBLINGS AND PARENTAL CHILDREN

The fear of abandonment is very real to all children, not just the children of divorce. They realize at a young age how dependent they are on their parents. The fear of losing the security and happiness parents represent has caused many a childhood nightmare. Like Hansel and Gretel, whose father fell under the evil influence of his new wife and left the children alone in the forest to be rid of them, ACDs fear scary images and shadowy dangers of the unknown.

The tale of siblings clinging to each other for support was repeated often during the interviews. A brother or a sister can be a tremendous wellspring of love and succor, for both the older and the younger children, for the weaker and the stronger. Their presence can relieve tense moments. Randy said, "Right before they separated, Mom and Dad yelled a lot and they even hit one another. When the fights started, I used to go to my sister's room. We just sat and held on to each other, real tight. Sometimes we kept score of who was winning the insult game." Siblings may not be a complete source of nurturance; yet they become vital sources of love, and sometimes the only constant in a child's life.

The Child as Parent of a Child

The oldest child often emerges to lead the way, or is given the mantle of authority by the parent. "The care that I received from my fourteen-year-old sister and sixteen-year-old brother gave me the guidance I needed to end up in college. My sister taught me how to wear my hair and makeup. My brother helped with homework, impressed me with the importance of keeping up my grades, and planned the college-prep courses with me," said Valerie.

Some parental children take on responsibilities well beyond those of latchkey children, who simply wait for a parent to return from work. They are true parental substitutes at astonishingly young ages.

What makes the eight-year-old accept the job of a parent? And just who *are* parental children?

- Parental children have to perform the tasks of a parent with regularity, instead of playing.
- Parental children have to be continually responsible for the welfare and safety of others.
- Parental children are treated by their parents as equals, without regard for generational boundaries.

Children rally to the call and become the parental child for many diverse psychological reasons. Some of these reasons include:

- protecting the parent
- pleasing the parent
- expressing empathy for their siblings
- demonstrating competence
- cherishing the parent's image
- dominating their siblings
- keeping the parent functioning and healthy

The last item on the list is the most powerful source of motivation. Children will go to almost any extreme to comfort a parent or to protect him or her from psychological collapse.

HEALING JOURNAL EXERCISE: FINDING THE PARENTAL CHILDREN

Check the questions in the following list that apply to your childhood.

_____ Did you have to perform day-to-day parental tasks that prevented you from doing your homework or from playing?

_____ Were you continually responsible for the welfare and safety of others, before you were competent to be so?

_____ Did your parent treat you as if you were an equal, without regard to age boundaries?

_____ Was there no adult supervision or inadequate supervision?

_____ Were you on your own a great deal?

_____ Did you feel smarter, stronger, and more capable than the adults who cared for you?

_____ Did you have to perform tasks that you felt were too difficult or too time-consuming for you?

_____ Did you often wish that there were someone to take care of you?

When you have to parent yourself, you are just as much a parental child as when you have to parent another. Sometimes that is even more difficult because of the loneliness involved. If you checked any of the questions above, chances are you were a parental child.

Bill, whom we meet next, may have taken his responsibilities to extreme measures. He offers us a glimpse of what drives the child to become the parent, and how it can affect the ACD's development.

BILL: TEAMING UP TO FIGHT THE WICKED STEPMOTHER

When nine-year-old Bill was called to head up his family, he became responsible for the children: Tracy, seven; Audrey, six; and Appy (called that because she was the apple of their father's eye), five. Bill could have been the contemporary version of Hansel.

Bill's parents married when they were both very young, much too young in retrospect: his mother was eighteen and his father was twenty. Nine months later Bill arrived. Then came four more children in quick succession, the last of which was stillborn.

As the stream of children arrived, Bill's mother, who seemed robust at eighteen, began to suffer emotional problems. Recurring depressions plagued her, eventually becoming severe. Bill's father, a young and fun-loving man with an eye for the girls, wasn't prepared for all the responsibility that went with such a large family. He stayed away more and more, and eventually came home only long enough for his wife to get pregnant.

After the stillbirth of the fifth child, Bill's mother suffered her most severe depression. She became overwhelmed by physical and mental exhaustion, just barely dancing on the edge of competence. To protect her children, she turned them over to their paternal grandparents, and checked herself into the mental hospital. The children lived with their grandmother for a year, and then were sent to live with their father and stepmother. They loved their grandparents, but didn't know their father very well and didn't know their stepmother at all. They were awash with anxiety and trepidation.

As their mother became more and more incapable, Bill had risen to act as surrogate head of the family. He was given responsibilities even before he had given up his "blankie." At three, this "mother's big boy helper" could change a diaper and feed a baby; at five, he made lunch and did light chores regularly.

Bill still wore his cloak of responsibilities when his little squadron arrived at the father's house. There, a test of authority ensued. They were raised by a woman they considered their wicked stepmother—Leona, their father's "woman." Their father's job required him to travel, and he was home only occasionally.

At thirty-five, Leona had never had children of her own. It was a mystery to her how to negotiate goodwill between herself and the children. She knew that in their father's absence she needed to exert some discipline, but the children rejected her authority, and vehemently denied her the right to be their mother. "In all fairness to Leona, we must have been a handful," recalled Audrey, a mother herself today, and the only one of the four who got close to Leona. "She wasn't a bad woman; she was just lost with us."

Leona didn't know how to earn the trust of this troop of children. She did not understand Bill's role and thought the children were just being bad. The children vowed that no matter what Leona did to them, they would remain loyal to one another. Leona and the children clashed, but Bill was her particular target. When Leona gave an order, the children checked first with Bill, even if it was no more than a quick glance for a signal. If he approved, they complied with Leona's demands; if he didn't, they resisted even in the face of a certain whipping.

And neither whippings nor other forms of punishment were spared. That's how Leona's frustration and rage were communicated: through beatings and lockups—sometimes, for weeks at a time, they were kept in their rooms after school—and other miscellaneous forms of discipline.

Bill waited patiently for his mother's return and his well-deserved rewards. In fact, the children's mother never did return. She checked on the children from time to time, but never asked for them back. That second abandonment, when the children learned that they would never go to live with their mother, was a more crushing blow yet. Thus each child, in his or her own way, had to make peace with living with Leona, but it was hardest for Bill, because it violated his perceived sense of duty.

The younger siblings are probably in much better shape today for Bill's sacrifice. Bill is not in good shape. The relationships among these siblings are marked by love-hate feelings toward one another. One reason for these feelings is that the parenting delivered by siblings cannot be complete, cannot be totally satisfying, because child caretakers are themselves not complete. Their charges need more than they can provide, and yet the caretaker is giving as much as he or she can give. The caretaking child himself has been abandoned by the parent, and at the unconscious core, the caretaker sibling feels angry, deprived, and bitter that he or she has not been taken care of. These feelings of deprivation and rage can suddenly surface in adulthood, and often are vented on the siblings, spouses, or children. These feelings are all the more confusing because these ACD caretakers see themselves as the competent ones, and have a difficult time admitting their neediness.

Bill today is still the victim of his past, having great difficulty with adult responsibilities and long-term commitments. Bill needs therapy but will not accept it, because he is still operating on the old messages from his mother, which demand that he be the giver. He has not learned to accept help. His ambivalence toward responsibility of any kind has been played out in his history of divorces, which came in quick order, with children left behind in each marriage. The other siblings, too, have on-again/off-again relationships with one another. The youngest, Appy, who was the most shielded by all her siblings, is the only one of the siblings who has not been divorced, and she makes a valiant effort to keep the family together. She is generous with the family, but the response of the others to her efforts is more mixed than she would like it to be.

HEALING JOURNAL EXERCISE: SIBLING RELATIONSHIPS BEFORE AND AFTER DIVORCE

The purpose of this exercise is to explore your own sibling relationships, and how divorce affected them. Start by making a list of your brothers' and sisters' names, their birthdates/ages, and birth order.

Next to each name write three descriptive words.

Describe your role among the siblings (for example, baby, sourpuss, scapegoat, the good one).

During and after the divorce. Describe briefly how your sibling relationships changed after your family split.

Describe how separations from your siblings felt.

Make note of any feelings of guilt or of glee, or of some advantage you obtained over a brother or sister because of the circumstances. These feelings may still be at work. Notice whether you have any anger or resentment because your siblings were better treated than you. What patterns do you see? Are those patterns still alive in your life today?

Stepsiblings and half siblings. List your stepsiblings' and half siblings' names, birthdates, ages, and birth order. Next to each name write three descriptive words.

How did you feel about each? Was there favoritism? Describe your role among your stepsiblings.

Many ACDs feel that there is a great deal of unfinished business regarding the unequal treatment of children in a blended family or a stepfamily. Do you have unfinished business with your stepfamily members?

The following questions may require some time to think them over. You need not answer them in writing, but thinking about the answers will help you reevaluate your relationship with your sisters and brothers.

- How are your relationships with your sisters and brothers today?
- Are they as you would like them to be?
- Do you yearn for better, closer relationships with your sisters and brothers?
- What is getting in the way?

Set goals for improving sibling relationships and work on them. You know how to make friends; you have done it all your life. You can use those friendship skills to make friends with your family.

Siblings and the Inner Self

Siblings are important in the development of one's inner self and one's concept of that self. Such notables in the field of psychology as Melanie Klein and Heinz Kohut have theorized that one's self-concept develops from one's early intimate relationships. According to this theory, called the *object relations theory,* each child constructs his or her own unique identity and self-concept, starting in infancy, by re-creating and internalizing images of other people, known as *object representations*. Thus the youngster's self-concept emerges from his or her earliest intimate relationships. Our selves are intricate, living tapestries, woven from dynamic interactions between these internalized people, our own personalities, and the unfolding of our psychological potential.

Although parents are the most important persons for their children, if they are not available, children turn to other family members. Among the ACDs I interviewed, siblings, who have long been underrated in psychological studies, made a very significant contribution. Yet it was not all love and roses. In some instances, brothers and sisters not only didn't make positive contributions but were competitive, and even destructive, with one another. This entire area of inquiry is even more important today, even in intact families, because with high-paced, two-career families, there is a great deal more reliance on sibling contacts.

HEALING JOURNAL EXERCISE: FINDING THE FROZEN CHILD WITHIN

If you assumed the role of the parental child, chances are you tucked away your own inner child and your own needs. The inner child goes into hiding at the time that a traumatic experience occurs. This child, frozen in time at the moment he or she was tucked away, lives within us.

Your child may have gone into hiding because the feelings became too much to handle. He or she may still yearn for love, safety, and protection. He or she may communicate with you through psychological symptoms, such as an emptiness in the heart or recurring depressions. He or she may communicate with you through physical symptoms, such as distress in the stomach, recurring headaches, or a craving for sweets. Whatever the symptoms are, they usually mean that the child needs attention.

In working through this book, you are making contact with that inner child, with the feelings that were put on hold, with the empty spaces in your soul, with the gaps where there should have been emotional development. By becoming aware of where those gaps are, you take a giant step toward filling the emptiness. By better understanding this part of your past history, and by giving yourself permission to unlock those emotions, you can heal that part of your tattered heart. Press onward with your feelings. What you are doing is good medicine.

Answer the following questions in your healing journal.

- Whose adult shoes were you wearing?
- Which of your sisters or brothers disappointed you?
- Whom did you imitate?
- How did you get your needs met?
- Do you feel the weight of responsibility for your siblings?
- Do you feel resentment that your siblings do not want to be responsible for you?
- What do you feel you missed in parenting?

Recall an incident when you needed your parents and they were not there. Notice what you yearned for.

Make a list of what you feel you missed. You may be able to do this by identifying what you yearn for today. Maybe it's simply someone to hold you and comfort you. Notice how that part of you feels that needs comforting. It is important to allow yourself to feel now what you felt then, because your hidden child can communicate through those feelings. *You are an adult today. You can comfort that child and allow him or her to feel secure through your care.*

Perhaps you learned about the feelings of your inner child through the previous exercises. Following is a description of Kelly's case, further illustrating how the departure of a parent can traumatize a child. Kelly was fortunate because, unlike many children, her symptoms of the divorce trauma were so profound that they had to be tended to by her parents. Despite the competent psychological help she received, she relied heavily on her sister to help her.

KELLY: MOTHERED BY A YOUNGER SIBLING

Kelly's story brings to light the role of a younger but stronger sibling. It is almost always the more stable sibling, no matter what the age, who emerges as the pretend adult.

Eight-year-old Kelly was the oldest of four girls and had been closest to her father, although both parents had been loving and affectionate with Kelly and her three sisters. The contrast between what had been normal in their family and what developed later was monstrous. Kelly recalled, "We went from a very happy family to a war zone with instant casualties."

Kelly's parents separated when she was in summer camp. On her return home her reaction was quick and blunt. "I immediately became hysterical when Mom told me," she said, explaining, "They had never fought, so I thought *I* did something wrong to break up their marriage." Her father, a divorce attorney, had a hidden weakness: women. He had kept his affairs quiet until he became involved with a client who was a well-known society figure.

The divorce between Kelly's parents was ugly, with retribution playing a major role. Kelly's mother, smarting from the indignities her husband had heaped on their family, subpoenaed her husband's paramour. Surreptitiously obtained pictures of intimate moments spent by the pair to prove the dalliance became tabloid favorites.

The effect of the scandal was profound. Already in the clutches of trauma, Kelly continued to develop psychological symptoms. She stopped eating. She couldn't sleep. She felt surrounded by a wall of fear, and could not be alone. She recalls, "I started to beat up kids at school. I would call mom fifty times at work, twenty-five times at my uncle's. When she came home, I would not leave her side. I would sit outside the bathroom when she took a bath. I panicked when she wasn't at home."

Her sister Janie was only four years old, but served to reassure her older sister: "Janie would come home from preschool and try to take care of me by saying, 'I will walk you to the neighbor's house so that you can stay there until Mom comes home.' Or she would say, 'Mommy is coming home and you don't have to cry.'"

Kelly saw a child psychologist for two years, and slowly overcame her emotional problems. But she will never forget the kindness Janie showed her.

Whether the younger child continues to rely on an older sibling, or an older child, such as Kelly, turns to the younger child, the responsible child will eventually feel burdened. When neither sibling can really get his or her needs met by the other, they both come up empty. When the older child leaves the younger child or children to pursue his or her own life, the younger ones feel, once again, abandoned and enraged.

Caretaker children can never be sufficiently paid back for their lost childhood, but they usually expect a payback and gratitude, which is rarely forthcoming.

Parental children are left with resentments that translate into: "Look at all I have done for you, and what are you doing for me?" The weight of those earlier years often lingers oppressively on their shoulders, and the anger long suppressed may break into the open at later, and often inappropriate, times. Thus what looked like promising, lifelong loyalties often turn into love-hate, on-again/off-again relationships among ACDs.

Sibling Rivalry

The competition to possess our parents is as old as the Old Testament. During the first few months after birth, the infant basks in the illusion that he or she possesses the mother exclusively. For the firstborn, this illusion persists until a tiny rival for mother's affection comes on the scene. The child who enjoyed this exclusivity has trouble giving it up.

Small children sometimes express their preference clearly and simply. A four-year-old of my acquaintance inquired of his mother, with storms gathering on his brow, "Mom, can't we give Jeffy back now?" These feelings may go underground, because children receive the parents' disapproval for feeling this way, but they may never leave entirely.

Not all sibling competition is undesirable, and most families realize this. The home as the main arena of sibling aggression—a safer place in which to experiment than the world of strangers—is an important social laboratory. But the rivalry, exercised in the name of building skills, has to be carefully mediated by parents in order to help keep it within acceptable bounds. Still, siblings who might beat up each other at home would unhesitatingly aid one another against outside aggressors.

Other circumstances will actually fuel sibling rivalry: favoritism, mishandled sibling conflicts, inadequate boundaries, and insufficiently available parents. For Jennifer, our next case, all of these elements intersected to create a brutally difficult life for her.

JENNIFER: THE ONE-WAY RIVALRY

Underneath her rivalry with and her utter dislike for her sister, Jennifer had one wish: she wanted her share of her mother's attention, attention that was directed to her older sister. Jennifer hated her because she felt that her sister was perfect.

> "She was always good in school, when I daydreamed. She was sweet; I threw tantrums. She never seemed to have any problems, while I wet the bed into my teens. My sister owned our mom completely. She had her approval, her praise, and her friendship. They were like best friends and always stopped talking when I came into the room."

> "I am not like my sister" became an important aspect of Jennifer. Although it met with disapproval, she felt a sense of satisfaction when she talked about this identity of hers, her "brattiness" accommodating her rivalry: "If you have the name you might as well have the game, I thought."

> "Still, I felt terrible about myself, because I had these murderous feelings toward my sister, and she was always so nice to me." Jennifer's sister, who possessed everything Jennifer needed, refused to fight. Indeed, she seemed perfect.

> To add insult to injury, Jennifer needed her sister because of the frequent and lengthy absences of their mother, who was either working or looking for her next husband. Their mother would travel to other cities, leaving the girls alone. During these absences, Jennifer's sister was a surrogate parent and the only family available to Jennifer. Her willing help was reluctantly accepted, but Jennifer hated the fact that she was dependent on her rival.

Caught in a catch-22 of conflict, Jennifer turned her rage on herself. Her conflicting feelings, combined with parental deprivation—she never saw her father—helped drive Jennifer into self-destructive patterns. She started using cocaine and marijuana. She drank. She was arrested twice. Her sister tried to help but couldn't get to first base with her.

The details of Jennifer's special life are hidden in a drunken, strung-out haze in her mind. She married once, but doesn't really know how that marriage ended. After a decade and a half of this "lost life," as Jennifer calls it, she moved back in with her sister. "Finally, whether with professional help or out of desperation, my sister said to me, 'Jennifer, I am moving and I am not going to tell you where I am going. I do not want you to contact me ever again.' Through the haze, I somehow understood that I had come to the end of the line. I remembered a friend who had once said to me, 'When you are ready, come to me and I will take you to a home where you can get better.' I found her and she took me to a home for drug addicts, and I lived there for five months and got on the road to recovery."

Five years later, Jennifer is an enthusiastic participant in Narcotics Anonymous, is living with a recovering addict, and is putting one foot in front of the other, still learning to build her life one day at a time. She learned photographic skills while at the home and is holding down a job, accomplishments she is still in awe of. "To get up in the morning at the same time every day is still so weird, but I am doing it and it's great!" she said. In a further unexpected twist of fate, Jennifer has become the wise member of the family. She marveled: "My sister and mom both come to me now for advice."

Jennifer's story of sibling rivalry underscores the importance of treating children equally before, and after, divorce. While it is not always easy, and because human nature sometimes allows a parent to prefer one child over another, it is still vital to a child's growth for him or her to have at least the same set of rules as the preferred child. It also helps for the parent to spend an equal amount of time with each child, minimizing favoritism.

The Child as Parent to the Parent

Thinking of oneself as a potentially giving parent is an important step toward emotional growth in childhood. Children cuddling dolls, or their baby brothers or sisters, are rehearsing for adulthood, just as they are when they're being mother's or daddy's helper. Such activities can even act as springboards toward competence and growth.

If, however, the well-being of a parent becomes a child's responsibility, and the child's dependence on the parent is distorted, the roles are reversed. In some cases, the child suffers from guilt and obligation, a one-sided bond that traps the child into caring for the parent. The child is thus prematurely transformed into an equal in the parent's view, and the parent relates to the child as to a member of his or her own generation.

You may ask if there is anything necessarily wrong with that. Children might indeed like to be elevated to the adult world prematurely. But let's see what actually happens.

The nearly universal image ACDs share is that of their father driving away from the house for the last time. The child often projects his or her own loneliness onto the absent parent and often thinks about him or her with concern. In an effort to compensate for that loneliness, we see children traversing great lengths to be fair to both parents, trying to be completely impartial in giving their attention and affection. If one parent gets two kisses, so must the other. Lauren, whose story was told in chapter 3, and who didn't see her father for almost ten years, translated her loneliness into the fantasy that when she grew up she would live in Denver, because it was geographically halfway between her two parents.

In the following story, we'll learn about Jennie and how she became a caretaker for her mother when she was just five years old. How her mother elicited this behavior is an example of just how distorted family relationships can become when roles are reversed.

JENNIE: HOW DID I BECOME MY MOTHER'S KEEPER?

Jennie, like a good parent, set aside her own goals until her child got better. The only twist is that Jennie's child was her mother.

> Jennie was only five years old when she first felt responsible for her mother. "I started to fantasize when I was five that I was going to be a doctor and buy my mother a house and take care of her so that she could be happy," she said. Her parents separated when Jennie was eleven. Jennie was not aware of her parents' problems—her mother had been physically abused by her father—but she knew that home was not always a happy place.
>
> Her father's childhood was crisscrossed with trouble. His par-

ents died when he was five, and before his adult half sister was awarded custody, he spent some time in abusive foster homes. He brought with him what he knew. As a grown-up, he demonstrated his love for the family by being responsible financially, but he thought nothing of being physically abusive.

In piecing together her early years, Jennie discovered that her dad feared that his wife was being unfaithful. This fear became magnified when he was drinking. He once found his wife in the back of the car with one of their bowling buddies. Jennie's father thought she had been necking with the man, and he became convinced that she was playing around. He beat her up and put her in the hospital. His favorite insult for her from then on was "you two-bit whore."

It's difficult to construct a true picture of Jennie's mother, because Jennie was so tied to her psychologically that her opinions have been colored. She has problems in assessing her father, because, since she was a small girl, she has heard her father referred to regularly as "an asshole" or "that fucker."

After the divorce, Jennie and her mom moved to the West Coast. Her mom took jobs as a waitress while Jennie took care of the house. She listened to her mother's problems, and helped her mother with her dating problems. Jennie washed and ironed her mother's clothes, and even hand-washed her mother's underwear. "I became a very good housekeeper," she said.

"What about *your* life?" I asked Jennie.

"My life was on hold. I could not really address that until my mother became happy," she answered. Jennie had two older brothers, and by the time they came to the coast, they were old enough to be on their own. They were unwilling to buy into the "Let's help Mom" lifestyle, so Jennie was it.

Despite the burdens she carried, Jennie was a good student, working toward her childhood fantasy of becoming a doctor. While in medical school, Jennie became aware of a strange anomaly: "You must understand that all medical students think they have all the diseases they are studying. If you study tuberculosis, you start coughing. If it's heart disease, your left arm and chest hurt. I was different. I never went through that. Instead, I always thought of Mom, I almost became Mom, and I thought my mother had those diseases because she was always having assorted symptoms. Her back aches, and she gets muscle spasms all over, and she can't lose weight. She would get headaches, her liver hurt, her stomach wasn't right. And she was tired a lot.

"My worry about her escalated because I had a couple of

dreams about her dying." Jennie arranged a physical examination for her mother with one of her professors. His findings shocked her: "Your mother has some minor physical problems, but what's really wrong with her is that she is not willing to care for herself."

"The news was like a lightning bolt from the sky," Jennie said. "First I was livid with him for telling me that. There *had* to be something wrong with her. But there wasn't. Then I realized the truth. She used her symptoms to get me to jump through hoops. She wanted to be waited on and she wanted attention. The truth was staring me in the face."

Why did her mother's prognosis come as such a shock to Jennie? "Because if she were healed she could love me the way I thought that she should have loved me and never did. If there was nothing wrong with her, maybe she just didn't love me." The doctor's findings had much more impact than a physical diagnosis. They provided the treasure map that showed where Jennie's childhood was lost: "It was a bitter pill to swallow. When I did, I started to lead my life for *me*."

Jennie's story illustrates that there is no end to the variety of things children will do to breathe life into the parent so that he or she can become the parent they need. Children may even become sick in an effort to invite the care they need by becoming more needy than the parent. Fawn, for example, came down with a rare childhood blood disorder at age six that required hospitalization. "I am sure I managed to get sick to distract my mother from her own unhappiness over the loss of the love to which she felt she was entitled," she said. "I had to do something drastic to get my parents' attention." Fawn had to be near death to accomplish that result. "Part of the reason that I got sick was because I could not decide how I could love my mother so much and love my father, too." By being sick she brought her warring parents together in a fragile truce and reduced her own stress.

Children are inadequately equipped to be caretakers. They can assist parents, but they ought never to have to carry the full weight of adults. Parental responsibility is not something that can be taken on suddenly, it must be learned via practice and over time.

THE DEATH OF CHILDHOOD

We cannot stay children forever. The death of childhood is a necessary loss. For the girl, the realization of that loss used to occur when, having walked down the aisle on her father's arms, she was given to her husband in wedded bliss. Although that moment was tinged with love, fear, and misgivings, the ceremony marked her transition to being an adult in charge. Today, with emancipation occurring earlier and marriage later, other events have taken the place of that rite of passage. The result is that girls may be better educated, hipper, and much more sexualized at an earlier age. Boys may be taller, stronger, smarter, and more well informed.

In divorced families the death of childhood is most often a premature one. By virtue of the split, the children become either more important or less important to each parent than they had been before. If the child becomes elevated by one or both parents to friend or caretaker, the price of that promotion is the loss of childhood, the loss of security, the loss of having a parent to turn to.

In movies, we've watched a number of fathers going off to war instruct their young sons about the changing of the guard: "Son, you are the man of the house now. Take good care of your mother." The poignancy of that moment rarely leaves the viewer dry-eyed. All of us feel the pain of a boy having to give up his birthright to childhood in order to rise to the monumental challenge of wearing his father's shoes.

Richard Jenny, who talks of his family's split in his stand-up comedy act, parodies this absurdity: "Sure, Dad, no problem. I'll take over. I have no wheels, no driver's license, no job, but I'll be the man of the house. I'll come home from school, put my feet up on the coffee table, and demand, 'Bring me my Ovaltine, woman.'"

Growing up takes several decades. Having to grow up suddenly leaves ACDs to operate without the needed learning. Mistakes made as a result come back to haunt them. These may include bad marriages, unplanned children, or the loss of an education or career.

Brother and sister relationships can indeed go far in maintaining a sense of family. Sometimes just knowing that someone else is sharing your pain is enough to allow you to face the challenges ahead. Parents should encourage their children to *be* children, with one another and with themselves, to help bridge the gap between intact family and broken family. Then, and only then, can the wounds of divorce begin to heal.

HEALING JOURNAL EXERCISE: SORTING OUT RESPONSIBILITY AND RESENTMENT

Growing up by leaving home is sometimes painful, but it is a normal journey toward adulthood. But growing up at home, staying at home, and becoming a substitute mother or father is an emotionally messy way of becoming an adult. Our emotional ties are confused, our loyalties are mixed, we feel trapped, powerless, and helpless because we sometimes despise the very people we love. Until we sort out those feelings, learn to understand them, and file them away consciously, we cannot outgrow them. Let us turn to that work now.

Some of those feelings may still play themselves out in your life today, and may be directed toward your spouse or your children.

Look over the following statements and check the ones you recognize as a part of your emotional portfolio.

_____ I feel that other people's feelings are my responsibility.
_____ I feel that other people's behaviors are my responsibility.
_____ I really don't like it when I have to consider other people's feelings when I make a decision; let them take care of their own feelings.
_____ I avoid responsibility for other people at all costs.
_____ I sometimes feel that there is nothing I can do.
_____ I sometimes feel that I am not able to do anything, that I pretend to know what I am doing.
_____ I secretly yearn for someone to come and take care of me.
_____ Life feels too hard, and some tasks seem insurmountable.
_____ I often resent the responsibilities of being a wife/husband.
_____ I often resent the responsibilities of being a mother/father.
_____ I secretly express these resentments by neglecting my spouse or my child.
_____ I yearn to be free of my family responsibilities.

If you put checkmarks beside two or three of these statements, you have unfinished business with your past that may need more attention than this book can provide. You may need to draw off the poisons from the past before they poison your life. You do not want to repeat your parents' lives, and you do not want to deal with family in the way your family dealt with you. Therefore, you need to free yourself from past relationship patterns and form new ones that allow you to be your best.

SORTING OUT FAMILY FEELINGS

If you were the child who was parented by a sibling, you transferred a lot of your natural parental attachment to a source that was too young herself or himself to be a complete parent. Your sibling, too, was growing up. *In order to complete his or her maturing, he or she had to leave.*

If you were the parented one and you resented the parental sibling for going away, recognize that those feelings do not belong to your sibling. You may question this statement, but your siblings do not deserve your feelings of resentment. If you could express your feelings, you might say, "I didn't receive the love or the attention or the care that I should have, *and no one has acknowledged that!*" If anyone deserves resentment, it is the adults in your life. Again, these adults may not have set out to hurt you. Still, your true feelings need to be spoken and acknowledged. Once they are acknowledged they can be put away, and healing and growth can begin. You are old enough today to be able to articulate those words. And you can do it!

One thing you will gain from working through this chapter is perhaps that you will be motivated to mend tattered relationships with brothers and sisters. The rough edges may no longer take their toll on your heart. The following exercise will allow you to come to terms with some of those relationships. You will find value in considering the following.

This is a powerful exercise in sorting out your feelings about your sisters and your brothers from those you have toward other family members. Even if no current relationship exists with those other family members, you may be carrying a residue of unfinished emotions in your heart.

Reminder: Although it may seem like some of these exercises have overtones of blame, they are not intended to create blame toward anyone. If blame emerges, anger is not far behind. If you can get in touch with the anger, perhaps you can also get in touch with the sadness behind the anger. It's time to release; it's time to heal.

HEALING JOURNAL EXERCISE: SORTING OUT YOUR FEELINGS

In your journal, write a letter to each sibling, but do not mail it. Tell each one how you feel about him or her today and how you have felt about him or her in the past. If your sibling has been generous with you, express your thanks. If he or she has been selfish with you, express this. Do not hold back. Be sure that you have a box of tissues next to you, because there may be a lot of tears. There usually are.

Read the following only after you have completed the letter writing. You will need highlighters in two colors.

Take each letter and change the salutation. Instead of "Dear Susie," alter the letter to read "Dear Mom" or "Dear Dad." Leave the body of the letter as it is, and reread the letter as if you had written it to your mother. Highlight with one color those statements that fit your mother. Then repeat the process and highlight with the other color the statements that fit your father. I believe that by doing this you will gain a greater understanding of your feelings and to whom those feelings may belong. You may want to share this book and copies of these letters with your siblings, if that is appropriate. You are now in a position to see more clearly, to start to release the unwanted feelings, and, if appropriate, to create good sibling relationships.

The Secret to Good Sibling Relationships

You are all adults today. You no longer have to wear the robes and roles that you wore as children. Each of you now has enough information to prevent the return to childhood, bringing your relationships up-to-date. Discuss with each other what you learned by reading this chapter and identify the circumstances that distanced you. Recognize that each of you did the best you could growing up. Set aside the blame and the bad feelings and start anew. It is a worthwhile endeavor. Create the sibling relationships you want.

If you are compatible and share interests, that's all the better—but it is not necessary. Love and caring are most important. You will find, as have so many other ACDs, that love will emerge if you allow the muddy waters to recede.

If all else fails and some of the relationships cannot be repaired, you will have done your work, and you can put this part of your life to rest. You will be more complete for having done so.

5

Surviving in a Hostile Environment: Drinking and Drugs

Like adults, children turn to drugs to relieve stress, to have fun, and to achieve social acceptance. They also turn to drugs to drown out insecurity, fear, and sadness. Drug use is frequently the sign of youth's rejection of moral and social values of the system under which they live. As parents play an increasingly smaller role in their children's lives, a cohesive, powerful peer subculture that is recognized by both youngsters and society at large moves in to fill the void.

ROBERT SCHWEBEL

Although experimentation with drugs typically starts in adolescence—an unstable period at best—all such experimentation does not lead to addiction. ACDs tell us that the breaking home did, however, cause them to turn to alcohol and other drugs. Many ACDs needed the quieting effects of drugs and alcohol to help manage their emotions, protect their budding identity, and hide from the conflicts of a divorced home. They also supplemented their minimum daily requirement of love in this way.

Other obsessive/compulsive behaviors also helped some ACDs create an illusion of control and predictability, and reduce anxiety in their lives.

What happens when an ACD is also an ACA (adult child of alcoholic)? This chapter will look at the parallel issues of these two groups. Through it all, the indomitable human spirit of ACDs shines through. Despite heavy odds, many pull themselves out of the clutches of their addiction, to build a new life of pride and accomplishment.

ACDs: THE HOOKED GENERATION

"Are you looking for more people to interview?" asked Sari, an ACD whom I interviewed a few months back.

"Yes, I am still interviewing," I replied.

"I can get you as many ACDs as you like. I'll just make an announcement in my twelve-step group. It is full of ACDs."

I declined her generous offer, because I did not want to use a source with such an obvious slant toward addiction. However, I was soon to discover that ACDs, driven by the need to protect themselves during unhappy times, often fall prey to regular use of substances. "When I did not want to hear one more bad thing my parents said about one another, I got drunk," said Mike, who started drinking soon after his home broke up.

"My dad didn't understand me and my brother," recalled Heather. "He either treated us like little kids, or he left us alone in his apartment while he went out on a date. We had nothing to do but watch TV. He had a pretty good supply of booze, and my brother and I took advantage of it."

Compulsive behaviors are evident among many ACDs. Often they began as ritualistic and habitual and later became fully obsessive and compulsive.

Among the ACDs I interviewed, I found the following variations:

- Kit was an exerciseaholic.
- Julia was a shopaholic.
- Louise was a workaholic.
- Josh was a rock-musicaholic.
- Kimberly became a sexaholic.
- Janie was a foodaholic.

- Steve was a religious-cult-aholic.
- Bob was a compulsive gambler.
- Jennifer was given to nail biting (more accurately, finger biting, because when there were no nails left, the tips of her fingers also fell prey to her habit).

Some of these behaviors went together hand in glove. "I thought about food and exercise all day long; I became obsessed with every crumb I put in my mouth," said Darcy, whom we will get to know later in this chapter. "When I was not thinking about food, I was exercising."

After such behaviors take hold, they become a driving force for ACDs, many of whom are the victims of more than one substance or behavior.

Why Some ACDs Turn to Drugs

What were the reasons most frequently given by ACDs for their use of drugs or alcohol? How do ACDs explain their obsessive-compulsive behaviors? There were many and various reasons: they provided relief, reduced anxiety, assuaged guilt feelings, and gave an illusion of control when the world seemed out of control. The use of marijuana appeared to help reinforce ACDs' courage. "After my dad moved out, my self-confidence was at such a low ebb that it was difficult for me just to show up at school," said Maureen. "When I smoked grass, I felt I was able to face going to school."

Narcotics may have been used to help conceal impermissible feelings, such as murderous rage or inappropriate sexual impulses. These narcotics may have been the best of the available choices—the lesser of two evils. The numbing effects of narcotics were also a means for ignoring contradictions in life.

Teens get lost in drugs when their defense mechanisms can no longer prevent unhappiness. Drug abuse indicates that more is needed to maintain psychic and emotional barricades.

Survival of the self is the highest order of business, whether you are a toddler, a teen, or an adult. Our drive for self-preservation and self-interest is usually much stronger than any tendency for self-annihilation. We don't run into fires; we run away from them. We don't jump out of airplanes (unless we have a well-functioning parachute securely strapped to our backs to guide us to the ground).

Maureen seriously questions whether she might have done something worse to herself had she not turned to drugs. "I had so much anxiety that there was a constant, loud noise in my head," she said. Her inner reality was in turmoil: "If I were to go to my doctor today and complain of the symptoms I had, I am sure he would put me on heavy tranquilizers." Her regimen of drugs took the place of a doctor's prescription.

Drugs and alcohol are, of course, not the answer to ACDs' problems. Nothing is said here with the intention of whitewashing drug use, and drugs are not the only way to escape from the postdivorce home, although the quick fix while waiting for life to get better is a powerful competitor. Some ACDs found the highs in achievement: Fannie buried herself in her books and became an outstanding scholar; Bobbie was a computer freak; Fred became a football player of note. Engaging in these activities, sometimes to great excess, was a way to assuage distress. They were, nevertheless, better equipped for life when they finally did emerge from childhood.

In the best of all possible worlds, the answer to any problem is resolution. The use of drugs of any kind only delays the inevitable need to confront the problem head-on and learn how to deal with it.

Becoming Addicted

No ACD took a drink or a hit on a joint with the notion that he or she would become hooked on the stuff. None intended to sign up in bondage to a slave master.

The first high, during a time of distress, promises a reliable and inexhaustible source of good feelings. The seductive availability of drugs and the fun they offer, coupled with a new group of friends bonded by this rebellious activity, makes drugs hard to fight.

Teenagers typically do not have clear insight about their drug use. They do not say, "Yes, I am doing drugs. I know that it is bad for me, but I do them because I am trying to stay sane and preserve myself." They cannot, without psychological help, undo the tangled threads of their psyche. What you will usually hear from teenagers is, "What do you mean, there is something wrong with drugs!?"; "Who, me? I do great!"; "Who needs that school shit, anyway?"

The drug, however, eventually becomes a moving force, replacing all other problems as the number-one problem. If any of the material in this chapter seems to apply to you, I suggest you return to your healing journal for some self-assessment.

HEALING JOURNAL EXERCISE: ASSESSING SUBSTANCE USE

Place a checkmark next to those areas that may apply to you. The answers will help you assess danger signs in your life. The choices below represent some of the typical symptoms of drug use.

_____ difficulty in thinking clearly and solving simple problems
_____ difficulty with managing feelings and emotions
_____ difficulty with memory
_____ difficulty with exercising good judgment
_____ difficulty with controlling behavior

How did you do? If you checked one or more items, answer the following questions in your healing journal about the use of substances or alcohol, or about obsessive-compulsive behavior.

- How often do you drink or use drugs?
- How much do you drink or do drugs?
- Do you drink or use drugs by yourself?
- Have you tried to stop?
- For how long did you stop?
- How many times have you stopped?
- Why did you return to it?
- Why did you start to drink or take drugs?
  (List as many reasons as you can.)
- Are those reasons still valid in your life?
- Do you have a habit that you have to engage
  in, whether you want to or not?

Look over your answers. Remind yourself that a shroud called denial may obscure the truth. It may try to convince you that your alcohol consumption is just for fun, or that toking on the weed is mere relaxation after a hard day's work. If your answers raised the least suspicion that the fun helps you avoid something you should be doing, or that the relaxation is becoming a substitute for life, pay heed to that suspicion. I can only open a door to the subject in this book, but I suggest that you get more help through one of the Anonymous programs, such as Alcoholics Anonymous or Cocaine Anonymous.

The next story illustrates freedom run amok in a search for limits.

DARCY: "THEY SHOULD HAVE ENFORCED THE RULES"

Darcy's tale is unusual because this petite, five-foot-two-inch brunette with a hesitant smile lived through an experiment with an alternative lifestyle—communal living—during the untamed sixties. But the too-much-too-soon freedom she spoke about, which left Darcy with the task of having to totally rule her own life, is a common theme in the stories of ACDs.

> Darcy was not yet fifteen when she ran away from home. She speaks of her mother and father as caring people. In the sixties, however, her parents moved the family from a comfortable suburban home in the Chicago area, and a traditional lifestyle, into a huge ramshackle ranch house in which ten other families shared an alternative lifestyle. The children were placed together in dorms, and all the parents' bedrooms were clustered far from the children's area. The parents laid down their authority and became "friends" to their children. Later Darcy's parents also cast off their marital bonds and, shortly after their experiment began, got divorced.
>
> "I had my first boyfriend when I was thirteen," Darcy said, "but soon I was with sex partners who were much older." Yearning for parental vetoes, Darcy invited a nineteen-year-old boy to move in with her. Heaven for a teenager? Apparently not. "I was hoping my father would stand up and keep me from doing stupid things," she recalled. She had what all teenagers *think* they crave: total freedom. But, as teens often do, Darcy went on a search for boundaries by becoming more and more reckless.
>
> For Darcy, *reckless* meant going to a park in a bad part of Chicago, where the "lowlife" hung out, and doing drugs and having sex: "They took us to remote places and they would do—whatever." Darcy paused with her eyes averted. "I don't like to think about it anymore," she said. Darcy's experiments went from bad to worse. She stole cars and was arrested. "It was just dumb luck that nothing happened to me when I hitchhiked."
>
> Finally, she and a girlfriend ran away. "We thought that the three hundred dollars we had saved would last," she said, her face darkening at the thought of the unpleasant adventures these two fifteen-year-olds had. Darcy finally settled in with a man who took

care of her, a laborer who soon moved her to Georgia. "I didn't know how to stop him from hitting me," she said. It was during this time, when she felt trapped and completely out of control, that Darcy became obsessed with food and exercise: "I became terrified that my body would get out of control, too."

Finally, Darcy either had to call her parents or suffer greater indignities. Darcy feared that call, but to her great surprise, her parents welcomed it and urged her to return home. "I guess they did love me," Darcy said.

Today, Darcy still fights her symptoms. She also suffers from episodes of rage that usually spring into being when she starts to like someone. Her anger always wilts budding relationships. Darcy is making headway with her therapy, but she knows she still has a long way to go.

The belief that a community of peers rather than just two parents can better prepare a child for life essentially created a vacuum of authority around Darcy. Such a vacuum is often present in the divorced home, where either the rules become relaxed or there is no one to enforce them. There are often not enough adults around to properly supervise and teach the youngsters life skills through day-to-day contact.

Isn't that situation similar to any home in which both parents work? Yes, there are similarities between the divorced home and the two-career family, but there are also profound differences. When both parents work, the rules remain consistent, and the presence, support, and controls of both parents are felt. A break in the parents' relationship compounds the problem because it implies a break in respect for the home as well.

SELF-CARE

Despite our ability to sense dangers around us, we are not born knowing how to take care of ourselves. Freud said,

> It would have been a very good thing if [children] had inherited more . . . life preserving instincts, for that would have greatly facilitated the task of watching over them. . . . The fact is that children . . . behave fearlessly because they are ignorant of dangers. When in the end realistic anxiety is awakened in them, that is wholly the result of education; for they cannot be allowed to undergo the instructive experience themselves.

In the first decade of life, the parents' teachings focus not only on physical skills, such as learning to drink from a cup and walking, but also on avoiding physical dangers, such as not playing with matches. In the second decade of life, and equally importantly, adolescents need to be taught how to care for their emotional, psychological, sexual, and moral selves.

It is not enough to know that if you run in front of a bus you may die; it is just as important to know how to handle obscure dangers in the realm of human relationships. The farther teenagers venture from home, both geographically and psychologically, the more they need to know about the perils of adult activities. Some of these lessons are absorbed by adolescents who observe their parents in any given situation, and some are learned by open communication.

Learning emotional and sexual rules can become more complicated when parents are divorced. For example, teenagers whose divorced parents begin dating again have, in a sense, had their own developmental tasks—the period of testing and exploring their sexual potential—preempted. The decision of whether to sleep with a new boyfriend or girlfriend is far different for the parent than it is for the teenager. But teenagers don't always accept this and often have great trouble in dealing with their parents' sexual activities.

What struck me most in listening to the stories of ACDs who were substance abusers was the loss of their childhood lessons in self-care, those lessons that most of us take for granted. They also lacked adequate ability to self-soothe. Instead of looking inward for the answers and for comfort, these ACDs as children and adolescents looked outward, and many still do.

Why ACDs did not absorb the lessons of self-care or why they threw them away is not totally explained by divorce. But it becomes evident that when teenagers don't feel cared for, they often come to believe they are not *worth* being cared for.

HEALING JOURNAL EXERCISE: ASSESSING YOUR SELF-CARE LEVEL

Is proper self-care an issue for you? Do you know which self-care skills you may need to improve? Place a checkmark next to those items that apply to your life.

_____ I can realistically anticipate danger in situations, and I respond appropriately to my internal warning signs. (This statement refers to physical, emotional, and mental hazards. Can you judge people or situations correctly and recognize relationships that are potentially bad for you?)

_____ I can distinguish between momentary pleasure and its harmful consequences. (This question underlies the basic rationalization of drug use. Are you truthful about the dangers of drug use and abuse?)

_____ I can renounce those pleasures that offer harmful consequences. (Can you say no to temptation? If not, do you avoid situations in which such temptation would arise?)

_____ I can measure risk. In doing so, I logically explore a situation through its probable conclusion and then decide if the conclusion is healthy. (Weighing pros and cons is an important part of basic decision-making skills. Do you weigh the pros and cons of a given situation before reaching a decision?)

_____ I take pleasure in learning to master risky situations. (Do you look to your own inner reward system for taking risks? If you are motivated mostly by approval, acknowledgment, or gratitude, you may not be taking appropriate risks.)

_____ I can withstand peer pressure when it conflicts with what is good for me. (Everyone has occasional difficulty resisting peer pressure. However, it is important that you believe in yourself more than you believe in your peers.)

_____ I continue to gain information about the world at large and my place in it. (The mature, healthy person expresses an interest in areas outside his or her domain, and welcomes information as part of the learning process.)

_____ I continue to develop the ability to be self-assertive and self-protective. I find ways to speak up and ask appropriately for what I need. (With this skill you are able to monitor healthy limits for yourself.)

_____ I continue to develop the ability and skill to choose friends who will not be abusive. (This means selecting *out* those people who hurt you, who do not respect you or your opinions, or who are abusive *in any way at all*. It means selecting *in* people who value what you have to offer.)

_____ I am regularly self-soothing in an appropriately self-nurturing way. (This means that when you are feeling distress, you are able to calm yourself. You are able to soothe yourself in a convincing fashion. For example, "I may not like the fact that this relationship [or job] didn't work out, but I am going to be all right anyway. I know that I have to make some mistakes in order to grow. I will not use these lessons as ammunition with which to beat myself up.")

Select two checked items from the above list. Then select an incident from your life that most fits each item. Next, create three self-soothing statements designed to make you feel better. Repeat these each day until it becomes second nature to you to do so. This is a terrific technique for keeping your anxiety in check.

WHEN DRUG USE BEGINS FOR ACDs

JACK: WHEN LIFE STOPPED MAKING SENSE

The story of Jack gives us some insight into a young man whose love for a sport might have protected him from the temptations of drugs, had it not been for some life changes due to his family's divorce at a crucial time.

Divorce portends endings and beginnings. For Jack it meant saying good-bye to a special skill and hello to drugs. When he moved to a new junior high school, an important part of Jack's life was lost—one that, to a teenage boy, meant the loss of an image, a devastating blow to his self-esteem.

Though an exceptionally sensitive thirty-two-year-old man, Jack reverts to a teenager's lack of insight and teen phrases when speaking of the past. He names monotony as one factor in his starting to take drugs at fourteen: "It was the unhappy monotony of school: it was the same each day. It didn't seem to mean anything."

Jack had been a good student, and so his feelings about school, coupled with his growing sense of futility, represented a change of attitude. Jack's identity as a young golfer had been firmly rooted in his sense of self. He felt special: It was a source of pride, and it gave him a unique identity among his friends. His friends in school were chosen from the jocks, a drug-free group. Then, due to the divorce, he, his mother, and his siblings moved away. He had to leave behind a golf course and a group of friends who knew and liked him. Jack tried to maintain the sport after his family moved, but the closest golf course was just too far away. Personal pride was replaced by emptiness, and he stopped hanging out with kids who were involved in competitive sports. "It was easier to break into the drug group in school. They accepted new kids," he said.

Looking beneath Jack's words, we can see the real story. What Jack called monotony was really sadness, the sadness of a boy who lost something essential in his life. He took the drug route to feeling better.

ACAs and ACDs

ACDs who grow up with alcoholic or drug-abusive parents are at an even higher risk for doing drugs and alcohol than other ACDs. The child of an alcoholic who is also a child of divorce faces many additional problems. An alcoholic custodial parent becomes an immense burden. The alcoholic visiting parent does not present a day-to-day issue, but visitation may become a harrowing experience. In either case, the child fights a lack of dependability, predictability, and consistency.

In Table 5.1, attributes of adult children of alcoholics are compared with those of adult children of divorce. If you are an adult child of divorce *and* an adult child of an alcoholic, looking at these lists will help you gain more clarity and perhaps a new direction in working through the residue of the past.

The ACA portion of the table has been taken from Janet Geringer Woititz's book *Adult Children of Alcoholics*. The ACD portion is based on my own research.

You may relate more closely to the attributes in one column than the other, or you may straddle them. To clarify your place, do the following exercise. Avoid being critical of yourself as you sort through the subtle differences.

HEALING JOURNAL EXERCISE: ACA OR ACD?

This exercise will guide you in discovering whether you conform more to the ACA or the ACD pattern. Identifying your patterns is essential, because recognition helps replace feelings of helplessness with the determination that change *will* occur. You may find that, depending on the circumstances, you conform sometimes to one, sometimes to the other. If your patterns fall more squarely into the ACA category, I recommend you attend meetings of a self-help group called Adult Children of Alcoholics in addition to doing this work. Bear in mind that the fact that you are at high risk does not mean you have to fall into

TABLE 5.1. ACAs AND ACDs COMPARED

Adult Children of Alcoholics	Adult Children of Divorce
1. ACAs guess at what normal behavior is.	ACDs guess at what normal behaviors in romantic relationships are.
2. ACAs have difficulty following through on a project.	ACDs have difficulty following through on life's project.
3. ACAs lie when it would be just as easy to tell the truth.	ACDs present facts manipulatively to gain a desired effect.
4. ACAs judge themselves without mercy.	ACDs are highly self-critical but to a lesser degree than ACAs.
5. ACAs have difficulty having fun.	ACDs do not.
6. ACAs take themselves very seriously.	ACDs do not take themselves seriously enough.
7. ACAs have difficulty with intimate relationships.	ACDs have difficulty in allowing closeness in romantic relationships.
8. ACAs overreact to changes over which they have no control.	ACDs must control and create changes for no apparent reason.
9. ACAs constantly seek approval and affirmation.	ACDs constantly seek a reflection of themselves, whether it brings approval or disapproval.
10. ACAs usually feel that they are different from other people.	ACDs usually feel an inner sense of alienation.
11. ACAs are super responsible or super irresponsible.	ACDs also are super responsible or super irresponsible.
12. ACAs are extremely loyal, even in the face of evidence that the loyalty is undeserved.	ACDs are too loyal, or not loyal enough.
13. ACAs are impulsive. They tend to lock themselves into a course of action without giving serious consideration to alternative behaviors.	ACDs are impulsive, mostly about starting or ending relationships.

the habits of your parents. Many have proven that you can avoid following your parents' examples.

Who Is Most Likely to Become Addicted?

Perhaps Christine should have become addicted. She is at high risk on two counts: her father was an alcoholic, and her parents divorced when she was eleven. She talked with me about her drug involvement:

"In high school I tried everything—LSD, speed, alcohol."

"To what extent did you do these drugs?" I asked.

"I would get drunk and drugged out most weekends and during vacations," she replied.

"Would you consider yourself an addict?" I asked.

"No, amazingly not," she said. "I stopped the minute I found out that I was pregnant, and I have never craved drugs or done drugs since."

For the last forty years, researchers have tried to understand the riddle of who is most likely to become addicted. Experts are sharply divided on the portrait of the typical addictive personality. One school of thought favors a psychological model with predisposing factors: anxiety, depression, low self-esteem, an inability to control strong feelings, antisocial behaviors, and difficulties in establishing meaningful relationships.

Another group of researchers blames it all on chemical dependency. Addicts, according to this model, are no different from the rest of the population until they drink or take drugs. Then, due to a chemical predisposition in their bodies, they develop a dependency on the substance, which in turn can cause a change in their personality.

I believe that in only a very small percentage of cases is addiction purely an either/or proposition. In most situations, the two causes overlap. Taking to drugs is probably caused by a combination of factors, including heredity and environment, social acceptability, peer pressure, levels of emotional maturity, and self-esteem.

As substance abuse can take hold gradually, so can a relapse occur after a period of abstinence. In the next segment we look at signs that may provide guidelines for detecting backsliding.

Warning Signs of Relapse

If drugs were a problem in the past but seem to be under control now, ask yourself the following questions.

- Do you feel a heightened sense of unease?
- Are you denying that there is anything to be concerned about?
- Are you starting to worry about the sobriety of someone else instead of your own?
- Are you becoming more compulsive or stuck in the ways you behave?
- Are you becoming more impulsive?
- Are you feeling immobilized?
- Are you getting confused?
- Are you afraid you are losing control of your life?
- Are you thinking about drinking or doing substances "just a little?"

If you had any *yes* answers, consider a further evaluation. The easiest time to stop backsliding is at the first sighting of warning signs.

"You cannot help an addict until they are ready to help themselves" is the dictum of Narcotics Anonymous and Alcoholics Anonymous. Sometimes the willingness to help oneself is not apparent until that powerful force of nature, the instinct for survival, takes over. If the user is lucky, this occurs at the point of no return as reality drowns out bravado with the realization "I may die from this."

Maureen was plunged into that realization, and when she reached that milestone, she turned her life around and never looked back. With survival as her driving force, she discovered that her addiction, though severe and debilitating, was something she had learned, and that as a learned behavior it could also be unlearned.

MAUREEN: A CASE IN POINT

"I was at a friend's house, freebasing cocaine, for about a day and a half," Maureen recalled. "I went to the bathroom and looked in the mirror. No one looked back at me! In a shock I realized that the blank mirror was forecasting my death."

Maureen left immediately and hid at her home for five days, thinking that she would die. Finally convinced that she wouldn't, she got herself some help. After some time spent in therapy, she picked up her life where she had left off. She went back to school, and got a job. She hasn't touched cocaine or alcohol since.

Maureen rebuilt her life and is successful, on her way up in her career. She is sober, but she has a lot of work to do. That she has to catch up emotionally is brought home to her by the men she dates: "My love life is a mess, because men my age don't like to put up with my childish needs." She said, "I am retarded compared to my friends. I need more reassurance than anyone I know. But if I could kick cocaine I can do the rest."

Though quitting is a harrowing first step, it is not the most difficult time. This occurs when sobriety returns, when the bright light of day is no longer diffused by the wafting clouds of potent smoke. It comes when ACDs look into the mirror to see themselves naked, without the mask that mutes the harsh vision of their scars, of their inadequacies, of the raw search for who they are. It is a very painful time of self-reproach, and as they walk around they feel as if the skin had been lifted from their backs.

FROZEN PSYCHES

ACDs, like other recovering addicts, discover that with sobriety they return to the maturity level they were at when they first started using drugs. Thirty-year-olds may find themselves stuck at the age of ten in some aspects of maturity. All the distress they were avoiding, all the youthful conflict they felt, which was temporarily muffled by the effects of the substances, is alive, fresh, and hurtful once again.

Those who were using substances often emerged from their tunnels in their thirties and tentatively approached sober life. Often, they found they did not like what they saw. They became self-blaming and self-deprecating for the wasted years and for the missed personal development. They became their own harshest critics.

Unfinished Teen Tasks

Surviving the twenties can become an overwhelming challenge for ACDs. The twenties, writes Gail Sheehy in *Passages*, are supposed to be as "enormous as they are exhilarating."

> To shape a Dream, that vision of ourselves which will generate energy, aliveness, and hope. To prepare for a lifework. To find a mentor if possible. And to form the capacity for intimacy without losing in the process whatever consistency of self we have thus far mastered. The first test structure must be erected around the life we choose to try. Doing what we "should" is the most pervasive theme of the twenties. The "shoulds" are largely defined by family

models, the press of the culture, or the prejudices of our peers. . . . One of the terrifying aspects of the twenties is the inner conviction that the choices we make are irrevocable.

Sometimes not choosing becomes a choice. Will, whose life we examine next, is a young man with a willful, strong mother and a weak, alcoholic father. We witness his strategy in trying to cope with his panic attacks and other emotional problems.

WILL: STRAIGHT TO TWENTY-ONE, THEN PANIC ATTACKS

"I was always very straight," Will said about his years of drifting after high school, starting college, then dropping out. Will blames his mother for spoiling him and being excessively lenient: "She demanded nothing from me and my brother, probably to compensate for her guilt because she sent away our father."

Meanwhile, Will had little guidance: "I got no direction from my parents. No one drummed into my head the value of education." In this state, Will stumbled into his twenties feeling unprepared, helpless, and lost. Then, when he was twenty-one, three powerful events converged and nearly brought Will to his knees. First, his brother almost died in an automobile accident. Then he visited his father, who was hospitalized at the county general hospital. "Not a pleasant place," Will wisecracked. In a serious vein he added, "No one warned me, and I walked into my father's darkened room and there he was in restraints, in the midst of alcohol withdrawal." And finally, Will's uncle, with whom he felt a strong bond, underwent bypass surgery.

Soon after these events, when Will went to Yosemite, "my favorite place in the whole world," he started to feel what he subsequently found out were panic attacks. "I felt so anxious that I thought I was going to die. I didn't scream, but the ensuing emotional tailspin was powerful enough to make me feel like throwing up. I had to go home and stay there."

The attacks continued and a friend suggested that Will try Quaaludes. "They worked. They put me in this euphoric state," Will said. Having crossed the threshold of sobriety, smoking marijuana followed, and soon Will was getting high every night. He worked erratically, because "drugs were my priority. I was living for getting high in the evenings."

Will was thirty when he reached his lowest ebb with drugs, feeling helpless to quit because he feared the return of the panic attacks. The turning point occurred when a mentor came into his life: "He must have known that I was in trouble. He started to take me out to lunch once a week and would ask me questions like 'Where will you be ten years from now?' or 'Have you ever thought about going back to school?'"

Trying to think through a hangover haze wasn't easy, so Will started to think about answers while cutting down on his drug habit. Soon he quit. With his friend's encouragement, he returned to school in the evenings while working a full-time job, and now he is nearly finished with an undergraduate degree in chemistry. He wants to go on to an MBA. His pride shines brightly as he mentions his 3.9 grade point average.

Will's panic was unleashed not only by his fear of life's ending, but also by his feelings of uselessness. He had no direction, and he felt helpless in the face of these merging forces. "I never saw myself as a druggie, yet I became one," he said. "It never really fit for me. That's probably why I was able to stop."

The twenties can be a treacherous time if we are not equipped to face their challenges. Tasks of the teens revisited in the twenties feel out of place. Sometimes even later years witness the return to earlier passages. Such was the case with Kit, who didn't rebel when it was time for her to rebel. So she is rebelling in her thirties by starting to drink.

KIT: DRUGS AT THIRTY, A DELAYED REBELLION

Unlike Will, Kit was a bright, happy-go-lucky type of child, "the baby" in a family of five children. She avoided the pull of drugs completely until recently. With her petite frame and little-girl ways she looks no more than twenty, a full ten years younger than her true age.

Kit took her first drug on her thirtieth birthday. "I want to try marijuana next," she volunteered. "I have three to four drinks a week. It doesn't sound like much, but I do not like how sloppy I get," she readily admitted.

"Why did you start now?" I asked.

"I am rebelling against my age. I don't to want to be thirty. But if I am going to be thirty, I want to know what I missed at sixteen." She no longer feels like the baby, although at times she still feels very needy and often very young.

Perhaps Kit is rebelling against more than her age. She may be rebelling against never having rebelled. Back then she learned to stay the baby to avoid spankings at her father's house, where her grandmother ran the home through rigorous physical discipline.

Kit avoided the wrath of her grandmother and got everyone to take care of her.

So now, when she should be traveling another of life's passages, she is involved in what seems to be an untimely rebellion. Because she is thirty, we can hope that Kit's experimentation will be contained and that it won't lead her down the road to addiction. It doesn't have to.

ACADs: ADULT CHILDREN OF ALCOHOL AND DIVORCE

ACD/ACAs whose custodial parents were impaired by substance abuse spent their childhood worrying about their parents. I call them *observer children*. When interviewed about their feelings as children, they respond with information about their mothers and fathers rather than about themselves. These children watch the parent's antics; that's how they try to make sense of the world. They observe more than they participate. The parents' lives become the focus, and the children become their parents' historians.

One might think that the case of Madeline is an exaggeration, yet stories similar to hers abound. Parents often tell time by how old their children were when certain things happened. ACD/ACAs tell time by recalling how their parent was when a certain event transpired.

MADELINE: AN ALCOHOLIC PARENT DISTORTS
A CHILD'S WORLD

From Madeline, we learn just how distorted a child's view of the world can become when he or she is influenced by an alcoholic parent.

Addiction was handed to Madeline along with her morning juice and the afternoon vitamins. She has a snapshot of her mom posing in front of the kitchen window, the sill crowded with prescription drugs. She recalls once taking a sip from her mother's can of 7-Up on a hot summer day—only to discover that it was filled with booze.

Madeline and her siblings—six children in all from four different fathers—were given their vitamins after school. Then they were often told to get into their pajamas and go to bed. They didn't mind, because the sleep felt good. "I thought everyone did that until I went to live with my dad when I was twelve," Madeline said. "He laughed and said, 'What are you doing in your pajamas at three in the afternoon?' I was humiliated."

It wasn't until much later that Madeline found out what her vitamins really were: "I was working in a doctor's office doing inventory, when I spotted our vitamins on the shelf. I felt pretty stupid discovering that what I thought were vitamins were Dramamine [an antinausea medication that produces drowsiness]."

In her mother's custody, Madeline and her siblings lived a sequence of strange lives, in a series of towns, with a string of men. "We never knew when we would get a new stepdaddy. My mom said that she married them all, but I doubt it."

The more isolated the children of a substance-abusing parent become, the more likely it is that they will absorb a toxic worldview. Madeline's mother was always highly suspicious of people, who she said would victimize you if they could. Others were always at fault: angry landlords who wanted their money; fathers who wanted their children; lovers who demanded fidelity. During a period that Madeline calls psychedelic, her mother's girlfriend threw them out the week before Christmas. This girlfriend, Madeline later found out, was her mother's lover. This was apparently the mother's only homosexual relationship. Madeline best remembers this affair because the children had to leave behind the presents under the tree and because the home was bizarre: "One wall was blue and white polka dot, one wall was black and white stripes, and the beanbag chairs were red." She did not know until much later the cause of their sudden departure: her mother had become pregnant while living with her gay lover.

Craziness can be contagious when the influence of the close-knit relationship is strong and when family relationships are isolated from others. *Folie à deux* is the name given by psychiatrists to such shared craziness.

When Madeline was thirteen, she lived with her father and spent only every other weekend with her mother. By now her mother's paranoia was in full bloom. She told Madeline that the house in which she lived was haunted by the ghost of the landlord's wife. Her mother finally found the ultimate fall guy: the Devil. She said he visited the house and made her scribble his plan to capture souls. Heavily influenced by her mother, Madeline herself witnessed the Devil's presence when she saw boots make their way through the house without the benefit of anyone wearing them. She swears she also saw her mother levitate two feet above the bed in the middle of the night.

Madeline survived this surrealistic time. Fortuitously she and her sisters all had responsible fathers. From what Madeline could piece together, these fathers apparently chased after their children and, from time to time, succeeded in regaining custody of them. Although Madeline had to overcome her mother's hatred and fear of her father, she nevertheless admits that he provided a stable home for the balance of her growing-up years.

When she struck out on her own, Madeline started to repeat her mother's life: she had her own heavy episodes with alcohol, and married a hopeless drunk at eighteen. With her second husband, at age twenty, she found her way into a strict religious cult. Though she could not tolerate the cult's view of women as subservient to men, her time in that cult helped her quit drinking.

Madeline has a driving need to become whole and to remain healthy. She is doing this for her children now, but I trust that, with time, she will also do it for herself.

Madeline is still readjusting her picture of the world, a picture based on her mother's perceptions. She is rebuilding her twisted self-image, which bears the marks of her mother's drunken insults, unfair criticism, and distorted labels. She is trying to dislodge her expectation that the people she loves will become unpredictable and confusing.

When the parent is paranoid, the child's world is more dangerous. When the parent acts mad, the child's world becomes desolate. Despite the Roman saying *in vino veritas*, I don't believe that wine brings out the truth, that true feelings emerge when the brain is soaked in alcohol or something more potent. I believe that when the body chemistry becomes indisposed, so do objectivity and judgment.

HEALING JOURNAL EXERCISE: FORGIVING YOURSELF

This exercise is for ACDs who are in recovery or have recovered from substance abuse or other addictive behaviors. Its purpose is to make peace with the burdensome memories of excesses. You may have done work in this area, but a review may uncover another layer that needs handling.

Have you worked with your body? Your body has its own memory. To make peace with past memories, it's important to create forgiveness toward yourself and toward others.

Forgiveness cards. On three-by-five cards describe an incident about which you feel regret or shame. First write a brief summary of what happened. Then write:

Am I willing to forgive myself for _____ *[name the incident]*?
If the answer is yes, write:
I forgive myself for _____ *[name the incident], and I will stop faulting myself for having done that.*

Then see if that rings true. If it doesn't, there may be a need to complete something. In that case write:
One thing I need to do before I forgive myself is _____.

Then ask yourself, Am I willing to do that? If you are, go ahead and do it, and then forgive yourself. Once the process is completed, take the card to a safe place where you can make a small fire, like your backyard or the kitchen sink, and burn the card. This little ritual will complete the process of letting go of a part of your past that you no longer need.

FEELING BETTER OR FEELING LESS BAD

It's important to realize that the same motivation that moves you to achieve your best can also steer you down a self-destructive path. Quite simply, the bottom line about what motivates us is this: *we want to feel better or to feel less bad.* The Dalai Lama, the spiritual leader of millions, touched on this point at the beginning of his first address in the United States in several decades. To this gathering, all expecting exceptional wisdom from his eminence, he said, "We are more alike than we are different: we all want to feel good and we all want to avoid feeling bad." The truth is simple. We all want to feel good. We all want to feel less bad.

Let's see how you manage periods of feeling bad. Write in your healing journal:
One way I manage feeling bad is _____.
Another way I manage feeling bad is _____.

We can learn to create natural, drug-free good feelings, but we must harvest them from our achievements, our personal victories, our self-mastery. When we earn our highs, our brain responds to our victories by pumping out the chemicals of reward, the endorphins. It's important to accept that we cannot expect to feel good all the time. Nature will not constantly activate the pleasure center. When the pleasure center is stimulated by learning and achievement, its rewards are slower acting, but they don't exact the price that artificial chemicals do.

HEALING JOURNAL EXERCISE: CREATING GOOD FEELINGS

In the following exercise, you will learn how to create behaviors and activities that feel good. With your eyes closed, recall a time when you felt good without the aid of chemicals. Recall it in great detail—what you did and how you did it. Did something you achieved make you feel good? Notice whether you want to credit someone else with making you feel good. That is not what we are looking for. In this exercise, the more specific you can be, the better the results. Then, when you find such a time, become aware of why you felt good. Then complete each of the following sentences in three different ways.

One thing I did that made me feel good is _____.

One thing I achieved that made me feel good is _____.

One piece of life mastery that made feel good is _____.

If you have no trouble completing this list, you have come a long way in taking charge of your feelings. If you have problems with it, then, based on what you *wrote*, complete this sentence in three different ways.

One thing I need to do more of to give me feelings of accomplishment is _____.

Waiting for Life

Some ACDs live life as if they were in between, or waiting for something. They may feel like they are between jobs, waiting for a better one. They may feel like they are between relationships, waiting for a better one.

Life is what happens while you are in between, waiting for life to happen.

Life is what happens while you are waiting to get better.

Life is what happens when you are in transition.

Life is happening now.

Don't wait to get better to live life. Do not wait for a romantic partner to absolve you of your past mistakes. Don't wait for a boss to help you reach your potential. Although another's love can cleanse and sustain, and a mentor can help provide guidance, you must do your part. Today is life. Live it now.

As we have seen, ACDs fall victim to many things, not the least of which are addictive behaviors. *Addictive behaviors need not take a lifetime to overcome.* They yield to the sincere intention to lead life with dignity.

6

WHO AM I? ACDS AND IDENTITY

I keep creating myself; I am the giver and the gift. If my father were alive, I would know my rights and my duties.

JOHN-PAUL SARTRE

Me. Myself. I. Self. Ego. How you see me. How I see myself. How I think you see me.

What of this is our identity? How does a splitting family affect individuality?

It seems so deceptively easy to just be yourself, but in this chapter we come to understand why this is so difficult to do. We will briefly follow the progress of identity to see how our unique selves unfold. We will explore how our parents and families help this self grow. We will become acquainted with *identity builders*, factors that nurture growth; and *identity busters*, agents that thwart growth.

By tracing the influences that shape personality and sexuality, we will see how ACDs handle the special challenge of developing a sexual self in a disintegrating home. We will look at how to integrate and reconcile conflicting voices. And I will offer an Identity Bill of Rights, a reassertion of ACDs' right to be who they are.

HOW IDENTITY IS FORMED

A fully formed identity doesn't spring into being with a baby's first breath, although babies quickly start to reveal their unique tendencies, traits, and characteristics. For more years than any other creature on earth, almost two decades, children walk in the shadow of their parents and families. Then they are expected to emerge in their own right and begin to cast their own shadows.

By no means, however, are we passive recipients of influences in this process. Nearly from the starting point we begin to sculpt ourselves. We constantly sort through attitudes and behaviors around us, adopting some, rejecting many. We use as models our parents, brothers, sisters, peers, mentors, heroes, and even fictional characters. From the dawn of separateness, we interpret events around us, asking, "What does that mean about me?" We also rehearse behaviors as a forecast of ourselves in the future. What child hasn't played house, passionately arguing about the right to play mommy or daddy?

The drive to distinguish ourselves from others is important, too. "My older sister was real sweet. I was good, too, but no one paid any attention to me for that. I had to be the clever one," said Sophie, explaining how she gained a special sense of self.

The younger we are, the more fluid our identity, and the more we need the security of a safe harbor: the reflected identity of our parents. "My daddy is *thi-i-i-s* big," says the four-year-old boy to his new playmate, hoping to appear more formidable. "My mommy said!" says the child, taking on the cloak of ultimate authority.

Not all children are born with the same strength of character. Responsive parents and strong families provide a powerful safety net for faltering identities. Even children born with the potential to be strong pay a price for failed families. Their search for a replacement might find them drawn to highly structured groups, worthwhile or destructive, such as gangs, religious groups, or the armed services.

Identity: The Continuous Self

Having an identity means, according to the psychologist Erik Erikson, "to experience one's self as something that has continuity, and to act accordingly." This sense of self is not dictated by others, but is "a subjective sense of an invigorating sameness and continuity." He refers to the "unity of personality," which includes enduring values, cohesive attitudes, and dependable behaviors. We color all the roles we play in life with that personality.

Our favorite heroes provide a clear lesson in consistency. Whether we agree with what the heroes of the world stand for or not, they are clearly identifiable. Comfortable in their own skin, they act the same, regardless of whether they are with children or adults, with paupers or kings, with unknowns or celebrities. There is great comfort in knowing how they think, what motivates them, how they react to the world.

When our parents are our heroes, we gain more than comfort, because we do more than observe them. We emulate and idolize them; we revel in their successes; and we inherit the privileges of adulthood with clear choices. From their examples we know what we might choose to emulate or to discard. It is much more difficult to come of age when our parents, our patterns for being, are changing faster than we are growing.

Building a Sense of Self in a Divorced Home

There are many reasons why building a cohesive sense of self is a much more difficult task in a family split by divorce. Some of these are set forth on page 125, in a list of things I call *identity busters*, but two reasons are worthy of separate mention.

One reason is that parents, particularly mothers, go through profound psychological changes themselves because of the demands of the divorce. "Many women are completely different people ten years after divorce," Judith Wallerstein observes in her book *Second Chances*. Some women deteriorate because, having lost the identification stemming from their marriage, they lack the inner resources needed to adjust to single living and single parenting.

The second reason is that not only are the children the symbols of the failed marriage, but they are often the focus of continuing disagreement. For the child trapped in the middle, the battle doesn't have to be great to be traumatic. Just being the messenger—"Tell your father you can't go this Sunday"; "Tell your mother she is wrong when she doesn't let you . . ."—makes it hard to strengthen a sense of self.

Identity Builders

Identity builders are ingredients that serve to build and reinforce our identity. Some of these are:

- involvement of two loving parents
- consistency in values
- adequate feedback and solid boundaries
- appropriate models for male/female behaviors
- attitudes that confirm, assist, and support

- respect for each family member's uniqueness
- demonstration of respect for authority
- being acknowledged for special skills and talents
- religious/spiritual identity

At least a few of these conditions have to be present for a child to be able to build a reliable system of internal reality.

The Changing Identity

Our self-concept continues to be permeable for the first decade of our lives, with our family members being its most important shapers and movers. We may or may not take to heart the words "Don't do that"; yet we do take to heart their emotional content. Those words, barked in an angry, scolding voice, are likely to tell us, "You are bad." When a pleasant voice says, "Thank you for picking up your room; that is very helpful to me when I am busy," we are given a reason why we are valued, which is confirmed by the pleasant tone in the words.

During the second decade of life, the teen years, peers take over as the movers and the shapers—much to the chagrin of parents. Identification begins to shift; to belong to a group of peers, to conform to prevailing codes of dress or codes of behaviors—torn jeans, purple socks, or nose chains—is everything. Most teens will be partly upset that parents hate the way they look, behave, and speak; but at the same time they are perversely proud of their own modest declaration of independence. Some psychologists call this critical period the second major thrust toward the formation of our identity: we die as children and are reborn as adolescents.

In the third decade of our lives—sometime during our early twenties—we are supposed to step into socially acceptable roles as workers, parents, spouses, and so on and move toward our life's work through a purposeful identity. In the recent past, preparation for adulthood and maturation has become slower and more meandering. Perhaps today, in an era that requires more preparation for a complex world, and when life expectancy may soon touch the century mark, it ought to be considered normal for adolescence to persist into the late twenties. Certainly if any childhood trauma has led to a slowing of maturity, this would hold true.

Am I Thirty Already?

Thirty seems to arrive overnight. For young adults, but particularly for ACDs whose adolescence has been extended, thirty becomes a watershed age. If the answer to the question "Who am I?" is still actively being sought at this time, a surprising urgency to find an answer becomes apparent. Between thirty and thirty-two, the inner voices question us relentlessly: "What about marriage?" "What about having children?" "Am I doing my life's work?" "Why is everyone else married, or in a successful job or career, when I am still dating and trying to decide what I want to do when I grow up?" Many ACDs feel conflicted; their inner thrust toward establishing their lives confronts the pressure of their unfinished past, which urges them to wait until their emotional growth is completed. "I feel like I am several years behind my peers" is a statement I often hear from ACDs.

Two Ways to Arrive at Identity

You can arrive at your own sense of identity either by progressive evolution or by sudden revolution. Identity can be shaped by a series of small decisions and small events, none seemingly traumatic in itself; or it can be shaped by an internal earthquake, in which earlier aspects of the personality are shaken apart and reassembled into a new and unforeseen pattern. The latter is very often the experience of ACDs. Engaged in internal combat, ACDs may be besieged with doubts about established values and family expectations that are not necessarily consistent. Just about when the intensity becomes unbearable, choices emerge, the upheaval magically subsides, and presto, your *identity* springs into being.

ACDs have to fight the identity battle not only through the typical issues, but also in order to deal with their own special issue: fighting off the effects of identity busters. Next, let's return to the healing journal to explore how *your* identity was shaped. You may find it fascinating to recount the journey of how you became who you are.

HEALING JOURNAL EXERCISE: WHO ARE YOU?

Let's begin with a two-part exercise that's deceptively simple yet very challenging. Write the following question in your healing journal:

[Your first name] _____, *who are you?*

Then answer with:

I am a person who _____.

Continue writing until you've answered the question in five different ways.

If you find focusing on yourself difficult, use this trick: go to a full-length mirror, look at yourself as if you were seeing yourself for the first time, and then ask the question aloud. If still no answers come to mind, complete this sentence:

The reason I do not answer the question "Who am I?" is because I am afraid I will reveal _____. Remember, fears can keep you from telling the truth. Be courageous. Do not let your fears dictate your destiny.

In the second half of this exercise, follow the same procedure. In your healing journal write the following question:

[Your name] _____, *who are you not?*

Then complete the following sentence in at least five different ways: ·

I am not a person who _____.

When you have finished, complete this sentence with five different endings:

One trait I have is _____.

Look over your list and decide whether you *value* these traits. Then sort the list into traits you value and traits you do not value. If it is difficult for you to identify traits, ask friends to help you. This exercise, along with the others, will allow you to expand your view of yourself. The better you know yourself, the more easily you can accept and value yourself, or even change yourself.

HEALING JOURNAL EXERCISE: EXPLORING THE DOMINANT INFLUENCES ON YOUR IDENTITY

In the following exercise you will explore some of the influences in the development of your sense of self in order to deepen your understanding of who played a part in helping you learn about yourself.

In your healing journal, complete each of the following sentences with five endings.

One thing I learned about myself before my parents' divorce was _____.

The person/s from whom I learned that was/were _____.

Some of the people I imitated were _____.

One thing I was proud of was _____.

One thing I was ashamed of was _____.

Then repeat the exercise for each five-year segment of time after your parents' divorce. Then skip to today, and answer these questions:

- Who influences me today?
- In what way do I allow myself to be influenced?

These last few answers probably allowed you to identify pre- and postdivorce forces that shaped your personality. Note whether the people whom you selected to influence you today are different from the people in your past. Then move on to the next exercise.

HEALING JOURNAL EXERCISE: IDENTITY BUILDERS

Referring to the list on pages 117–118, name five identity builders that affected your life. Notice how each guided you toward becoming who you are today.

Perhaps answering the questions has provided you with a new angle on your childhood or adolescent behavior. Perhaps you understand better why you did things that were labeled bad or why you did things that were labeled good. You may see who helped empower you, and how you gained your strength of character. Discovering the connective threads in the formation of your personality will more than likely strengthen your belief in yourself.

Like Parent, Like Child?

Ira Progoff, the author of *At a Journal Workshop*, and an important force in advancing the psychology of self-healing, speaks of stepping-stones of inner growth and awareness. He suggests that seemingly disjointed events in our lives can be strung together by common patterns, which serve as stepping-stones to understanding ourselves. Such stepping-stones in personal discovery come from the drawing of comparisons between our parents and ourselves.

Whether our parents divorced or not, we do not necessarily want to own up to being like our mothers or our fathers. In fact, it is the test of adulthood to "be your own person." Having been hurt by a parent or having seen parents as weak or destructive because of the divorce crisis during childhood, ACDs often reject the idea of being like their parents.

"I am not like my mother," Tess shuddered. "My mother was

weak, and I vowed *never* to be like her. I am strong!" Tess proudly declared, pointing to her accomplishments: a master's degree in urban planning and a job with an architectural firm.

Bill said, "I would never treat my family the way my father did. If I thought I was like my father, I would really hate myself."

If you have some shared trait with the bad parent, you may deny large parts of your own personality, or if you admit them, you probably hate them in yourself. Neither attitude is necessary. Even if you sound like your mother, even if you are quick to laugh just like your father, *you still are not your parent*, and you are not apt to behave as your parents did. Even if you inherited many personality traits, those similarities are simply your starting point. All the factors that shaped you created a one-of-a-kind *you*. You are the most important influence in your life.

Just as it is difficult to see yourself clearly, likewise it is difficult to see your parents accurately. Because we look at family members through our emotions, drawing a good likeness of them is a tricky task. How do you separate the real person from the person whom you see through filters of love and admiration or anger and resentment?

In the following exercise I urge you to become more acquainted with your parents and to see how you may be similar to and different from them.

This exercise will help you see your parents outside their roles as your parents, though it may stir up intense feelings. For anyone, comparing oneself to one's parents raises feelings that may range from nostalgia to dread. For ACDs, who may have been torn too soon from their moorings, revisiting their parents may be a challenge, but a worthwhile one. At this point, you might ask:

- What useful purpose is there in having a keener sense of my parents and in making these comparisons?
- Why is it important to tell fact from fiction?
- How is this a part of the healing process?

Let me answer these questions in reverse order:

- It is part of the healing process to see your parents clearly.
- It is important to separate fact from fiction because, once you draw your parents' profile distinctly, you can also draw with great precision the line around your own personality.
- By completing this separation you snip the restraints on your

growth and development, and gain a keener sense of your true self.

In doing the following exercise, you will have an opportunity to see whether your eyes are clear or clouded. If your eyes are clouded by filters of emotion, a tearful cleansing may be the best remedy to clear them, so get the tissues ready. This segment was written for you.

HEALING JOURNAL EXERCISE: DESCRIBING YOUR MOTHER AND FATHER

The following sentence-completion exercise will guide you in describing your mother in the past and in the present, before and after the divorce. Answer regardless of faded memories, inaccuracies, or lack of information, because it's what you have in your heart and in your mind about her that counts.

In your healing journal, complete each of the following sentences in five different ways:

- *In recalling my mother, I think of a woman who was* _____.

- *In recalling my mother before the divorce, I think of a woman who was* _____.
- *In recalling my mother after the divorce, I think of a woman who was* _____.
- *My recollection is that my mother changed in the following ways:* _____.

- *In thinking of my mother, I think of a woman who today is* _____.

Then complete the following sentences with five endings.

- *One trait my mother has that I value is* _____.
- *One trait my mother has that I do not value is* _____.

Look over what you've just written, and then list the similarities between your mother and yourself by completing the following sentences.

- *The following are similarities between my mother and myself:* _____.

- *When I look at the similarities between my mother and myself I think* _____.

- *I do not like the following similarities:* _____.
- *The way I would like to change is* _____.
- *I value these similarities:* _____.

What are you feeling as you contemplate these similarities? Whatever the feelings are, let them be, and allow them to spend themselves.

- *The following are differences between my mother and myself:*
_____.

What are your feelings when you contemplate the differences? Whatever the feelings are, let them be.

Now, in your healing journal, complete the preceding sentences in reference to your father in five different ways. Again, you do not have to be completely factual, because the picture you carry within you is the picture to which you are reacting. Describe what you *think* he was and is like.

When you finish, look back over what you have written and let the effects of the work flow. Then answer these questions:

- What have I learned about my parents?
- What have I learned about myself?
- What new patterns have I seen that I had not noticed before?

Discoveries may be joyful, providing a valued bond, or they may unearth old resentments. You may also find that the illusion of similarities dissolves under the light of awareness. Remember, once you identify something in yourself, you can take charge of it. If you don't like it, you may change it or shed it. If you like it, you may keep it and you may value it more. It's only the unseen traits, the unexplored memories, that we have no control over. In any event, this work will help clarify and strengthen your sense of self.

This is not necessarily a speedy process; separating tangled psychological threads takes time. The process moves in its own good time.

HOW IDENTITY IS DISRUPTED

I call growth-hampering forces in the environment *identity busters*. In addition to divorce itself, many such forces are typical of divorced homes:

- fights over the children
- rejecting, unavailable, or distant parents
- overly critical or permissive parents
- overly attached parents; diffuse boundaries
- discarded lifestyle/changed beliefs
- banishment of certain family members
- distorted or absent feedback
- loss of family identity
- physical/sexual/psychological abuse
- shame over family members or self
- fear of loss/need to please
- addiction to a substance or a behavior
- parents' disparagement of one another

In the intact home, there may be implicit permission to be like mom or to be like dad. In the divorced home, not having that permission has to be dealt with. Faith told me, "Every day of my life my mother told me my father was a jerk. She used more colorful language, however. Why would I want to be like that?" But she inherited some of her father's ways, and this made Faith dislike herself: "I wanted to be different from both my mother and my father."

One ACD, Gail, in her search for differentness, became a minister. Others chose to be different by making sure they had a steady marriage, a successful career, a lack of dependency. Are you different? What does this mean for you?

HEALING JOURNAL EXERCISE: IDENTITY BUSTERS

In this healing segment you will look at your own identity busters and see how you coped with them. Did you have identity busters that are not included above? If so, list these in your healing journal.

The question to ask yourself in locating identity busters is "What stopped me from expressing myself when I was growing up?" Another question that may trigger recognition is "Why was I unable to learn who I was?" Then consider these questions:

- Were identity busters always part of your life?
- When did you first recognize them?

If you often ask yourself, "Who am I today?" you may still be forming yourself. The following list may help you clarify in your own mind the extent to which you have arrived at an acceptable identity. Check those items that apply to you.

_____ You flounder on your path.

_____ You avoid responsibilities and don't make commitments.

_____ You make frequent, sudden, precipitous changes.

_____ You are restless and have to keep moving from job to job, from one woman or man to the next, even from place to place.

_____ You invite others to control you, to define you.

_____ You have trouble forming and maintaining intimate relationships.

_____ You are drawn to strict disciplines that define you.

_____ You are always looking for the perfect way to live, the perfect woman or man.

_____ You step into the identity of others or attach yourself to others who seem to have a solid identity.

_____ You see yourself very differently than others see you.

If you made more than one checkmark, this area of work is one that may merit your attention. You may need to rethink your professional endeavors, or your life may need some fine tuning to best express who you are.

Who we are is a grand topic and a continuing inquiry: even in childhood we have fantasies about it. It is good to get back to those early ideas about yourself, because those thoughts contain some essential truths. Revisiting them strengthens and reunites forgotten or disowned parts of yourself. Complete these sentences in your healing journal:

- When I was a child, I thought I would become a _____.
- When I was a teenager, I thought I would become a _____.

Notice whether your life contains some of the adult activities you envisioned for yourself. See how your ideas about yourself have changed, and write down the reasons they changed. As you think about those early ideas, they may regain their strength and validity in your life.

Having done the work in this chapter, think about what you have realized. You may well be pleased by your answers. Some aspects of yourself may have displeased you, however. Write a short paragraph discussing new ideas about continuing to develop yourself and about fine-tuning your life to best create opportunities for self-development.

SEXUAL IDENTITY

An anomaly kept reappearing in my interviews with ACDs. The men tended to possess qualities that, in America, are more typically thought of as feminine, and the women often had traits more often identified as masculine. Divorce, especially when the children were in their teens, seemed to cause sexual-development issues to go awry, partly because identification with the appropriate parent became more troublesome. Girls emerged more tough-minded and sexually precocious in divorced families that split up while they were adolescents, while boys, who generally maintained a closer connection with their mothers, and tended to use them as models for behavior, showed more nurturing qualities and sensitivity, even more than their sisters.

Does growing up in a divorced home cause a child to overcome sex-based differences, or does growing up with divorce prevent the timely, full blossoming of masculine and feminine aspects of ourselves? I suspect that the latter is closer to the truth, but it is up to each ACD to decide for himself or herself.

Why We Start Out Differently

Even an environment carefully controlled so that boys and girls are treated equally can produce boys who exhibit more aggression than girls. The behavioral differences between boys and girls generally begin to show up soon after the second birthday.

Boys and girls become men and women by following different paths to sexual identity. Dependency is a comfortable part of female identity, as is intimacy. Boys, on the other hand, have to make themselves powerful and independent in the world, and many start doing this at an early age. Boys are fascinated by the men around them; they try to imitate them, because that is their promise of manhood. "They grow toward them," says Robert Bly, whose sensationally successful seminars about manhood have captivated men of all ages.

There is no question that we all have both masculine and feminine aspects, and that we should be free to express them. As boys can play with dolls, and girls with trucks, and still grow into men and women comfortable with their sexuality, so can women think logically and incisively, be good in math, and still be nurturing mothers and feminine women. Men too can be nurturing with their infants, as many of today's young fathers are, as well as artistic and poetic, and not be less manly. Today, in America, we are allowed to appreciate men who can show their feelings and openly cry.

Becoming a Man

In order for a boy to become a man, he must be included in a man's world. Freud said, "Little boys manifest a special interest in their fathers; they want to grow up like them, be like them. Boys eventually turn to their fathers for self-definition." Robert Bly claims that boys have to be in the presence of men because a silent exchange takes place between boys and men: "When a boy stands close to his father, something passes between them," something that allows the boy to learn "the male way of feelings," which "gives the son a certain confidence and knowledge of what it means to be a man." Bly says it is like emotional food being passed from the father's body to the boy's body. Sadly, he claims, there is not enough contact between men and their sons.

In primitive tribes, initiation rites were conducted to break the boy's powerful infant ties to mother and womanhood. Today boys have few rituals to become men, even in intact homes. But in divorced homes, where sons typically live with their mothers and have only intermittent contact with their father or a father figure, growing into a man becomes even more problematic.

Constructive Fathering

When a boy needs constructive fathering, mothering can't help him. He's outgrown it. As stereotypical as that sounds, boys are still tested, as they have been for thousands of generations before them. What happens to Johnny when he gets beat up by the class bully and his father is not there to say, "You just fight back," and maybe even give him pointers on how to win? Mother's well-intentioned counsel may be: "Johnny, you just stay away from that troublemaker." Even if she tells him to fight back, she cannot show him how to do it. Besides, boys don't want to fight like their mothers; they don't want to be mommies' boys! When the boy is taught mostly by his mother, he faces the prospect of learning the "woman's way." The later he learns the "man's way," the more awkward those ways will feel, and the task of becoming a man becomes that much more difficult.

What did ACDs do to create their personal rites? How did they supplement the missing male model? We are going to see how two ACDs did it, Mark through intuition, and Brad through the love offered by a mentor, his coach at school.

MARK: DOING IT ON INTUITION

Growing up in a home in which he was outnumbered by females—two sisters, a mother, and a grandmother—Mark hungered to be admitted into his father's aura of maleness. But his father's apparent indifference plagued Mark, and when the family split up, he felt deprived of even this infrequent contact. Though Mark was always a good student, his grades went on the skids in high school. Therapy offered a temporary respite, enabling Mark to better his grades and enter college.

Mark was still disturbed by what he felt was a silent curse on his manhood because his father did not properly acknowledge his achievements. At nineteen, Mark was driven to seek challenges: skydiving and sky jumping; a rigorous year away from the comforts of the known and familiar to endure the toughest physical jobs he could find, shoveling snow and digging ditches; living in a rented room far away from home, "faceless, in a world of men." Mark's trials strangely resembled the initiation rites of primitive tribes. Was it some ancient knowledge that was operating to thrust Mark toward manhood?

Mark, though temporarily satisfied now at thirty-five, still finds that he is at his best when he returns to self-imposed challenges when things get too comfortable. "I think that's how I keep the old self-doubts under control," he said.

The Father's Criticism

A boy may turn to his father only to face another identity buster: criticism. After divorce, the boy and his father may be more awkward with each other because of the estrangement. Fathers who find it easier to parent through criticism may increase their criticism at this time, driven partly by guilt toward the son, partly by the fear of losing the boy to feminine influence. The son's awkwardness may fuel the fire; the father doesn't like his perception that the boy is becoming a mama's boy. The father's anger toward his wife may be delivered through criticism of their sons.

A boy can accept and profit from criticism when it is counterbalanced by benign day-to-day contact, or when an occasional "Well done, son" is forthcoming. Without that, and with decreasing contact with his father, self-doubts may trail the boy of divorce for decades, as they did Brad.

BRAD: A COACH'S LOVE AND ENCOURAGEMENT

"I was a really good athlete, but I didn't have anyone to encourage me. On the contrary, I was always run down by my grandfather," Brad said. His grandfather, the patriarch he was named after, never forgave Brad for being the product of his favorite daughter's indiscretion after a wedding reception at which too much vino was consumed. The shotgun union that followed did not have a chance, and soon after Brad was born, Brad's dad was asked to leave the huge family home in which three generations lived.

"My grandfather kept saying: 'You no good bastard, you're just like your father.' I did look like my father, different from anyone else in the family." Brad's doubts about himself were expressed in a recurring nightmare throughout adolescence: "A deformed person was chasing me. Even though I was a very fast runner, my legs were like lead and they wouldn't move.

"I learned what a man's love can do for a boy when my coach came on the scene. That's what heroin must feel like! I was high on his attention." The coach's affectionate support and his belief in Brad paid off. Brad's endless workouts proved what someone's belief in a person can do: Brad won an Olympic silver medal in wrestling. "I know that it was my coach who gave me the power," he said.

Despite heroic efforts, mothers cannot be both mother and father to a boy. So the boy looks for a counterbalance to the female influence. Can that male influence be the boy himself, advancing to the role of the man of the house, as he is often invited to do?

A Boy's Dilemma: Feelings of Aggression and a Sexual Taboo

Without his father to model manhood for him, a teenage boy can easily become overwhelmed by his aggressive feelings. He may feel a lot of rage toward his mother, feelings that may or may not make sense to him. He also detests himself, if he is not brave enough to satisfy himself. Dan felt totally humiliated: "I felt like a complete zero; I could not be like other boys." When he'd get home, he would foist all his anger onto his mother "for not being the father that I needed."

The boy whose parents are divorced solves the confusion safely by pushing away all these feelings, becoming passive and frequently depressed. He often lacks energy and enthusiasm, and either retreats to his room or vegetates in front of the TV, waiting to grow up. So the tasks of late adolescence—a period that according to Erik Erikson is a "time of ascendancy" and "an essential bridge between childhood and adulthood"—are put off to the next decade.

Another dilemma that the boy may face is a belief that if he chooses to clothe himself as the man of the house, he takes on the right to be aggressive and sexual toward the woman of the house—his mother. The incest taboo is so strong that boys must suppress their mothers' sexuality at any cost, even if they have to delay their sexual growth during important developmental years. "I must be some kind of monster," the boy thinks with great shame if his sexual urges include his mother. One way he can solve this problem is by allowing himself the expression of his more feminine aspects, which do not clash with the incest taboo. Or he may turn to hostile, acting-out behaviors that he cannot explain.

Daughters of Divorce

What about the girl? Why does she grow tough-minded in the split home? There is nothing to prevent the girl child in the custody of her mother from trying on the missing daddy's empty shoes. It may feel strange at first, but the mother's neediness and the brothers' avoidance of maleness leave a vacancy to be filled.

The father of the intact home stands guard psychologically over the girl's vulnerabilities. The man of the house is often respected by other males differently than is the woman of the house. He represents the potential for anger and aggressiveness. He can fight a boy on his own terms. The teenage girl may fight the restraints that these qualities bring, but secretly she also feels protected by her father. When he is not there, she soon feels unshielded from the world and has to protect herself.

Divorced fathers, without a mother's presence, are sometimes confused and frightened by their sexual responses to their little girl who is now capable of arousing them. With an appropriate sense of sexual boundaries, they will do everything in their power to rid themselves of unacceptable impulses. One way they do this, and one that puzzles teenage girls, is to hold their daughters at arm's length, no longer wrestling with them or allowing them to sit in their lap. When they have these unsettling feelings, they are more likely to become angry at any other male who finds their little girl attractive. "Who is that stupid-looking boy?" they ask. "How can he show up at our house looking like that!" These are fathers' less than graceful ways of communicating with their daughters and validating their womanhood as deserving of protective boundaries. The mothers' point of view is different from the fathers'. They often do not see anything wrong with that "awful boy."

"I never could understand why my father one day just stopped being affectionate with me," Wendy said, feeling rejected. During visitation, men often feel the need to create a shield against the discomfort of being alone with their daughters by bringing along their girlfriends or other people.

Observing their mothers weakened by the divorce, girls of divorce often strengthen themselves by refusing to identify with this example of womanhood. "This will never happen to me. I will never be like her," they defiantly proclaim. "I got my MBA by the time I was twenty-one because I was never going to be financially dependent on anyone!" said Vicky. "I wanted to get married, but I decided to first provide financial security for myself," said Bev, who started a chain of ice-cream stores while in college. Determined that the same fate will not visit them, the girls also put up emotional walls, banish vulnerability, and become more controlling.

Other research has characterized women from divorced homes as solitary, lacking empathy, and relatively detached from interpersonal relationships. Adolescent girls often interpret the ending of their parents' marriages to mean that they must become more oriented toward themselves.

The Search for Father Replacements Via Sex

When their fathers are not around, girls of divorced homes become sexual earlier and with more partners. Looking back at the boyfriend she had at age thirteen, Melanie said, "I was looking for a replacement for my father." Thirteen-year-old girls' bodies may be able to have intercourse, and even bear children, but their psyches are far from able to handle the feelings that are aroused by adult sexuality. "I was a mess when I found out that my boyfriend was also having sex with an eighteen-year-old friend of his," said Dianne. "I was too young to handle it."

Many girls of divorce have difficulty saying no to sex because they have difficulty valuing their bodies. Girls' sexual behavior is also fueled by hunger for acceptance by males. Their teenage male counterparts are now the men in their lives and their guides for what is appropriate. They often emulate these boys and their more detached sexuality.

We must never underestimate the importance of the father in the growth of a child's sexual identity. All the evidence points toward the conclusion that for a boy to become a man and for a girl to become a woman, they need a mother and a father. The most surefooted leap into manhood or womanhood is accomplished with the healthy participation of two parents.

HEALING JOURNAL EXERCISE: A LOOK AT FAMILY SEXUALITY

Your family's sexuality can be characterized in many ways. Take a few moments to go through the following list of words to see which ones apply to your family. Please note that these qualities are not unique to the male or female side of a family, but apply to both areas. In your healing journal, write down each word that applies to your parents, and next to each such word write either *M* for mother or *F* for father. If some of your siblings were influential in your sexual development, you may also write their first initial. Not all pairs of words are exact opposites. If there are adjectives or descriptive phrases not included here that characterize your family, add them to the list.

puritanical	relaxed
secretive	open
hidden	evident
blatant	appropriate
ashamed/unspoken	comfortable/spoken
clear	diffuse
abnormal	normal
highly sexual	normally sexual
promiscuous	asexual

Then place your initial next to each word that describes you.

Now answer the following questions in your healing journal:

- Do you share more characteristics with your mother or with your father?
- How do you feel about that?
- Do have sexual problems?
- If you do, describe them.
- In what way did your family relationships contribute to them?

Your answers will enhance your thinking about your sexual identity.

RECONCILING YOUR PARENTS' VOICES

Probably, without realizing it, you've tried to reconcile your internal mother's and father's voices and merge them to reduce conflicting feelings about yourself. As an adult, you can release conflicting loyalties in your head and become free to have one voice—your own. To what extent are you still acting out of a need to either oppose your parents or to please them?

If you choose to live the way you do because of, or in spite of, your parents' dictates and teachings, they may still have too much voice in who you are. While it is appropriate to use them as your primary gauge earlier in life, when it is time to create your own life, you need to follow your own dictates. Of course, you may choose to adopt your parents' suggestions and make them your own if you decide that they are right for you. It takes time and patience to fully discover yourself.

Why You Continue to Struggle

Are you still struggling with your parents' controlling voices? Do you have a running argument with voices in your head about what you should and should not do? Without your even realizing it, those shoulds may be the stone walls you run into when making choices for yourself.

Part of being a rebellious teenager is defiance, or the game of "Don't tell me what to do!" When that rebellion spills over into adulthood, the game becomes self-limiting. If you avoid doing something you want to do just because your parent would also have wanted you to do it, you are still a slave to that game. By holding on to the game, you are also holding on to the relationship with your parent. So you may unconsciously fear that when you let go of the game, you may be letting go of the parent. Don't ignore this fear or dismiss it too quickly.

When we let go of opposing our parents we also recognize that our parents are not as smart or as powerful as we thought they were. This is the moment of truth of adulthood, and it is the moment when we stop feeling shielded by our parents.

If you haven't contemplated these ideas to any extent, it may take some time to recognize their value in your life. Their recognition, however, will become a freeing experience. Please consider opening up to these ideas. Let them take hold.

Once you have let go of defensive identities, you may feel more vulnerable, but also more open to change. This is important. *Once you let go of the need to oppose your parents, or please your parents, you can sort through your parents' legacy, adopt what you like, and throw away what you don't want.* You can select from a whole universe of new qualities, adopting those that have special attractiveness for you, or you can retain traits that are familiar and comfortable.

You know that your identity fits when your behavior, thoughts, and feelings harmonize. With consistency, you will not spend as much time suppressing and hiding parts of yourself. You will be willing to open a window to your deeper self to the people around you. You will feel lighter.

It is a freeing experience to discover that with the coming-of-age of our identity, not only do we gain self-confidence, but the childlike dependence or slavish rebellion we thought was our permanent companion vanishes. Alternately, without that sense of self, we have problems maintaining our boundaries and therefore our independence.

Freedom to be who we are springs from the following realizations.

- You probably have a better notion of who you are than you give yourself credit for.
- You do not have to be either the same as—or different from—your parents.
- When you allow yourself to stop needing your parents, you can choose to love them.

THE ACDs' IDENTITY BILL OF RIGHTS

The following rights apply to everyone, but they are sometimes overlooked in the midst of family upheavals. You were born with these inalienable rights, and you still own them.

1. As an adult, you have the right to be whoever you are and to define yourself as you wish.

2. You have the right to be mentally and emotionally healthy.

3. You have the right to be like your mother or like your father or like either side of the family and be pleased about it.

4. You have the right to be proud of yourself.

5. You have the freedom to choose your own destiny.

6. You have the right to break the cycle and have an enduring marriage.

7. You have the right to avoid your parents' mistakes.

8. You have the right to a relationship with each of your parents *without taking sides.*

9. You have the right to make honest mistakes and you have the right to recover from them.

10. You have the right to communicate all your choices to anyone.

HEALING JOURNAL EXERCISE: GETTING TO KNOW ALL ABOUT YOU

As we move into the last four chapters, which deal with love and romance, it will be helpful for you to think about your sense of self in regard to romance. Look over the following list of words:

marriage
romance
sex
personal relationships

Then, in your healing journal, complete the following sentence:

One way I know who I am in regard to _____ [fill in one of the words from the above list] is _____. Complete this sentence for each word in the list.

There is no final, definitive *you*. A healthy, confident identity is not unremitting. It is fluid, changing, and forever growing, although its foundation is firm.

7

THE ABILITY TO LOVE: ARE YOU LOVE-ABLE?

When I broke up with the first woman I loved, it felt like an anchor chain was being pulled through my chest. I felt I would die.
DENNIS, ACD

S igmund Freud spoke about love nearly a century ago in this way: "We are never so defenseless against suffering as when we love, never so helplessly unhappy as when we have lost our loved object or its love." Rarely does the unhappiness become more acute than when a child loses his or her parents. Love is so vital that the lack of it can actually make a baby sick, or leave a child mentally or physically stunted. To give and to receive love is to quell our soul's thirst for intimacy, one of life's greatest rewards. When parents' love ends in divorce, the child is taught that love ends. With that lesson, trust withers.

To help understand love, it is fruitful to look at the love bond between parent and child, and at its role in other relationships. What happens if this direct channel to the heart was shaken during the family breakup? Perhaps the result is psychic numbing—children turning off their hearts. Perhaps a damaged love bond leads to codependency, or lessened love-ability. The ACDs who will help us understand the intricacies of this topic are Dennis, who used sex to appease love starvation; Valerie, who tells us about her first encounter with real love and with obsessive attachment; and June, whose story informs us about a typical ACD's ambivalence towards monogamy. Because solving yesterday's lessons of love will help lead you to mastery of your heart, we will examine your love bond and love-ability, and see whether you defend against love.

THE LOVE BOND

As mother and father watch their miraculous creation emerge and take its first breath of life, they are enveloped in awe. Curiosity and the wonderment of birth slowly simmer into a powerful, enduring, and deep connection with the child: the love or attachment bond.

The joyous love bond is nature's gift. It is usually anchored so deeply in our infant hearts that its loss feels life threatening. Along with creating the pleasure of connectedness, it also brings a child a sense of ownership: "my mommy," "my daddy." Later, that first bond and the pride of ownership resurface in adult love with "my man" or "my woman."

The love bond provides the underpinning on which a man and a woman's love for each other can rest. It has many tasks:

- The love bond must be enduring enough to withstand temptations.
- The love bond must provide a resilient foundation that can endure the jolts and jostles of life.
- The bond's embrace must be flexible enough to stretch when separated by distance, frayed by illness, or tested by career setbacks.
- The love bond provides a sense of union, as if two could become one, though adult love can never duplicate the bond that starts with birth.

The love bond in adulthood and in childhood has similarities and differences:

- Infancy's love bond is created out of the greatest possible intimacy—oneness. It then grows, gradually but inevitably, toward separateness.
- Adult love is created out of separateness, and grows toward greater intimacy. Although *codependency* often means an extreme form of dependency, appropriate mutual dependency is an essential ingredient of enduring love.

- Childhood's love bond carries with it an end to dependency and eventual separation.
- The adult's love bond is characterized by a growing dependency and the potential for permanent togetherness.

The Birth of Adult Codependence

The love bond is injured in childhood if the parents divorce. It becomes injured because:

- The child fears the loss of love and becomes protective of his or her feelings toward the parents.
- The child feels rejected and unlovable: "If my parents loved me enough, they would work it out."
- The child's bonds with the parents, particularly the separating parent, usually weaken.

For the love bond to grow into adulthood in a healthy way, it must mature with the child as the process of becoming an individual takes place. During this long incubation, the bond thins, in preparation for being withdrawn. In the transformation from love with dependency to love without dependency, the love bond becomes transformed.

When this process is interrupted, the child arrives at adulthood with an impaired or immature ability to bond. *Often the development of the love bond is stalled, and the bond becomes frozen at the age of the injury.*

Codependency and Other Problems with the Love Bond

By their very nature, children are dependent. They must depend on the parent for survival. If the love bond is disturbed and dependency threatened, the child may feel imperiled and may, in fact, be in peril. As we have seen in chapter 4, children will do anything, even sacrifice themselves, for the nurturing rays of love or to help maintain their parents' competence.

The sudden impairment, or premature ending, of the love bond causes a childhood pattern to continue into adulthood—one that we call *codependence*. Of course, divorce is not the only way that codependence can be created. It can also come from growing up with other types of dysfunction in the home. But it is an almost certain outgrowth of divorce, as the high percentage of Codependents Anonymous participants who grew up with divorce will testify.

Codependency is not the only dysfunctional bonding pattern that divorce creates. Other common patterns that emerged from the ACD interviews include:

- the illusory love bond: it looks like an attachment, but it is not
- an aversion to bonding; an inability to form love bonds
- partial bonding; being more comfortable with part-time love relationships
- temporary bonding ("I am yours forever," but the definition of forever may be a week, a month, or a year)
- fear and distrust of bonding; an unwillingness to form a love bond

Are these styles of bonding familiar? You may recognize some of these patterns in your life. All of us go through periods in our lives when we are not yet ready to settle down. These patterns become troublesome when people are *never* ready to settle down, or say they want to marry, yet never form a lasting relationship.

SHUTTING DOWN THE DIRECT CHANNELS OF LOVE DURING DIVORCE

It is not only the parent that may pull back from the child during divorce. The child, and particularly the adolescent, plays his or her part in the distancing, too. The ability to influence, and to be influenced by, people is a key component of love. These influences are transmitted through the direct channels forged by the love bond to our hearts and minds. They carry rewards, punishment, love, and nurturance. Unhappily, these channels also become conduits for conflicting or poisonous messages. Caught in family wars, children often find it impossible to screen out only the unwelcome messages and allow the good ones to penetrate. Instead they block everything, the nurturance and teachings as well as the conflicts of painful reality.

DENNIS: HUNGRY FOR LOVE

ACDs often arrive in adulthood incomplete and feeling starved for love. Dennis tried to mold himself to the expectations of his mother and stepfather to gain morsels of attention and approval.

Dennis's love bond was severely injured before he reached age five. Torn between openly warring factions, he was twice surreptitiously spirited away by his father's family and taken to Canada, where his grandparents lived. It wasn't until much later that he pieced together the facts. He was apparently returned to his mother by court order at the end of this turbulent period, but this decision cost him his relationship with his father and his father's entire family. They disappeared until Dennis was sixteen.

Dennis didn't get the reassuring attention of his mother, which he sorely needed. He rarely saw her because she was busy making ends meet. She then married a wealthy man Dennis tags as a playboy, who brought into the home a robust social life and the people who went along with it. Dennis felt he was getting lost in the wake of all these new people now in their lives.

Dennis earned attention and approval by becoming a chameleon, assuming attitudes and opinions he thought were expected of him. As his individuality slipped away, he grew more and more distant from his feelings and lapsed into a frightening sense of alienation. In his teens, Dennis found a refuge from this estrangement from himself: sex. Physical intimacy became the organizing energy for his scattered self.

Sexual contact, he professes, performed incredible feats: "It took away fear and confusion, and balanced the 'shit' things in my life." When asked to explain, Dennis blurted out, with surprise in his voice: "Sex! Romantic, sexual love made me feel like I was valuable, there was nothing wrong with me, and I was this incredible human being. It's the only place I got that."

Beyond nature's ingenious design, which makes sexual intimacy exciting, pleasurable, and validating, for Dennis, sex was no less than emotional survival. There were only two things, he believed, that pulled him together and jarred him into life: the first was the kiss of the "princess," that fleeting first moment in the arms of a woman. "I had this big set of armor. Just at the point of making love I would open up and connect, then close up again." That contact was pure oxygen to a drowning man. The second activity that breathed life into Dennis was testing survival: "I never drove less than twice the speed limit, and played poker with drug kings and murderers."

But his addiction to sex was the focus of his attention. He slavishly fed his habit with a daily fix: "When I met a woman, I would perform a snake dance to get her attention and to win her over, and ultimately the most powerful thing—to get her to make love with me." Boasting, without a trace of modesty, he said, "I did it very well, and I could break through all barriers to sexual love in a short period of time."

To insure a daily supply, Dennis became a virtuoso in playing the field: "I had phone books dedicated exclusively to women. In the morning I would start with the highest-caliber woman, but I would settle for someone needy at the end of the day if I couldn't arrange anything else." Although his tone was one of telling knee-slapping "war stories," it was apparent that it was more than mere sexual escapades Dennis was after. His brand of sex-as-life therapy could not tolerate distance. His partners had to be fully there for him in order to receive the needed supplies: "I could not be with a prostitute. And if women split off—you can tell—I could bring them back and make them present."

I asked Dennis, "When you were not close to people, what was your view of yourself?" Almost before I could complete the question, Dennis's answer came tumbling out, revealing a man doubting his own existence: "I was not experiencing myself."

Were these fleeting moments of closeness akin to love? I believe that for Dennis, the reassurance of sexual touch brought him as close to love as he could allow himself to get. Still, Dennis tried marriage three different times, and each lasted less than a year. The ending of these marriages hardly made a ripple in his life, since the Dennis version of the love bond easily falls away. Dennis fleetingly touched the lives of countless women, and he assures me, "I loved them all."

Dennis is in recovery today, as he begins his second year of celibacy to regain control of his sexual behaviors. When I last spoke to him, he was gradually reentering the world of dating.

HEALING JOURNAL EXERCISE: SEEING YOUR LOVE BOND

This exercise is designed to help you visualize your love bond so that you can better understand how you relate to others. This sort of exercise works well if you record the instructions in your own voice. Following your own voice, the voice with which you are most familiar, is very reassuring. You may do the exercise either by closing your eyes and visualizing the love bond, or by drawing with crayons or pencils. Notice what responses arise in you and write them down.

First, choose a person whom you readily identify as someone you love. This may be your spouse, your child, a parent, or anyone else to whom you feel an attachment. Select a comfortable chair to sit in. Be sure that you do this exercise when and where you are not likely to be interrupted; when you sink deeply into the stillness of your mind, an interruption can be jarring. You may start the exercise here. (If you record the instructions, start here also.)

Close your eyes. Let your breathing slow and your body become relaxed. Allow your breathing to deepen. Release the tension from each part of your body. Focus on relaxing and letting the tension leave your body. Then, as you continue quieting down, see yourself as you sit there in your mind's eye. After you are comfortable with seeing your own image, bring into that picture the other person to whom you feel bonded or attached. Ask him or her to sit down across from you. Describe the person to yourself. What is he or she wearing? What is the expression on his or her face? Keep noticing the details of how the person looks sitting across from you. Now recall the love you feel for this person. *Feel* the love you feel for this person. Feel the love *more*. Feel that love as you sit there. Then feel the attachment. Feel the bond that ties you to one another.

When you are in touch with your feelings, try to visualize the bond that exists between the two of you. The bond may feel so real that you can nearly touch it. Try to touch it while looking very carefully; try to see the physical shape of the bond that runs between the two of you.

What do you see? Can you see the tie that runs between the two of you? Keep looking, and examine what you see. You may see it as a ribbon, as a chain, as a solid metal rod, or as something less physical, such as a series of clouds or a veil that envelopes both of you. The picture of your bond is uniquely yours. Accept what you see.

- What do you see?
- Describe the shape, the length, the texture, anything that you notice about the love bond.
- How long has it been there?
- Is the bond flexible? Does it bend or stretch? How far does it stretch?
- Is it an enduring bond? How long will it last?

When you are ready, rub your feet on the carpet—this sensation helps return you to a normal state of consciousness—and then slowly open your eyes. (You may stop the tape now.)

This exercise can be very powerful—one picture is worth a thousand words—so allow time to be with your feelings. Then review the questions, and write answers to them in your healing journal.

If you visualized your love bond, you probably gained additional understanding of your relationships to loved ones. For example, if your love bond looked rigid, like iron, you may keep certain loved ones at a distance. If your love bond has a lot of elasticity, you are probably able to feel connected, though far apart. If your love bond looks foggy, you may need more definition and clarity in your relationship.

You may repeat this exercise with each person whom you love. When visualizing a love bond that has suffered some upheaval, add the following:

Describe the love bond. If your love bond looks tattered, injured, or interrupted, describe what that looks like. Don't try to make sense out of the description; just accept what your mind conjures up. This process does not necessarily operate in a logical way. While you are trying to see your love bond, other people may come into the picture. Allow it. Describe it to yourself while your eyes are closed. Then, when you are ready, move your hands, rub your feet on the floor, and open your eyes.

Describe in your journal what you saw. Pay attention to the emotions and memories the exercise triggered. Allow them to flow. Then record them in your healing journal. When you are ready, read on.

VALERIE: DAMAGED BY AN "EASY" DIVORCE

What are the effects on the love bond when the divorce is handled with velvet gloves? Does such caution avoid all injury? Valerie's story shows that even the most intelligently handled divorce may not leave a teenager unscathed.

At five feet, nine inches, Valerie's lanky frame nearly filled the doorway of my office. Her outstretched hand and firm handshake when we first met said, "Take me seriously." A beautiful woman, Valerie was stylishly dressed. Her delicate nose and sensuous lips were framed by a halo of tousled hair. Her presence was intriguing.

Valerie's parents treasured their only child. There were no drugs, no alcohol, no open discontent or financial problems. They were strict, but not too much so. And there was trust. "I always accepted that my parents knew what they were doing," Valerie said.

When the divorce approached, the parents turned to a psychologist, and, with his help, the breakup proceeded smoothly. There was no visible hostility or tears. Valerie would always be welcome in each parent's home. Her mother remarried a well-to-do, decent man, and Valerie was always included in their trips and generous lifestyle. Perfect! Right?

One would expect that twelve-year-old Valerie, popular with her peers, would continue to brim with self-confidence. But no. Soon after her parents parted, the obedient, unquestioning child disappeared, and a furious teenager emerged.

Valerie's furor ignited in full force when her mom talked to Valerie about her plans to remarry. "Jim wants me to marry him. But I will leave the decision up to you, because your feelings are very important to me. If you don't want me to marry Jim [a man Valerie had met and didn't dislike], I will not do it," she said. In telling me about this, Valerie became angry: "Why did she have to put this decision on my shoulders? How could I deny my mother her happiness? So I said, 'Sure, Mom, that's okay.' Then I went into the bathroom and bawled."

What was Valerie feeling? She is still puzzled. She was treated with such loving care during the breakup that she didn't feel she had the right to be angry or sad. She felt that there was something wrong with her. Without siblings with whom she could compare feelings, she pinned her rage solely on her mother's asking her to make the decision.

Feeling estranged from her mother, Valerie started to behave like an unwanted puppy: 'I would fall madly in love with guys whom I always loved more than they loved me. I was a sucker for 'If you love me why don't you?' because I thought that there had to be a good reason not to." Then at twenty, she graduated to "real love."

Valerie ignored the warning signs and fell madly in love with a man who had another girlfriend and a reputation for being disloyal. Valerie admits she was reckless: "We were in Boston and she was in Florida, so who cares? She could only visit occasionally."

John was a short man—five feet, four inches—whom Valerie described as a "teeny little guy, an intellectual, and very much on his own path." Valerie admired his "unique strength of personality." In its magnetic allure, she lost herself. His opinions became her opinions. His wishes became her wishes. Her surrender became complete with her first orgasm: "I basically wrote myself off." When his other girlfriend came to visit, Valerie allowed John to pretend that she did not exist.

Why did Valerie subject herself to living in John's shadow? Valerie's murky sense of self is unmistakable: "I believed that only one person could have an identity in the relationship, and that identity had to be his."

What has happened so far in Valerie's case? What went wrong? Does true love demand that you become an ego-absent slave, that you submerge your own needs? Emphatically *no!* Love makes us vulnerable, and vulnerability can tempt even the most courageous into cowardice. But love thrives when you express your true self fully. And no matter how strong you feel when you enter a relationship, *if you sacrifice self-expression, the relationship will weaken you.*

Most of us fall in love with an illusion: the hero or the princess. The illusion is a vestige of childhood, a time when we feel safe because of our parents' omnipotence.

The illusions of childhood allow young children to reconcile the loving parent with the punishing parent. Not yet capable of complex thought, the child solves the apparent duality by splitting the parent into a good parent and bad parent. As children mature, and their perceptions of parents slowly transform, the illusions vanish. They learn to see the parents as human beings who are sometimes good and sometimes not so good. In accepting this duality, the maturing person also learns to accept his or her own personality.

Unhappily, divorce interferes with childhood's illusions. ACDs' precious sense of safety is questioned, and the perception of parents' power and competence is replaced by a sense of impotence and helplessness. The decline of trust becomes an enduring companion that haunts ACDs' love affairs.

Valerie agonized over her love for John because she was not equipped to handle his loss. The potential of failing at love was devastating. For most ACDs, the first struggle with love becomes their second heartbreak. The pain of the first heartbreak—the broken family—surfaces during the first failed romance. It's a great deal to handle. Now there seems to be no one but oneself to blame. Messages of inadequacy drone on in the mind: "I am not okay. I will never be lovable. I always suspected that I am not desirable; now I have proof."

To delay the inevitable, Valerie held on tightly. John wanted to break up, but Valerie would convince him to stay. Then his other girlfriend threatened suicide, and John finally made his choice and left.

Valerie fell apart: "I was totally devastated for the whole summer." When she returned to school, she was haunted by a compulsion to see him. She would wait to catch a glimpse of him. "I wanted to keep tabs on him. I was sick for him. I thought that it was my destiny to think about him for the rest of my life."

Her release from her obsession took place over time. It helped that John moved away. Being enslaved forever by John's memory was not to be Valerie's destiny. Two years later, when John refused to see her for lunch, his "venomous" response to her invitation suddenly freed Valerie. "I lost something that I've never felt since," Valerie lamented.

Chastened by her experience with John, Valerie dated men she didn't trust. Settling for what you don't want is a way of feeling safe. Such a safe experiment was Valerie's gay relationship.

Valerie's relationship with Sandy began easily: "I gave Sandy a ride one night after we'd had a lot to drink at a party. After I pulled up to her house I leaned over and kissed her. I was excited by my daring and we soon slept together. She was tender and very feeling. She knew what she was doing—she had all the same parts," Valerie added rather clinically. "I didn't like it more, though, than sleeping with men."

In talking further about that experience, Valerie became un-characteristically defensive, as if she were going to be taken to task: "I know you will ask me why I had to do it, so I will answer it in advance. I was in search of a mother's love and approval. And it must have given me that, because it was the most secure and sat-isfying emotional relationship I ever had."

Valerie's hunger for a mother's love and affection was fed for two years by this willing surrogate; then it was over: "I started to miss men, and I started to miss maleness. I wanted someone who could pick me up and throw me on the bed." Valerie ended her gay relationship by becoming involved rather hastily with a man, get-ting pregnant, and becoming infected with herpes all at once. "I feel bad that I hurt my lover. I didn't mean to," she said.

Valerie is ashamed of the way she handled herself. Like Den-nis, she now feels more grounded, because "I have taken myself back." She is working on healing and is beginning to see that hav-ing a healthy relationship will require her not to give away the store, but to become partners in it.

What did Valerie lose in her relationship with John? How did she go so far afield? Valerie's love was an immature, young love, a love that fuses, a love that cannot set boundaries. When Valerie relinquished her self for love, she violated these fundamental truths about love relation-ships:

We must be more responsible for our selves than we can expect anyone else to be.

The dignity, or lack of dignity, with which we treat our selves will set an example for others.

When we forsake our integrity for love, we forsake our selves.

I have talked to many ACDs who appear to have little trouble choosing love partners alternately from either sex. What is often a gut-wrenching personal decision for most people may be a casual detour for some ACDs.

ACDs such as Valerie often feel mismatched, with different aspects of self maturing at different ages and stages. Are you mature and competent in one area, such as in your career, while feeling young in love? Or vice versa?

HEALING JOURNAL EXERCISE: HOW OLD ARE YOU WHEN YOU LOVE?

We love differently at various ages of our childhood. Even after we are grown, we can love with a love appropriate to each age that we have traversed. There can be the trusting dependence of a three-year-old as well as the maturity of grown-up love.

During divorce we shut down and often anesthetize our feelings, consequently missing growth in love. This response is called *psychic numbing*. Our feelings become preserved under a covering of icy numbness. Love performs the incredible feat of thawing the ice of the psyche, allowing an amazing archaeological expedition in our hearts, as both our love bond and its injuries are uncovered.

Talking to June during her interview, I asked her how old she felt when she fell in love. She thought for a minute and replied, "I get this giddy, silly, thirteen-year-old response to love." Predictably, that was the age at which her heart shut down because her parents split up.

But doesn't everyone feel young and silly when they fall in love? It's true. No matter how old we are, we profess to feel like teenagers when we start to like someone in that way. The reason is that the teen years, especially ages sixteen to eighteen, are typically when we turn away from parents, detach emotionally, and move toward experimentation with love. But if divorce, death, or other trauma causes an earlier emotional shutting down, the love age is preserved, only to reappear when you fall in love. For example, if you were eight when your parents split, many emotional components of the eight-year-old will reemerge.

To measure your love age, recall the last time you fell in love. Though this is not a guided fantasy, you may want to close your eyes after reading each question to observe your response more closely. Then complete these sentences:

- The last time I started to like someone, I felt _____ years old.
- The time before that when I started to like someone, I felt _____ years old.
- When I start to fall in love, I feel _____ years old.
- When I was most intensely in love, I felt _____ years old.

Next, describe in your healing journal what took place in your life at the ages you have listed.

When you become familiar with how your childhood injuries influenced your adult love bond, you will also realize that as that joyous emotion visits you, the pain from the past becomes mobilized. What do we do with this? We need to complete love's unfinished transactions. We will say more about this later in the chapter.

JUNE: AMBIVALENCE ABOUT MONOGAMY

The availability of many love partners is reassuring to ACDs, and therefore a commitment can be a frightening prospect. June's knotty attitude is typical of some ACDs' feelings.

June's family, which carried on a musical tradition from generation to generation, produced several world-class musicians. June fondly remembers get-togethers at Christmas, with strains of Mozart and Beethoven resounding through the house. Then the music stopped. June's mom had been having an affair with an impresario, and she eventually left to move in with him. June was thirteen years old when her family scattered.

Trying to find out June's personal values about relationships is like chasing a mouse through a complex maze. She distrusts her sexual attractiveness: "I don't trust people who want to love me because I don't see myself as attractive or desirable." Yet unless people first prove that they like her, June cannot warm up to them.

When people show her affection, it triggers fears of abandonment in June: "If people show that they like or love me, I am afraid their feelings are going to change."

Despite all this, at twenty-nine she managed to fall in love and into a live-in arrangement with a man. "Tony would be a hard act to follow if we broke up," she said. "I can't see being with anyone else." Still, she is far from making a commitment. Her guidelines are dizzying: "I have no trouble being monogamous with him, although I don't see myself always being monogamous. I don't think that is really normal." Yet June demands fidelity from Tony. Jokingly, she says, "I tell him, 'If you sleep with someone, I'll kill you.'"

"Would an affair not affect your emotional bond?" I asked her. In one breath she claims that such an affair would not injure anything, and in the next she contradicts herself by saying that she cannot have sex without some emotional value in it, which she realizes may become more than a distraction. She wants to have children, but she doesn't think of marriage as being an *enhancer:* "I don't care. It has never been a fantasy of mine to be married. I think of the relationship as the most important thing, not the marriage certificate." The catch-22 becomes complete a few moments later when she admits that she would not have children without getting married.

ACDs who have seen the destructive force of extramarital affairs are often ashamed of their families, and deeply desire to interrupt the cycle of family infidelity. Embracing monogamy, however, is very unnerving. "Monogamy makes me feel as if I am at another's mercy," says Jodi. "I would feel trapped if I had to give up all other women!" says Jeff. For anyone, making a commitment of exclusivity is a big step. For some ACDs, however, putting all their eggs in one basket seems like high-level risk.

HEALING JOURNAL EXERCISE: HEALING YOUR LOVE-ABILITY

In everyone's heart, there is a deep desire to love and to be loved. We are biologically and psychologically programmed for it. We must love, we are loving creatures. Love is what gives our existence its full meaning. Then why do we set up roadblocks when we try to love or allow another to love us?

Have you ever contemplated the following questions? Write about each one in your healing journal.

- Are you free to love?
- If not, what keeps you from that freedom?
- What is more important to you, giving love or receiving love?
- Has your ability to love grown as you've matured?
- Do you become protective of yourself when you feel love approach?
- Do you test people to make sure they really love you?
- Do you suffer anxiety about love?

False notions about love. On the following list, check those items that you think are true.

_____ "Love is fragile, and if you disturb it, it will disappear."
_____ "If someone loves me, he or she should know what I need without being told."
_____ "If I show him or her the true me, he or she will go away."
_____ "I can't ask for what I need, because I risk losing love."
_____ "If I show how much I want to be loved, he or she will surely go away."
_____ "If I love someone, he or she will control me."
_____ "If I don't get what I want from love, that means I am not lovable."
_____ "If I don't control the person I love, he or she will go away."
_____ "If I were lovable, everyone would love me."

Each and every one of these statements is false. If you marked any of them, take another look. Most of the ideas in the above list result from defensive thinking. Love is simply an emotion, but the ability to feel it is often clouded by the past. *A simple definition of love-ability. Love-ability is:*

- the ability to feel love
- the ability to give love
- the ability to accept love

Love is merely an emotion, and you do not need anyone's permission to feel it. The ability to love is nature's great gift, and no one can take that away from you except with your permission. This information may come as a shock to people who associate so many other things with love that they lose sight of its simple truths. Where do you stand with love-ability? As you answer the following questions in your healing journal, you will learn more about your relationship to love.

- How often do you feel love?
- Toward whom do you feel love?
- Do you feel love only for safe objects?
- How often do you feel love for yourself?
- How do you show your love?
- Does it feel risky when you show love to others?
- Do you limit your love because you fear that the person you love is going to run away with it?
- Can you love without attaching a large part of your self-esteem to the emotion?
- Do you recognize others' love for you?

The answers to these questions probably allowed you to see that you create invisible boundaries and limits. You may also begin to realize that you could feel love more often if you were not so protective of yourself. Have you thought about what love means to you? Read on.

HEALING JOURNAL EXERCISE: WHAT LOVE MEANS TO YOU

The many hidden meanings we associate with love reside deep within us. One way to unearth these meanings is through word association. To gain better insight of your love profile, complete the following exercises. Say the word *love* aloud; then write down the first word that comes to mind. Let the words emerge quickly, if possible, without trying to guide or censor your answers. The words that come forth may or may not be relevant. Don't judge or evaluate them.

In your healing journal, complete the following sentence in twenty ways.

- *Love is* _____.

You may reply that love is simply *wonderful,* as some do, or see that it's *powerful.* You may associate it with *marriage* or *obligation,* while others will see it from the point of view of *sex.* Typically *spending time* and *giving attention* show up on most such lists, but *exchanging gifts on special occasions* is nearly as popular. Each of us surrounds love with expectations, but rarely do any person's groups of expectations coincide completely with anyone else's.

To continue your love profile, complete each of the following sentences with ten different endings in your healing journal.

- One thing love means to me is _____.
- When I love someone I always _____.
- When I love someone I never _____.
- Those who love me usually _____.
- Those who love me rarely _____.

Perhaps you found out some surprising things about yourself. You may have discovered a streak of generosity that you didn't realize you had, or a wall of expectations that would be difficult for anyone to penetrate. Perhaps you saw how someone can unlock the gates of the wall. Having identified some of your own attitudes surrounding this emotion, you can communicate them to others, which will become very useful in avoiding disappointment.

HEALING JOURNAL EXERCISE: DEFENDING YOURSELF AGAINST THE THREAT OF LOVE

When love starts to thaw hidden corners of our hearts and mobilize their contents, we may defend against love to avoid pain. Have you tried to hold love at bay by doing any of the following? Check those that apply to you.

_____ Creating illusory relationships, those that fade away.
_____ Never giving yourself completely; always holding back.
_____ Unwillingness to be monogamous; keeping your options open.
_____ Engaging in bisexual relationships as a way of avoiding commitment, even to a sexual preference.
_____ Always having other possible relationships in the wings.
_____ Moving in and out of relationships; moving from place to place, from city to city, or even further to avoid commitments.
_____ Finding something wrong, being a perfectionist, nitpicking, or making unacceptable demands.
_____ Hurting the ones you love.
_____ Selecting love partners who are sure to hurt you, or provoking them into hurting you.

If one or more items on this list applies to you, see whether you realized before how you defend against love. It's possible that you may not be ready for a deep romantic involvement. I am not suggesting that you should move into a relationship before you are ready for it, but you ought to be clear about where you stand. Then you can determine whether you are allowing yourself to clear your life and grow toward settling down.

Learning to Love Again

ACDs generally take one of two routes to loving again. They give themselves completely, like Valerie did, thinking that lessons of self-discipline don't apply to love, or else they refuse to take any chances, not allowing anyone to matter. These ACDs may be sexually active, but sex becomes a substitute for intimacy. People whose love lives are devoid of love, even when they have one or more partners, often come up empty. They eventually feel victimized by others and by life.

Between these two extremes, there are a lot of variations. If you cannot love yourself, you will always feel needy, and that neediness will distort your love relationship. Don't look to others for what you cannot give yourself. *If you cannot treat yourself with love, you may not be able to trust the love you receive from others.*

To discover willingness to love yourself, do the following exercise. You can begin the process as follows:

- Write yourself a note of appreciation every day. Buy yourself a friendship card you wish someone else would send to you.
- Give yourself recognition. Compliment yourself on meeting a deadline or getting in touch with an old friend.
- Give yourself small rewards regularly—an extra movie, a ball game, a shirt you've been wanting, a phone call to a friend who lives far away.
- Write affirmations. Put a note on your bathroom mirror that says, "The person in this mirror is great!" to remind you to be confident and self-assured.
- Criticize yourself less. When you find yourself being particularly critical of yourself, stop. Tell yourself that you may think that critical thought five times and then no more. Then refuse to allow that same thought to mar your day again.
- Do something each day that you can be pleased with. It may be something as simple as remembering to say hello to a neighbor or starting with the most difficult task of the day. Then allow yourself to feel the pride that comes from the extra effort.

Treating yourself with love is an important step toward clearing the road toward a mutually loving relationship.

Having done all this preparation, there is one more step left. Love is the most healing potion there is. To heal the past, you must allow love back into your life. Mental rehearsals such as therapy, twelve-step programs, or other support groups are necessary to work through to the threshold of love. Working through your memories can move you to a higher level of understanding yourself. But there is only one way to complete the job: *you have to be in a relationship to finish healing.* In order to reach your deepest understanding about relationships, no other preparation or drill will suffice. You must allow yourself to be touched by love.

Six Steps for Learning to Love Again

Following are the steps in learning to love fully.

1. Select, and allow yourself to be selected by, someone who is not a safe, controllable person, but someone who will matter to you. This person will have the capacity to win your heart and touch your soul. This person will be someone with whom you can celebrate life, someone whom you could respect and admire, and someone whose loss would be deeply felt. Otherwise there is no risk and no growth.

2. As you move toward a relationship, allow your attraction to grow slowly. By making your investment in another person gradually, you can retreat gracefully if you decide the choice is not right. If you move too quickly, you may get swept along, and then it's much more difficult to retreat. You wake up one day only to find yourself in a wrong relationship, which you will then have to reshape to fit your needs.

3. Learn how to interview properly, before your judgment becomes clouded by affection or sexual desire. Even if you have never had a sexual love relationship before, in everyday life you have had to form judgments about people ever since you were a little child. Use these same skills in this realm. *The best time to evaluate a potential love interest is when you first meet.* Use that time diligently. Much of the information you need is generally there at the start if you just pay attention. Heed not only your head, but also your instincts about what you hear and see. Most people spend a great deal more time researching to buy a new car than preparing to find a love mate, though rarely does a disappointment over an automobile result in heartbreak.

4. Approach each nuance of love and each sense of discomfort with openness, and examine whether the discomfort belongs to someone from the past. You will learn to trust yourself if you can differentiate old, held-over feelings from current, new feelings. Is it your new friend who is bringing out these feelings, or is your past intruding into your present?

5. Avoid casting stones if a relationship does not work and you need to move on. *There need not be anything wrong with either you or your love choice for the relationship to end.* Learn to be nonjudgmental. "We did not fit" or some such remark is much better than castigating a failed love. By taking a neutral attitude you save yourself a lot of grief, and you preserve your faith in yourself and in the opposite sex. You also appear safer in the eyes of a potential new love partner.

6. Keep track of your emotions. Start therapy if you need help with your feelings. People start therapy when they leave relationships, but therapy can be immensely helpful to sort through the confusing feelings in a budding relationship as well.

In traveling the path of life, we bump into all types of people, and get bruised by the jagged edges of disappointment. It's easy enough to hold someone else responsible: it's harder to accept your part in what happened. Yet the latter is better for *you*. As the saying goes, "Forgive and forget." You may not forget, but you ought to forgive, because forgiveness releases you from that past hurt. You free up a corner of your soul and, by discarding the bad feelings, make room for the good feelings that await you. Unforgiven hurts bind us to the past and blind us to the present.

Now that you have finished this rather comprehensive look at you and love, identify the two or three most important points you have discovered about yourself. You may have always known these things, but perhaps you have discovered a new depth of understanding. Jot down in your journal the aspect of this chapter that provided you with the most healing, and then move on to chapter 8.

8

How to Court Love and Translate It into Marriage

Love is a free exercise of choice. Two people love each other only when they are quite capable of living without each other but choose to live with each other.

M. SCOTT PECK

Neither infatuation nor love is enough to create a marriage. Launching a good marriage requires many skills, not the least of which is a positive attitude toward marriage itself. ACDs often view marriage with doubt and find it difficult to believe that marriage will take care of their needs. Therefore even the courtship process is viewed with suspicion.

I have devoted this chapter to those ACDs who want to sharpen their skills in gaining a love partner. I have included only short quotes from interviews, and have emphasized information and exercises about courting. Together we'll explore the stages of dating and mating, from courtship through living together and commitment. We'll see how marriage can actually help achieve personal growth. In the healing sections, you will test your own marriage-ability quotient, to see if you don't need an attitude adjustment.

Through positive imagery and reinforcement, you'll learn how you can turn your own personal roadblocks, like codependency, fear of intimacy, and fear of abandonment, into green lights to future happiness. By learning to pay heed to your body, you will have a heightened sense of awareness in the entanglements of love.

HOW ACDs LOOK AT MARRIAGE

The views of the following three ACDs share a common thread: each ACD thinks of marriage as a tremendous risk and approaches it rather gingerly. They all admit that they want successful marriages, but they are not sure what that means.

Raised by her mother from the time she was seven years old, Mandy, twenty-seven, never envisioned a man in her perfect family. Rather, she pictured it as a mother and two children. After falling in love and marrying, she is rewriting her definition of family to include the man she loves as the father of the children she wants.

Tom, at thirty-seven, has had three marriages, all of which sound more like brief sexual interludes than committed relationships. He never believed in marriage, and he keeps proving that marriage doesn't work for him. Tom was used to changes, because his mother and father racked up seven marriages between them, and he was moved from parent to parent at least that many times.

Marianne has spent many years entertaining potential candidates for marriage. She has been close to the altar a couple of times, but hasn't yet felt confident that she was with the right man, one who wouldn't leave her. Had she found him, she thought, she could avoid the risk of failure. Marianne is finally realizing that she is divorce phobic, and at age forty-four she is again trying to adjust her views of marriage to accommodate a potential life partner.

Most ACDs not only want to be married, but also want to have the perfect marriage that eluded their parents. Often they set marital standards so high that they alienate all potential mates. Marital partners are not failure proof, nor, unfortunately, do they come with satisfaction guaranteed or your money back. ACDs fervently wish they did.

Most ACDs do not feel secure enough in their resolve, or confident in their abilities, to create an enduring marriage, so they look to their future mates as guarantors of marital bliss. They need to overcome the distrust of continuity learned from their divorce-caused childhood changes. So what and whom can you trust? How do ACDs learn to trust marriage when they know more about its failures than its successes?

The selection of a marital partner involves risk. Good judgment and promising candidates are only a part of the equation. Courage plays a leading role in the selection process; trust runs a close second.

The Courage to Marry

ACDs often possess ample courage when it comes to starting a business, running for public office, climbing the career ladder, or engaging in physical dangers by seeking outward-bound experiences. Yet some of these same grown men and women, once their professional persona is set aside, become frightened little girls and boys in the face of love. "I can do anything, but don't make me face those fears of abandonment," they might plead. Yet it is on the trail of love that courage is most needed.

The longer ACDs wait to get married, the longer their shopping list becomes. Their list may include characteristics that they must have in a mate, as well as characteristics, called nonnegotiables, that they will not tolerate. Attractive traits may include appearance, financial stability, and even desired locale, while nonnegotiables may range from being a smoker to not wanting children. But instead of becoming more and more selective, ACDs need to learn to take appropriate risks. They must stop looking for assurances outside themselves. They must trust that *they* possess the very ingredient that will help fulfill their dreams—their own abilities to make their marriages work.

No one can tell you whether you should marry. But there must be some good reasons why marriage, which faced the assaults of the liberation movement and the predictions of its demise in the sixties and seventies, has enjoyed a resurgence. Since no one is coercing people to marry, marriage must still be the best lifestyle for the majority of people. Many people still believe the best way to live is in a loving relationship. When we love one another, the natural tendency is to create an entity, such as marriage, to hold and preserve that love.

Yet love does change with time. In a good marriage, a variety of emotions is enjoyed. The first stage is almost always infatuation—that giddy, head-over-heels feeling that washes over our every thought, word, and deed. When this infatuation abates, a deep, genuine fond-ness ensues and grows into everything that love encompasses—re-spect, joy, communication, trust, mutual support, and much more.

Love has the ability to move from the headiness of mutual dis-covery to the comfort of shared good times and even bad times. It is the richness of these shared memories, of a common history, that makes your past real and fills you with a sense of continuity. A decades-enduring marital partnership that has come through the good and bad times is a proud example of the potential of love.

"I figure we have had seven different relationships in our thirty years of marriage," said Stan, an old friend. "Sandy keeps changing, so it's never dull." Sandy's dynamic life often clashes with Stan's steadi-ness, but their differences, though at times bothersome, have also re-mained attractive to each of them.

From examples of long-standing, happy unions we learn that the most reliable way—albeit not a perfect one—to weave two lives to-gether is by marriage. Despite convenience foods and apartments that are designed for people living alone, society still supports marriage in many ways. Houses are not built for one, nor are cars. Studies show that married people are happier and healthier than their single coun-terparts. Being single for a lifetime is very demanding. All the respon-sibility rests on one's own shoulders, with little of the burden shared by others. It *is* possible to develop a wonderful support system, through mutual goodwill, regardless of one's marital state. But the marriage bond, which creates the family, binds more securely and makes it more difficult to drift apart.

Your love bond is nature's gift to you.
You were born with it!
You had it as an infant;
You can re-create it as an adult!

HEALING JOURNAL EXERCISE: CHANGING YOUR MIND ABOUT MARRIAGE

For ACDs who want to get married, an attitude checkup may be in order. Are your negative attitudes standing like so many little soldiers, guarding your vulnerability? If you have become invulnerable, it's dif-ficult for anyone to know you, much less love you. Protective attitudes may have been useful in the past, but after a while they can become a habit. See whether these culprits are familiar to you.

DO YOU SAY THIS?	DO YOU REALLY MEAN?
Marriage is a trap.	I don't trust the institution of marriage.
Marriages don't work.	What if I fail? I don't want to be responsible for a divorce.
Marriages may work, but only for a short period of time.	I don't trust myself or anyone else to be faithful for very long.
People I love leave me.	I don't believe that anyone can love me.

If any of the right-hand statements are true for you, write them in your healing journal. Now search your mind to see what hidden meanings may lurk within you regarding the following statements, and write them in your healing journal. You may also want to create your own list.

- I don't know what makes marriages work.
- I have doubts about anyone being a good marriage partner.
- I doubt that the right person will choose me.
- Love brings pain.
- If a relationship doesn't work, there is something wrong with the other person.

These or similar attitudes, which are probably the vestiges of a childhood in one or more failing marriages, can't help but affect your search for a mate. Once you have recognized these skeptical attitudes, seek out people with working marriages and ask them how they handle these concerns. Read biographies of couples whose marriages withstood the test of time. If you search for answers, you will develop a can-do outlook about long-term relationships.

Checking up on Your Intention

Intentions are very important ingredients in achievement. If you intend it, you can achieve it. If the intention is firm, it becomes a beacon in the darkness of uncertainty and fear.

Are your intentions clear, or do they need clarifying? Do you say things like: "I don't care if I get married" or "I think I want a serious relationship, but I don't know if I want to marry"? If you applied for a job with such uncertainty, chances are you'd bungle the interview. ACDs with uncertain relationship goals bungle opportunities, such as first dates, blind dates, and contacts with people who are good potential mates. I am forever surprised when ACDs tell me about dates on which, without realizing, they behaved in a way sure to chill another's interest.

Relationships don't just happen, as romanticists might suggest, especially when we walk around being defensive. Relationships develop gradually, a blend of people's thoughts, feelings, and sexuality. Your attitudes start to communicate themselves immediately, and if you remain positive about being a Mr. or Ms. Right, you are much more likely to get positive results in return. If you harbor negative thoughts, you will appear defensive, no matter how well you think you hide it. Consider this:

> Honesty invites honesty in return.
> Emotions invite emotions in return.
> Thoughts invite thoughts in return.
> Intimacy invites intimacy in return.
> Defensiveness invites defensiveness in return.

If you see someone backing away from you, looking defensive, ask yourself: "How was I being defensive?" When your invitations bring the desired response, your budding relationship may look like this:

CYCLE OF SUCCESS

As mutual intimacy is shared, love develops.
As trust and intimacy grow, love grows.
As intimacy is respected, trust grows.
As love and trust grow, you want to be together, perhaps
for a lifetime.

With your vision sharpened by clear intention and the willingness to risk, you will be able to see through the defenses of others and become aware that behind many of the frog suits of defensiveness hide beautiful princes and princesses.

HEARING JOURNAL EXERCISE: BANISHING NEGATIVE ATTITUDES

If you feel good, chances are you will look good. And if you feel and look good, people will notice the wonderful attributes you have to offer. By the same token, when you feel bad, you are much more likely to project a poor image to the world.

Gloomy attitudes set people up for failure and the depression that follows. Pessimistic attitudes eat away at your ability to succeed. Banish the pessimistic attitudes that worm their way into your mind. You can work on them in two ways: first, identify your pessimistic interpretations of events and reinterpret them in a new light; second, write marriage affirmations. Affirmations are powerful tools that reach deeply into our brains and slowly replace unwanted thoughts and modify troubling emotions. The repetition of positive thoughts, while countering their negative counterparts, affects the emotions, replacing fear with hope and making room for love. Write each of these statements five times in your journal.

- Marriage works for me.
- I can create a strong, enduring marriage.
- I am an attractive, desirable marriage partner.
- I deserve a good marriage partner.
- I can keep the commitments I make.
- I can choose someone who can keep his/her commitment.
- I do not have to repeat the unwanted examples of childhood.
- I will have an enduring marriage.
- I can let go of relationships that don't work.
- I am able to trust.

What I am about to suggest next may sound strange to you: take turns writing with each hand. Because the hands are controlled by opposite hemispheres of the brain, this initially awkward exercise will more fully bathe both sides of your brain with the affirmations.

If this is the first time you have done affirmations, you may find that doubts emerge in response to affirmations. For example, writing "I am someone people want to marry" may trigger this negative response: "Sure I am. Then why aren't I married?" Write down the response, then write the original affirmation again, until no further negative thoughts come to mind. At that time all opposition is spent for the moment.

"I was able to slide into a new relationship almost effortlessly," confided Teddy, a young ACD. She works on her affirmations whenever she has a few moments. She writes them on three-by-five cards, which she carries with her. "I flip through them while waiting for red lights to change and when standing in lines," she said. As Teddy knows, sometimes when we are caught up in our daily rush, it is good to remind ourselves of a new point of view that we are nurturing.

Courtship

Why is it important for ACDs to learn more about courtship? Courtship, an old-fashioned word—as time honored as marriage itself—allows lovers to try out potential mates and assess them for enduring value. But it is difficult to handle deep anxieties about relationships while allowing a courtship to progress, as ACDs must do. Perhaps by focusing our attention on how best to align two lives, we can better understand how to deal with our doubts and move toward a happier beginning.

Initially, while the hearts of lovers fall into a like, private rhythm, fantasies are spun of a private world built only for two. If the rhythm is mutual and the beat persists, the relationship will grow. Not every courtship is successful, because we may be briefly attracted to many people who are ultimately not appropriate for us. The courtship may also be unsuccessful because the rules of courtship are obscure.

"Do you understand the rules of courting?" I asked Bette during our interview.

"No, I don't," she replied. "I always call my friends to ask things like: 'What does this mean and what should I do: Bill hasn't called.' We analyze what was said and what was done to the finest detail to try to decide what the other's conduct means."

What should Bette do if he calls again three weeks later, as if the interlude of silence had never happened? Today there are few firm rules, and about some things there are no rules. Men likewise puzzle over such on-again, off-again questions. They don't know whether to pursue or not. Will the woman like it or not like it? How many times should they call before accepting that "I just don't have time because of work, or family" means "It's been nice to know you."

With confusion and misunderstanding about how to behave, we often chase one another in all directions. Not having dependable rules affects our willingness to be honest, open, and ethical with each other. Being stood up on a date no longer surprises those who have dated a lot. Disappointments and distrust are epidemic. But the question of who should pursue whom seems most troubling: "I have called men and I have initiated different types of get-togethers. But there is a fine line between initiating and chasing. I don't know where that fine line is," said Donna. Some men like to be chased; others may be flattered at first, then become confused, and, in the end, lose respect for women who act aggressively.

It takes a strong heart and a firm resolve to get through false starts and to let go of the bitterness of near misses. You will avoid many bruises, however, if you try not to fight yourself while you are putting out feelers.

HEALING JOURNAL EXERCISE: DATING AND COURTING

Dating can be particularly difficult for ACDs. Many, in fact, dislike dating intensely. For them there is no such thing as a casual date because ACDs feel judged, evaluated, and, if the relationship doesn't continue, discarded. They'd rather go out with a group of friends than spend time on a date. Even more difficult is moving through would-be relationships, starting and ending attachments.

Still, with the proper mind-set and an openness to growth, dating and courtship can be eye-opening and beneficial. Recovering from the inevitable bruises along the way provides the means through which strength and self-confidence grow. Dating can be a lot of fun if people allow it to be just what it is: a look-see, the sharing of a few hours, an easy testing of mutual chemistry.

In your healing journal, in two columns labeled *Traits Desired* and *Traits Offered,* make a shopping list of attributes you desire in a romantic partner, and of those attributes you would like to contribute to a love match. Think back to people you have known, or to whom you've been attracted, and identify characteristics that were particularly attractive to you. The people don't necessarily have to be love interests. They could be family members, friends, or even fictional characters. Ask yourself, In whose company did I feel good? In whose company did I feel most like myself?

It is much easier to know what we want in someone else than it is to assess what we have to offer someone. In the *Traits Offered* column, list any and all of your characteristics that it would be important for someone else to know about. Then pair the traits. Do the columns promise a good blend? If not, rethink what is needed. For example, if in your *Traits Desired* column you list someone who is athletic, yet that does not appear in your *Traits Offered* column, think about how you would participate in someone's life whose interests include time spent in athletics. Are you a spectator or a fan? Do you desire to learn sports?

If not, are you prepared to spend weekend hours alone while your husband or wife is playing golf? The more your interests mesh, the fewer the differences that will have to be negotiated.

Remember, you are not looking for someone who merely turns you on sexually, or who can contribute to your standard of living. You are also seeking a potentially good parent for your children, a good companion, and a soul mate. Is there a good match? Once you are clear about what it is that you would like, you are much more likely to gravitate toward the person who is right for you. Doing your homework—a small price to pay for a potentially lifelong partnership—will result in enduring benefits.

Why Not Just Live Together?

Marriage is a deeper commitment than any other relationship of choice. Society has created special rules for starting or ending a marriage: marriage licenses and divorce decrees. Many legal rights flow from marriage, one of which ACDs are only too familiar with: the division of financial assets and obligations upon divorce.

There are other reasons for marriage as well. The emotional bonding of marriage is like no other chosen bond. The decision to take someone into your life as your most intimate family member is a decision that brings profound changes into all aspects of your life. In moving toward marriage, each step in your relationship should promote the proper perspective.

- Dating is a rehearsal for a monogamous courtship.
- Monogamous courtship is a rehearsal for a live-in relationship.
- A live-in relationship is a rehearsal for marriage.
- Marriage is not a rehearsal; it is the *real thing*.

HEALING JOURNAL EXERCISE: SETTING GOALS FOR PERSONAL GROWTH

You cannot predict when you will get married, but you should learn to use the process of moving closer to that time as an opportunity for growth. Make a list of goals for growth in your healing journal. What is it that you want to change or improve in yourself? You may select from the following list, or you may have a list of your own special goals. It may be simple:

- I want to improve my ability to judge and evaluate people quickly and accurately.

- I want to be able to go on a date and stop thinking that the other person is judging me.

Or your goals may be more lofty:

- I want to be able to control my urgency to get into a relationship.
- When I discover I like someone, I want to move slowly. I want to discard old patterns of trying to bind them to me.
- I want to become clear about how I push people away.
- I want to learn to control my anxiety.
- I want to stop trying to control others.
- I want to behave in a more sex-role-appropriate fashion.

Then answer these questions.

- Do I feel young when I start to like someone? *What do I do to compensate?*
- What doubts do I have about myself when I start to like someone? *What do I do to compensate?*
- What am I afraid of when I start to reveal intimacies about myself? *What do I do to compensate?*
- Do I reveal too much too soon to a date? *What do I do to compensate?*
- Do I feel distress when I start to like someone? *What do I do to compensate?*

In your answers to "What do I do to compensate?" you may find enlightening information about your own responses to the beginning of relationships. For example, you may have become Mr. or Ms. Motormouth on a first date, unable to stop talking about yourself, your job, your friends. You may have become embarrassed by this and, because of that embarrassment, started to find fault with the person you were with. Once you see that, the changes you need to make become evident. Perhaps liquor loosens your tongue; you can switch to mineral water. Perhaps you will consciously start asking questions about your date to divert attention from yourself. In any event, working on these issues will help you define your dating goals.

Avoiding Codependency

We should not be terrified of dependency. We need to avoid coloring all dependency with codependency hues. In her book *Codependent No*

More, Melody Beattie defines a codependent as one who has "let an-other person's behavior affect him or her, and who is obsessed with controlling that person's behavior." When the term *codependency* was first coined and recognized, people responded in droves, ACDs among them. ACDs are beset with issues of control, as is anyone who has ex-perienced family chaos during his or her formative years. The normal response to a world that is threatening to disintegrate is to try to con-trol it.

Who among us has not been affected by our loved one, and who among us hasn't tried to control our spouse or other loved ones? Too many mistakenly identify themselves as codependent, and too many, likewise, consider it imperative to avoid *all* dependency like the plague. *Codependent no more* to some translates as *married no more* because they can't figure out how to be married without being dependent.

You cannot have a healthy marriage without healthy dependence. Marriage without interdependence is not marriage. In loving attach-ments, dependency is a valued asset. Other components of codepen-dence, such as having influence over one another and trying to please one another, are also important components of marriage. In all loving attachments, the desire to please one another is a healthy sign. In lov-ing attachments, it's as much a joy to adopt each other's tastes as it is to share each other's things. That sort of influence is a sign of love. Thus we are molded by this mutual influence, and fit together more snugly.

The appropriate level of dependence varies from couple to couple, and even from one phase of the marriage to another. The secret to the proper amount of dependence is that we must be able to depend on each other while maintaining our own identity, integrity, and self-respect. We must retain our healthy personhood while supporting the other's as well. We must be able to support the *we*-ness while clearly maintaining a *me*-ness.

Unmarried ACDs often profess to be codependent because they have trouble both in becoming attached and in letting go of attach-ments. There is a way to avoid becoming too dependent: by working toward becoming what I call *co-active.*

Becoming Co-Active

What is *co-active?* Being co-active is being active with each other in order to build a true partnership. When you are being co-active instead of codependent, you work for the *we* without giving up the *me*. You decide on and work for partnership projects.

Being co-active means you support your own identity—you maintain your hobbies, your friends—as well as your love partner's identity by participating in both separate and joint activities. Following are some tips for becoming co-active:

- Build a partnership. You will build a partnership when you take an equal hand in creating and maintaining the relationship.
- Build a friendship. Use your friendship-building skills to strengthen the friendships in your romantic relationships.
- Monitor the power; keep it in balance. Be sure that the power is kept in balance, because a love partnership needs to be a balanced unit.

HEALING JOURNAL EXERCISE : ATTACHMENT SKILLS

Recall your past relationships. Evaluate yourself in your healing journal in terms of the ease of those relationships, using the following scale: very easy, easy, difficult, very difficult.

- Starting attachments: _____.
- Continuing attachments: _____.
- Ending attachments: _____.

You most likely wrote *very easy* or *easy* next to one or two items, but not all three.

Now answer the following questions:

- How would you have scored five or ten years ago?
- Are you moving in the direction in which you want to move?
- Where do you stand today?
- When did you last have a serious romantic attachment?

From these results you will be able to see where you need to create movement in your life. If you scored *difficult* or *very difficult* in starting attachments, you don't take enough risk there. If you scored *difficult* or *very difficult* in keeping attachments going, either you are selecting people who aren't for you, or you are unwilling to take the risk of deeper intimacy. If you scored *difficult* or *very difficult* in ending attachments, you are not willing to handle feelings of loss.

It might be very helpful to reconsider whether your separation from your parents has been completed. (See chapters 2 and 3.) Your willingness to risk is a measure of your attachment skills, and as it increases you will move closer to your desired goals.

Coping with the Dance of Uncertainty

The distance between people fluctuates from day to day and from week to week. I call the alternating steps of distance and closeness in courtship the Dance of Uncertainty.

New love magnetizes lovers and promises intimacy. Reality intrudes, however, and provokes the truth: hard as you may try, it is not possible to sustain the heady moments. Paradoxically, feelings of intimacy can best be preserved and repeated only if people are allowed their freedom. If you try to hold on to these moments, they vanish or become spoiled.

The need for distance or for closeness varies with the individual and fluctuates over time. The most comfortable level of closeness is often set by the style of closeness that was familiar in the family of origin. Those who grew up in families with a lot of touching and kissing will not feel at home with someone whose family was cold and did not touch or kiss. Nighttime snugglers will feel unloved with those who build an international border down the middle of the bed that can be crossed only with a visa.

There may be no discernible pattern to the fluctuations at first, and the distance is usually set by the one who needs it more, rather than the one who needs it less. There must be acceptance for pushing apart, as well as for coming back together. Eventually, a pattern emerges and becomes predictable.

For ACDs, the spaces created by these separations may bring pain, insecurity, and self-doubt. It is during these times that the fear of abandonment becomes a haunting presence. Yet it is in the pulling away and in the returning to closeness that love is reaffirmed. It is in the spaces that love gains urgency and the desire to be together becomes certain.

Still, it is always painful to let each other go, because although emotions have begun to intertwine, no one knows how deeply rooted they are. It takes time to know whether two people can return to each other with the same pleasure over and over again. And when perspective returns, the experience of courtship may fade into just another story, or perhaps a tender but brief adventure, or the decision, "It's not for me," or "I'm not ready for this."

But if the couple continues the courtship, dancing the Dance of Uncertainty with grace and willingness at the beginning will lead to a generous payoff at the end—a remarkable sense of security, and the permission to be free within the bounds of love.

During the courtship, both lovers must know that they can move away without penalty and be welcomed back, so that when they return they return out of choice, not out of obligation or bondage. We may not mind being in bondage to our own passion for another, but we mind desperately being in bondage to the dictates of the one we love.

Uncertainty in love is incredibly difficult for ACDs. As a result, ACDs often sabotage their own budding relationships rather than taking pains to muddle through them. To avoid the emerging pain, ACDs often make all the wrong moves. They pursue too intently: they become petulant when their friend is aloof. They create transparent excuses for making contact and rushed plans for future get-togethers. The more *right* someone is, the more *wrong* we can act.

Trying to avoid painful feelings triggers addictive or compulsive behaviors. There are impending danger signs to heed. Relationship addiction threatens when:

Our actions are driven and not chosen.
Impulses control.
We force contact out of weakness.
We become undisciplined in love.

These foreboding behaviors must be stopped right then and there, before they take root.

Later, if our expectations are not fulfilled or if pursuit doesn't bring the desired result, we may start to reexamine our love choice, and that creature who was so perfect a short time before suddenly appears to have giant flaws. Yet our new view may be only a projection of our own disappointment, fear, or anger. If we like someone, he or she is wonderful; if we are heading for disappointment, he or she seems defective. For us, that person can be only a prince or a princess, or a frog.

The "I'm Starting to Like Someone" Survival Kit

"It's so hard to wait to know whether he likes me or not that I'd rather end the relationship," said Cindy in a recent therapy session, as she realized that she doesn't really want to end the relationship she is involved in. What can she do to avoid the anxiety that causes her to want to throw in the towel too soon? How do you stay balanced while waiting for the relationship to develop? Instead of trying to figure out what the other person is thinking or doing, take this as an excellent opportunity to work on self-care: reassure yourself that you are indeed a lovable, marriageable, and worthwhile human being *with or without this person*. Here are some options that may help you survive uncertainty:

- During times of uncertainty and waiting, spend time with special friends or family who appreciate you.
- Work on fostering good feelings.
- Stop yourself from attaching meanings, expectations, and fantasies to the potential relationship.
- Recall what helped build self-esteem in the past, such as a particular sport or talent, and pursue that activity.
- Do something altruistic, such as feeding the homeless or volunteering at your local children's hospital.
- If you feel continuing distress, get into therapy.

If you maintain a good life, you will be just fine if the relationship doesn't work out. I don't mean a life that is so busy that it has no room for anyone else, but I do mean a life that is satisfying. Use your best self-care skills, because it is stressful to leave yourself open emotionally while feeling vulnerable to the dictates of another.

The beginning of a relationship is a great time to be in therapy. It is also a good time to do journal work. Unfortunately most people, feeling buoyed by romance, do not want to do anything they fear might jinx their feelings of excitement. They usually associate therapy with the ending of relationships. In fact, the start of a relationship is a great time to peel away the pain of the past from the emerging love of the present.

Difficult or not, we must master the steps of intimacy, and such mastery is necessary early in a relationship. The need for intimacy skills does not stop at the altar, either. In fact, the shorter the courtship, the more need there is to master these skills at the next stage—commitment. These skills are needed throughout your marriage, because intimacy fluctuates there, too. Without those skills, the relationship, sooner or later, will become distorted.

You must learn to feel safe when one or both of you push away, seeking distance from one another. You need to recognize that security comes from within. There is no other way. This on-the-job training takes place as the distance between you widens and the bad feelings start to emerge. *These feelings are more likely to be remnants of the past than a forecast of the future.* Each time your partner needs a little more distance, he or she is *not* commenting on your value, nor foretelling the end of the relationship. This critical lesson must be learned by anyone who has suffered losses in childhood.

There are effective ways to work on the anxiety that accompanies these fluctuations in relationships. One is by engaging in vigorous physical exercise that burns away the stress of anxiety. Another is by doing the following visualization exercise. It works very well for most people dealing with feelings of insecurity.

HEALING JOURNAL EXERCISE: GOING AWAY AND COMING BACK

Through visualization you will take yourself through an episode in which you and your love partner are pulling away from one another. You may find that doing this exercise regularly will reduce the frequency of your anxious moments. It is also designed to give you a sense of control in a situation, without your trying to dominate it.

Read through the following instructions completely before starting the exercise. You may prefer to prepare an audiotape of these instructions. In doing so, speak slowly, leaving several seconds between sentences to allow the images to catch up to the directions.

Then go to a room where you won't be interrupted. Close your eyes and relax for a few minutes. Take a few nurturing breaths. Starting with your feet, and naming each part of your body in turn, allow the tensions in your body to dissolve.

In this relaxed state, visualize your love partner. Visualize him or her walking through a day at work, and through his or her private life. Watch the comings and goings. Take a minute to do this.

Then visualize yourself entering into his or her life. Recall the last time you saw each other. Notice the intimacy you shared. Recall the closeness, and visualize it now. Get even closer to one another and enjoy the contact. Then, at the end of the scene, allow yourself to move away from one another. Let it happen! Support it! You are doing something valuable for the relationship. Create good feelings while you are watching the two of you move farther apart. The distance is as loving as the closeness. Fill the space with love. Fill it with contentment. Allow yourself to smile, and fill your heart with joy. Notice that you are moving even farther apart. Continue to feel good. When you can no longer see each other, notice that you still feel good. Now start moving closer to each other again and repeat moving apart again. Notice your good feelings and that you are feeling more secure. When you are ready, open your eyes.

Write a brief description of what you saw, sensed, and did in your scene. Include any unusual or surpising thoughts, visions, and feelings that occurred to you while you had your eyes closed.

This exercise has many benefits. Most importantly, it helps you through lonely moments and moves you further along in gaining a sense of continuity and security. Recognize that it is within your power to create feelings of closeness whenever you wish to do so.

Behaviors of Closeness: Enhancing Magnetism

Although no one person can be universally attractive, we have all known incredibly magnetic people who sometimes are not especially beautiful, smart, or sexy. Their magic often seems shrouded in mystery. Is there a common denominator among them? I believe there is. These people project a shared trait: accessibility. We feel that were we to reach out, we could touch them. Were we to talk to them, they'd welcome the contact. Although we cannot all be born with that special magnetism, we can practice some behaviors that develop accessibility and learn to avoid behaviors that create distance.

Magnetism-Enhancing Behaviors

- Accepting, accommodating
- Appreciating
- Complimenting
- Listening well
- Communicating openly
- Respecting others' points of view
- Being generous
- Being consistent

At the opposite pole of the magnet, there are people whom popularity evades.

Distancing Behaviors

- Rejecting
- Challenging
- Arguing
- Criticizing
- Talking too much or showing off
- Manipulating
- Being disrespectful of the wishes of others
- Being ungenerous
- Behaving unpredictably
- Being willful

For the next week, notice how many items on these two lists of behaviors are part of your standard way of being.

SEX AND THE SINGLE ACD

Perhaps it was easier to traverse the playing fields of courtship when lovemaking was a reward for having completed the other tasks of establishing a relationship. Did decisions about sex seem simpler when a woman regarded it as a treasure to share only with the man of her enduring choice? Perhaps, although such a rigid standard was by no means a perfect solution. Today we find it valuable to be sexually intimate with several partners before marriage. This brings with it many challenges, not the least of which is that romance—much desired by most Americans—is more difficult to maintain in an environment of sexual plenty.

Somehow the environment of self-control, of sacrificing the moment for enduring value, allows fantasies to take root and helps romance to blossom. Much of today's disappointment in romance is explained by this lack of self-control. "What romance?" I am asked. "It is hard to come by," I am told. It's clear that romance does not thrive in today's all-too-available sexual unions. Romance entails fantasy, fantasy thrives on mystery, and mystery is all too quickly exploded in the quick-to-couple atmosphere.

The too-early lovemaking causes barriers to crash and boundaries to disappear, and often creates confusing closeness. But closeness to whom? When naked skin embraces naked skin, will the aftermath of the pleasures of the body find a disappointing stranger in your life?

Doesn't it do everyone a disservice to try to shape this disappointing stranger into your Ms. or Mr. Right in order to retain what little the relationship has to offer?

There has been a reconsideration of old-fashioned values recently, partly because of the threat of AIDS. The return to a more level-headed approach to pairing may arise from a recognition that moderation works better, and the threat of AIDS may have merely given people a push in this direction.

Because society no longer metes out severe punishment for being sexually active outside of marriage, people must create those rules for themselves. For ACDs who are still working on setting appropriate limits for themselves, approaching sexual intimacy with caution is appropriate.

How far should sexual chemistry be trusted? Doesn't the physical attraction carry a promising message? Sexual chemistry should be trusted only as far as its message goes. Chemistry, our bodies' signal of attraction, should be heeded for what it is: physical attraction. Haven't we all been attracted to people who are not right for us?

In the playground of courtship, some people use their bodies as if they were big toys, and if the body objects, these objections may be drowned out by drugs, denial, or disbelief. The body's voice should be heeded. The body is the biggest sensor we have, and its messages are important. The body can sense things that our minds cannot. It can react to things that our eyes are blind to. It may try to tell us that someone is not appropriate for us or it can react to the messages from inside us: "You are not ready to touch or be touched."

Our bodies are our friends and our most important allies in life. If we systematically discount their opinions, we may weaken their powers and insult their integrity. It is important to clean up our relationship with our bodies and reestablish a supportive partnership with them.

HEALING JOURNAL EXERCISE: GIVING YOUR BODY A RIGHT TO SPEAK

If you have never done a dialogue with an object, this may seem a little artificial or silly; yet it is a very effective healing tool. Give your body a voice and it may impart good information and wisdom to you. In your healing journal, start a written dialogue with your body this way: "Hello, body." Allow time for your body to respond. Close your eyes, if you like, until you hear your body's voice. Give it enough time to recognize that it now has a voice. It might say to you, as it did to one of my patients, "It's about time you asked me for my opinion." Then you might continue as she did: "I am surprised that you are ready to communicate with me." Make up your own dialogue, and prepare a set of questions you would like to ask your body, such as: "How do you feel about sex? How about drugs?" You may want to ask your body about the different drugs you may have taken.

Be as specific as you want to be. Invite your body's opinions, but don't rush it. This exercise may release a lot of emotions. Take it slowly; you can continue the dialogue another day.

In subsequent exercises, ask your body how it feels about the care you have given it. If it feels bad, create forgiveness and thank your body for having supported you. In doing this exercise you will find that you and your body will become better allies, and you will function more fully as a team.

SELF-ESTEEM: THE PRICE ON YOUR HEAD

A discussion of traits that influence the creation of all relationships would not be complete without a few words about the importance of self-esteem. Self-esteem, more than any other personal quality, plays a crucial role in your selection of dates and mates. It plays a role in all other areas of your life also, but for now, let's consider self-esteem strictly in terms of selecting a love partner.

What is self-esteem? *Self-esteem is the price you put on yourself.* That price tag tells the world, "This is what I'm worth." This value shows up in the friends we choose, the work we do, the dignity—or lack of it—with which we conduct ourselves, and the respect we exact from others. The value is almost totally self-determined, though the origins are found in childhood.

Self-esteem defies exact measurement. Virginia Satir, one of the early practitioners of family therapy, in her book *Peoplemaking*, likened self-esteem to the stockpot her family kept on the stove, whose bubbling contents filled the pot much fuller some days than others.

Your Psychological Immune System

I like to think of self-esteem as our psychological immune system. If an invasion of your self occurs, your psychological immune system will marshal its defenses to surround the hurt. Think of all the defenses—

denial, repression, rationalization, and the like—as being like white cells. They help protect the hurt until you feel better.

When we are in distress, we may think that our pain will never end. But our psychological defense mechanisms, which you may think of as the mind's scab, are protecting the hurt. But because it is less visible and more difficult to interpret, we believe that the scab is our personality.

It may take our selves a long time to heal from childhood wounds. ACDs know this. We have the power to slow down healing, or we can clear the road for it to happen as quickly as our spirit allows. A friend of mine who knows much about healing—she is in the process of winning a second bout with cancer—likes to say, "If you have time to do things over, you have time to do them right."

To increase the speed of your healing, work on developing strong self-esteem. Strong self-esteem is like good medicine. How do you shore up sagging self-esteem? By taking the risks of being your best self. "What funny medicine," you may say to yourself. "Taking risks?" Yes. That's the best thing you can do for your self-esteem. One way you can prove this to yourself is to look back over your adult life and see when your self-esteem was in good shape. Around that time you probably accomplished something important to you that was the result of having taken a risk, of having reached a goal. Once your self-esteem is sound, it will not only help heal you from new invasions and help protect you by not allowing others to abuse you, but also make sure you are giving yourself the best possible care. It will also help prevent you from going too far off your true path.

Probably nothing in this chapter came as a big surprise to you. Some of the information about translating love into marriage, handling anxiety about becoming attached, and examining attitudes about courtship may have brought your ideas into clearer focus. And perhaps you now have a better idea of why you may have been stubbing your toes so often. As for the future, whether you end up marrying immediately, or whether you date and travel the road of serial relationships for a while, you will find that by using the tools you have gained, the experience will be more satisfying.

9

ACDs AND
MARRIAGE

There is hardly any activity, any enterprise, which is started with
such tremendous hopes and expectations, and yet which fails so
regularly, as love.

ERICH FROMM

In learning how to make love relationships work, it is useful to heed the lessons of failed marriages as well as successful ones. By identifying the mistakes, ACDs can take a more enlightened approach to their own love partnerships and, perhaps, overcome the pitfalls that can cause their marriages to end.

One such pitfall, which we will learn about in this chapter, is the *rebound effect*—the sudden reemergence of incomplete grief. We will discuss how it may threaten a marriage. The healing journal exercises will allow you to identify why you are attracted to the people whom you select as your love partners, and to explore the changes that take place in your relationships.

THE REASONS PEOPLE MARRY

Most people marry because they are in love and expect to live happily ever after. Although love brings people together, people also marry for many other reasons: they want children, their friends start settling down, they want the security of a double income.

Some ACDs whose marriages fell apart speak bitterly about their disenchantment and self-hatred for having married for all the wrong reasons, though they believe that their judgment had been impaired by love or by need. Not only do they feel disappointed in themselves and in their ex-spouses; ACDs often become disappointed in marriage itself, because it did not make up for their childhood unhappiness. Others, who viewed themselves more kindly, realized that, when they married, they were just not ready to undertake such a maturity-testing relationship.

The decision to marry was often influenced by some immediate need, such as a place to live or a safe sexual partner. Given such needs, doubts were easily swept away. Andrea told me about her husband: "Tim said that I talked him into getting married. I didn't know that he had grave doubts. He never told me. I thought he just had the typical cold feet people get before marriage. Later, he revealed just how casual he was about marriage. He told me he thought that if it didn't work out, he'd just split."

The reasons people gave for getting married often showed defiance and unhappiness. Following are some of the reasons ACDs enter unsuccessful first marriages:

- to break with the past by marrying someone totally different from the ACD's family
- to get away from a difficult home life involving conflicts with parents or stepparents
- to prove they are loved by someone
- to replace a lost parent or family
- to have a child to love

Some ACDs marry for convenience, and view marriage as a place to wait until real life begins, sort of a holding tank of life. Rose was such a person. Under her polished, near-perfect appearance lay a hidden anxiety that accompanied her rapid-fire words.

ROSE: THE FAILED FIRST MARRIAGE

Rose's story describes an awakening that took her from a duty-filled life to a life of freedom. While Rose was weighed down by her parents' needs, she was unable to make life satisfying for herself. That changed when her father died.

"When I think of my childhood, I sometimes go off by myself and cry for hours," Rose said. Her mother was raised to expect the best in life, but not to face problems. Rose's father was from a similar background, and was a successful "heartthrob, movie-star-gorgeous" Hollywood agent.

Other women found her father charming, and he responded to their attention with enthusiasm, an enthusiasm that filled Rose's mother with constant grief. It fell on Rose to become her mother's protector, and, in the meantime, Rose's needs got lost.

"I know that the only reason I became very ill at age five was to distract my mother from her enduring sadness," Rose said. She indulged her mother with exhausting empathy: "When she did not feel loved the way she felt she should have been, she would have crying jags that lasted for hours. When she cried, I would cry." Finally, after her father's indiscretions became obvious, Rose's parents parted, but Rose continued to function as the emotional anchor of her family. Throughout her young adulthood she cared for her father, who was suffering from a life-threatening illness. During this time, she also got married.

Rose describes her first husband, Steve, as a "take-charge man," and their marriage as "two years of walking through a bad dream." Her voice gets tough and detached when she talks about him. He was a good man and loved Rose, but for her it was a marriage rooted in boredom, monotony, and a mechanical existence. Why did she marry him? The explanation is not satisfying: "I couldn't get rid of him, so I finally caved in and married him."

This was in bold contrast to events leading to her second marriage. Rose is a stunning-looking woman, and men often approach her: "That was how I met my second husband, the man I truly love. He walked over to my table—he was there with his nine-year-old daughter—and said, 'This is really presumptuous of me, but I have been staring at you all evening and I had to meet you.' We soon fell in love, starting an exciting romance and a fifteen-year marriage."

One could argue that Rose chose to postpone her own needs as an act of personal altruism, but when you talk to her, you realize she didn't know she had choices. She was operating out of a half-aware state, what she calls a bad dream-state, from which she awakened only when her father's death freed her. Upon his death, Rose's family responsibilities ended. Her mother had passed away two years before.

A month after her father's death her life took a sudden turn. She went to see *A Man and a Woman,* "a beautifully crafted film about romance," and she was ready to hear its message. "I was stricken by what I suddenly realized I had missed all my life and I knew I had to find it. The urgency of what I felt made me leave Steve that night! I never loved him! I told him that! I became free to be me, and I had to do it quickly. I felt very guilty for not loving him, but I said to him, 'You deserve better, someone who loves you.'"

I asked her, "Is it possible that you did not have permission to love another man because you didn't love your father the way you think you should have loved him?"

Rose gasped, understanding me instantly. Her guilt about her feelings toward her father had kept her from loving anyone else. Such emotional tangles are difficult to sort out, but once that task is done, the truth brings instant recognition. "God, that's interesting," Rose blurted out. "Maybe my heart did belong to my father. Maybe I am my father's daughter."

Rose's story dramatically shows how hidden resentments toward a parent can create such tangled emotions of unacknowledged anger that they build a trap from which ACDs find it difficult to escape. The result may be the denial of one's right to love. This idea bears repeating: *When we don't love a parent the way we think we should, our conscience can stop us from loving freely.*

Fortunately, our parents do not have to die in order for us to become free. This book contains many suggestions for completing the parental separation and freeing oneself to love. Numerous examples show that neither emotional amputation—severing incomplete relationships—nor denial works. There is a vast difference between emotional amputation and proper separation. The attempt to bury the past prematurely may create enduring obstacles for ACDs.

Marriage is one of the most complex of human relationships. Having a successful marriage requires a certain maturity and a secure sense of self. When you know who you are, you can merge part of yourself into the *we*-ness of the marriage, confident that you are not compromising your *me*-ness.

Marriage is a partnership in all the highly emotionally charged areas of life, such as sex, money, and children—the three areas about which most disagreements take place. Having thrown these ingredients into the marriage vat, we then add other emotionally charged issues, such as

- relationships with one another's families and mutual friends
- dual careers
- the possibility of different personal goals

- expectations of each other and of the new family
- strange new ways of doing familiar things

Given all this, it is a credit to our human adaptability that enduring love partnerships ever succeed. But marriages do succeed, and many ACDs have happy ones. More than anyone else, ACDs deeply appreciate their wedded bliss, and realize not only that marriage is a great teacher, but that working at the marriage can yield generous dividends in happiness and personal growth.

However, the success or failure of most ACDs' marriages doesn't necessarily turn on individual differences of taste or the dictates of life goals. Marriages are sometimes injured by the reluctance to trust, or by the fear of loss. But most fail because the foundation is not solid; most ACDs simply enter marriage before they are ready.

It is difficult for any of us to know whether we will be able to give our marriages what they might demand. However, ACDs whose marriages fail often placed unrealistic emotional demands on their spouses. Some expected unconditional love, total acceptance, and complete generosity when they were not prepared to give the same. Brett and Megan were just such a couple.

Brett and Megan: A Marriage That Was Not a Cure

Brett and his wife, Megan, brought their ailing marriage to me because they were caught on the horns of a dilemma: they were unable to make their marriage work—they had been separated on and off during their marriage of barely two years—but they were unable to let go.

Falling in love had banished their frequent and recurring depressions temporarily, and they were lulled into believing that their relationship was the solution to their emotional problems. But when the infatuation wore off, depression returned, and they both became disappointed. They felt like failures, which added fuel to their problems. They were separated when they came to see me, and they were on the verge of trying to make their marriage work again.

As they sat in my office for the first time, I wondered whether I had seen Brett's stony face chiseled into a mountain range somewhere. An occasional smile softened his features, but mostly his gaze was fixed and his expression unmoving. Contrasted with Brett's stolid presence, Megan's tentative posture suggested that she could instantly yield to flight. Her expression said, "Don't prod me too much."

"I tried hard to live up to Brett's expectations, but he wanted more than I could give him. Brett wanted me to help him with his feelings and I was willing. But his anger is so big that it feels like he is going to blow the place apart," Megan said in a fluttery voice.

Brett acquiesced. He too described his temper as unpredictable and violent. He said he had little control when Megan angered him and that he would explode with unpredictable regularity: "I was willing to work on it but I needed help. I wanted Megan to defuse me. I wanted her to help me control my anger by laughing me out of it." Apparently, Megan was able to do this when they first met, but soon after they married she started to feel that Brett was punishing her; her ability to deal with his anger diminished, and she could not continue to be his emotional strapping.

Logically, Brett should have married someone who could provide him with unbounded maternal generosity. Instead, he married a shy and frightened young woman, who had been physically abused as a child. Megan soon realized that she needed to heal herself before she could give to anyone else. They decided, with a great deal of sadness, that they had married too soon and that the marriage had to end.

People typically select a partner who is at a similar level of personal evolution. Brett and Megan had a great deal of emotional development to undergo before they were ready for marriage. They had been in the dark not only about how to prepare for marriage, but also about good and sufficient reasons for divorce.

In some ACDs' marriages, the mismatched intentions are invisible: one partner does not care if things work out. To create a lasting marriage, both people must want it; one partner cannot accomplish that task alone, as we see from the case of Jason and Christine.

JASON AND CHRISTINE: THE STYROFOAM MARRIAGE

Christine married a man whom she misjudged completely. "How could I not see that Jason's commitment was as fleeting as the clouds above?" she asked me. She thought she had planned carefully. She and Jason were both products of Italian families, and even though both sets of parents were divorced, the families expected their children to return to basic values: you get married, and you stay married. Christine subscribed to that philosophy, and she thought Jason did, too.

Jason's work demanded that he travel about half the time, and he pursued affairs within the first three months of their life together.

His affairs were at first fleeting, on-the-road flings, but then he met an older woman, a client, whose knowledge and experience, both in the boardroom and in the bedroom, were very appealing. Soon they were an item, and he drifted further and further away from Christine. Eventually, he saw no reason to stay married.

What happened here? Why did this marriage break up before the last of the wedding gifts had arrived? Hadn't Jason loved Christine? He thought he did, but there was no enduring vitality to his feelings.

Jason felt that if he and Christine had lived together first, he might have seen that he wasn't ready for such a commitment. He had had fleeting doubts when they were selecting their wedding clothes, but he got caught up in the fun of the preparations and dismissed his doubts. Was he not bonded to Christine? No, he did not feel attached. Had he ever? Yes, a little. Although he tried, Jason could not explain why he began to feel detached from Christine and from their marriage. Letting go was as simple and uncomplicated as disposing of a Styrofoam cup.

The case of Jason and Christine teaches us that, for a marriage to get off the launching pad, both parties must share the same viewpoint on its importance. Both must agree that it is for now and forever. Otherwise, it is a temporary arrangement that has no more promise of permanence than does the relationship of two roommates.

Christine and Jason never argued, but some ACDs do. These arguments present a variety of difficulties, which become particularly intense when old wounds are opened, some of which have to do with trust.

Monica was a person whose marriage became permanently bruised by such an encounter. Her case illustrates that when a gold-star wife does not get her husband's praise and approval when she needs it to bolster her own self-esteem, old hurts emerge to pour forth their ancient poison.

MONICA: MARRIED UNTIL DISTRUST US DO PART

Trying to please was a familiar habit of Monica's from her childhood. At age seven, her mother, who had been divorced for a couple of years, left her at her father's house. "My dad's girlfriend, a tall, redheaded woman with long, strong fingers, grasped me, picked me up, and looked me over," Monica recalled. She apparently met with her approval because the girlfriend pulled the little girl's face to hers for a kiss:

"Her breath smelled of cigarettes, and it made me gag." Monica wanted to pull away, but she didn't dare for fear of angering her father.

When she describes the day she "went into exile," her emotions flood back. Monica recalls the little girl with a pain so big that it threatened to break her heart into little pieces. I waited while she cried heavy tears, hiccupping a quick "sorry" between sobs. She quieted slowly, then continued.

In the ensuing time, the new stepmother was decent to her, and Monica behaved like a model child in return—because, she reasoned, if she was really good and did nothing wrong, she could keep her stepmother from giving her away, too. She helped cook and clean, and spent her after-school hours being useful. Still, Monica was beset with fears of being sent away, and her mother did not show up to reclaim her. Monica feels that if her mother had come, she would have developed the ability to trust the power of love.

At age eighteen, Monica went to work for the local community center in the small city where she lived, and met a young man whom she married, in typical ACD fashion, after a month and a half. If they had been giving out superwife gold stars, Monica would have surely qualified. She worked two jobs, did the cooking and the cleaning, and still found time to make her husband's lunches. She would sneak away from her own job to take her husband's lunch to him and eat with him. She would do almost anything to please him.

She recalls that her husband accepted her extraordinary efforts and came to expect them without showing appreciation. Predictably, he also became spoiled and lazy. Still, Monica would have tolerated his selfishness had it not been for her loss of trust. Despite all of her efforts, she came to fear that he might leave her.

The terrible feelings she had from the time when her mother left were unleashed when, in the course of a particularly heated disagreement, her husband said to her, "We should never have gotten married!" That's all it took. Monica heard: "I don't love you, and I don't want you, either." His words shattered Monica: "I had to leave him and the marriage because my safe haven was no longer safe." It didn't matter that her husband took back his words and tried in every way he knew to apologize. The damage was done: "There was no way back for me. It made me realize how fragile my ability to trust had been, because I could not trust my husband ever again." That marriage lasted six months, three days, and two hours.

Monica went on a rampage. Although she did not vow to punish the world, she certainly acted as if she had. Young and pretty, she got busy dating. "You could call me promiscuous, I suppose. I was real bad," she admits contritely. How bad? She sat shaking her head, tossing a curious glance at me from under her lowered lashes probably to see whether I would judge her as severely as she was judging herself. "I did not care whether I broke someone's heart. I was one angry woman," she admits. Why? "Because I failed to please the man I loved and I felt like a complete failure. So I was not going to be nice anymore. It was my turn now to be pleased, and if they didn't please me, I took it out on all the men who liked me." This frenzy did not last forever, and the basically nice Monica returned. Being nasty did not suit her.

"Then I met Keith. I liked him in a different way and that scared me. He wasn't safe, because he could get next to my heart. He was a real man, and he did not play games. If Keith said, 'I will call you,' he did." ACDs who are short on trust search for this kind of reliability, and it is a real premium with them, although when it seems to be in the offing, they do not trust it.

Monica and Keith's relationship became a stormy clash of wills, with distrust pitted against determination. Monica would push him away and he would come back. She would lash out; he would lick his wounds and still come back. "I wanted to marry him, but I was real scared," she said. Keith got more of a challenge than he bargained for. Not only did he have to overcome her unwillingness to trust; he also had to overcome yet another family crisis—Monica's father's divorce from the stepmother. "It was real messy," Monica recalls. "My father and I had a real falling-out then because he came and asked me to spy on my stepmother for him. But she had been good to me, in her way, and I refused to do it."

Keith's good nature and determination get the credit for winning the battle of wills. With his steady presence, he proved to Monica that she could trust him. He promised that their marriage would become much more than a fleeting dalliance. Today, seven years later, they are still forging their promise day to day, but happily so, as the parents of four happy children.

THE REBOUND EFFECT

One of the most distressing phenomena of ACD marriages is what I call the *rebound effect*. It is a powerful earthquake of emotions that, when unleashed, tears through heretofore solid, often long-term, and seemingly happy marriages and blows them apart. This phenomenon appears suddenly, shaking what seemed to be solid ground, as if an ancient fault line in the family had suddenly been jolted and had broken open.

Measured by normal standards, those marriages that are affected are seasoned and apparently satisfying, without a history of major problems. The rebound effect is often triggered by a loss, and, once set into motion, causes ACDs to repeat their parents' patterns, often with stunning similarities. Sarah and Paul, whom we next meet, had a lengthy marriage that became the unfortunate victim of the rebound effect. Theirs was a marriage in which the patterns set many years before took over, triggering unexpected results.

SARAH AND PAUL: RELIVING THE PAST

Sarah came to see me while she was in the throes of her divorce. It had turned angry and contentious, and she could not understand why she felt so uncompromising, and why her husband, who had always been so sweet, was so tough to deal with. Why did their divorce become a bitter struggle after twelve years of marriage and a happy family life with two children? She was trying to gain more cooperation, but it seemed that it would probably take years to mend fences, and Sarah wasn't of a mind to make peace.

Sarah and Paul had been successful business partners during their marriage, and built a business with far-flung interests. They not only worked well together, but enjoyed their family together. If Sarah had a complaint, it was that she could wrap Paul around her little finger, that he gave her too much slack. But she enjoyed his gentleness and his romantic nature.

Sarah grew very close to her mother-in-law, Betty, who became more like a mother than Sarah's own mother. Betty helped with the children, caring for them when they were sick, and she showered Sarah with little thoughtful presents. Then, without warning, Sarah's world came apart at the seams. One morning she went to investigate why Betty hadn't answered her call and found her lying on the kitchen floor. Betty had been felled by a powerful stroke and was on the verge of death. Although she fought hard, she lost the battle for recovery. Her death was a mighty blow to Sarah. "Not since my father left, when I was eleven, did I feel so destitute," Sarah recalled.

Soon after this trauma, Sarah started to feel restless. The rebound effect was becoming unleashed and was starting to sweep Sarah's marriage away. It first appeared when Sarah was introduced at a family party to Roberto, twelve years her junior. Roberto was from Brazil and had come to the United States to attend medical school. Roberto found Sarah's red hair and fair skin irresistible, and she was intrigued by his youth, his intelligence, and his strength. He was different from Paul: Sarah could not have her way with this macho man, no matter how hard she tried.

Sarah was stunned by the fact that she took his flirtation seriously. She did not approve of the affair, and she could not really explain it to herself.

Had she been unhappy with her husband? No, not really. Were some of her major needs left unsatisfied? She shook her head no. Was sex bad with Paul? Again, no. Sarah was an action person, not given to self-contemplation.

The similarities between her actions and her mother's became apparent when, with my help, she started to delve into the past. When Sarah was eleven, her mother had deposed Sarah's father for a successor already waiting in the wings. Her dad had told her, as he was preparing to leave, "Sarah, your mother does not love me anymore. She loves someone else, so I am leaving." With that, he packed up and was gone. Within a few weeks, Stan moved in and the substitution was complete.

When I inquired about Sarah's feelings when her father left, she allowed that she had felt deprived and abandoned. She also spoke of feeling betrayed because he left her, because he wasn't strong enough to stay and fight. Like most girls who go through the divorce of their parents, Sarah had learned to repress and deny those feelings, although they were still there, sealed away in a hidden chamber of her heart.

Now, with the sudden turn her life was taking, she started to feel those emotions again, and as before, she wanted to have nothing to do with them. She became unhappy with Paul and became critical and angry with him. She no longer felt safe with this gentle man, and her sense was that she needed someone at her side who would protect her from losses. Roberto's youth and apparent strength promised that. She did not want to hurt her children, but it would be better for the children to know such a man, too, she reasoned. She left Paul and married Roberto.

The good life she and Paul shared, and their love for the children, should have created a buffer against outside temptations. But what they had was not strong enough to withstand the force of the rebound effect, which came from the reemergence of complicated feelings that had been held hostage for so long.

In its elaborate twists and turns, life ironically often presents us with the need to complete yesterday's tasks. Soon after she married Roberto, he contracted a life-threatening disease, which would have been incurable had it not been caught in time. The familiar panic that she had felt with Betty's loss was with her again, but this time, due to the understanding gained in therapy, she had a better handle on her feelings and knew what to do. She and Roberto were determined that he would have a full and complete recovery. Roberto fought his illness with relentless determination and, after a tough year of difficult treatments, became well again. Sarah, nearly overwhelmed by her feelings, briefly thought of running away, but instead vowed: "If fate takes him from me, I will learn to handle it."

The rebound effect in Sarah's life was bound up with her instinct for self-preservation. Her feelings told her to run, that she was not safe, but her head was saying, "You can't do that." Thoughts don't feel, and emotions are not smart; we are in a constant process of accommodating our thoughts and feelings and trying to find the right balance between them. Sarah found the right way for her by staying through the hard times. Some of us are dominated by our feelings, and we respond to them before we think things out. Others are dominated by logic and are reluctant to let our feelings have a voice in our decisions. We are always in the process of striking the best balance we know how.

HEALING JOURNAL EXERCISE: GETTING TO KNOW YOU

It is usually no accident that people choose one another. This exercise is based on the fact that people generally have good reasons for being attracted to one another, and that it is useful, from time to time, to remind yourself of those attractions.

This exercise is also based on the premise that you can see and sense more about one another at the outset than you give yourself credit for. The nucleus of the relationship—those parts that lead to growth and those parts that lead to problems (these are often identical)—is present in the first meeting. It is often supportive to a relationship to recall the feelings of those early moments.

Doing this exercise is enlightening—whether you are married or not, whether you are currently in a relationship or not. If you are not married, you can do this exercise by using a past relationship. This work may explain to you why the relationship did not work out. One of the benefits of this exercise for unmarried ACDs is that you may gain a heightened sense of awareness of first meetings. If you do have a current love partner or spouse, this is an easy and fun exercise to do together.

The first part uses guided imagery; then comes a written portion. Again, you may prepare an audiotape so that your own voice can guide you through the exercise. If you do prepare a recording, remember to speak slowly and leave pauses of several seconds between instructions. Pace yourself to allow plenty of time for imaging, because once your eyes are closed, time takes on a different meaning. If you do not prepare an audiotape, read through the instructions first, perhaps reviewing them a couple of times to fix them in your mind. Then start.

Now close your eyes, and take a few moments to relax. Still your mind. Then recall what you were like when you first met your love partner. (If you knew this person before, but you didn't really pay attention to him or to her, you may do this exercise twice. The first time will be at the time before your interest caught spark, and the second will be after that time.)

- Recall what you had been doing before you met.
- Explore what your life was like.
- What kept you busy?
- What were your goals?
- Did you have a direction?
- Were you happy or unhappy?
- How were you feeling about yourself?

Now recall the very first glimpse you had of your love partner. Roll back the time, as if you were in that scene right now. Describe it as if you were writing a play. Describe all the details you can—how your partner looked and acted, what was said, who made the first approach.

- What assumptions did you make about him or her?
- On what did you base those assumptions?
- What was his or her best attribute? Describe the main source of attraction in detail.
- What did his or her looks promise?
- What do you see?
- Whom does he or she remind you of?

Describe what you notice in the minutest detail. Take all the time you need—just keep noticing.

- What did you feel or sense about him or her?
- What did you feel or sense about yourself being in his or her presence?
- What were your very first thoughts about this person?

Your thoughts may have been positive or they may not have been particularly complimentary. Recall your thoughts. Also describe in detail your own emotions, body sensations, chemistry, and feelings.

- What emotions and feelings did he or she seem to have?
- How did your feelings start to grow toward this person?
- When did this happen?

(If you did the exercise in two scenes, examine the differences between them.

- What did you see and feel in the first scene?
- What did you see and feel in the second scene?
- What changed?

Sometimes we feel that in viewing the second scene a curtain was lifted from our eyes, or that we were looking through a special looking glass—as if seeing this person for the first time.)

- What did you determine about this person's character?
- Did you feel you could trust him or her? Why?
- Did his or her energy appeal to you?
- Did you respect his or her stability, fun nature, or looks?
- What was special about him or her?
- What warning signs of potential problems were present?
- What did you tell yourself about these potential problems?

When you are ready, open your eyes. In your healing journal, write down what you remember about the first time you met. Next, describe what it is about your love partner that you appreciate today and whether that quality was evident in your first impressions.

If you now have a love partner, when you have completed this exercise, share what you've discovered with him or her, if that feels safe and valuable.

HEALING JOURNAL EXERCISE: CHANGING AS YOU GO

Love relationships cannot stand still. Even if they seem to be standing still, they are probably moving forward or backward with the needs of the partners. A marriage that does not move and adjust becomes rigid and uncomfortable, and you feel as if you are wearing a suit of clothing that no longer fits: it may pinch and squeeze you every time you move. Healthy marriages mold themselves to the needs of the partners, just as a suit of clothing adjusts to fit the body.

In your healing journal, write recollections of the beginning of your love partnership, what it felt like at the start. If you are married, describe what it was like to play the role of husband or wife in the beginning. Consider these questions:

- Did you start to feel differently after you stepped into the husband or wife role?
- How did your feelings change?
- How did your attitudes change?

Create two lists in your journal. Head one BC (before commitment) and the other AC (after commitment). Then answer each of the following questions, stating what feelings or attitudes changed after you and your partner made a commitment to each other.

- Did who was in charge of money change? How?
- How did respective financial contributions change?
- How did the frequency or style of sexual contact change?
- How did time spent together change?
- Did physical or verbal expressions of affection change? How?
- In what way did your communication change?
- Did who made the rules and who decided what change? How?
- Did problem-solving styles change? How?

See whether the changes are leading your relationship toward more harmony. If they are not, you may want to redirect the flow of change. All relationships get stuck from time to time in one area or another. Having answered these questions, you can probably see whether you are stuck in the financial, sexual, or communication area, or in some other major arena. It is good to identify the area in which your relationship is lagging. Then, rather than having to work on your entire relationship, you can concentrate your efforts with precision.

The awareness you gain about your feelings and attitudes will also help forestall the power of the rebound effect if it starts to emerge.

SUCCESS AND FAILURE IN MARRIAGE

In surveys of couples, the types of problems faced by those whose relationships survive are similar to the types of problems found in relationships that end. Marriages fail not because of the problems, but because of the way people deal with those problems. Marriages fail partly because problem-solving skills are missing, and partly because the glue that holds people together is not as strong as it needs to be. *The one universal ingredient in relationships that survive is the intention to make them work.*

The intention to make a marriage last is tantamount to a periodic renewal of the marital commitment. The solidarity of the original commitment—the strength of the promises made—is the key ingredient in overcoming problems. When two people get together to form a bonded union, a great deal of courage and goodwill are needed to get past the potentially staggering initial adjustment problems, as well as to get through the various phases of marriage. Doing your best a day at a time, while looking at your life with a sense of humor, helps as well.

It may come as a surprise to people who have never had a serious relationship that living within the boundaries of a commitment yields freedom. It's freeing not to feel the need to decide whether you feel like being in this relationship. Instead, you just accept that you *are*. It's freeing not to have to decide if a new, tempting, trouble-free, love-'em-and-leave-'em sex partner could be more fun and should be sought. It's freeing not to have to decide whether someone else is more perfect for you. A firm commitment eliminates all those questions. The only question that remains is how best to make the relationship work in order to receive its greatest benefits—which, according to those who live happily together, far outweigh the sacrifices.

An enduring, fine love partnership is a glorious achievement. It is also hard work. But if you can grow and develop with the blessings of your partner, both you and the marriage will grow in stature.

10

MAKING MARRIAGE WORK

*I promise to give you the space to change and grow at your pace,
and if that's not at my pace I will still love you, accept you, and be
with you.*
MARITAL VOWS OF CHUCK AND LINDA

Keep in mind Norman Cousins's philosophy—"A problem is a solution in the making"—as you read this final chapter, which is specifically devoted to helping you strengthen your loving attachments. Who controls what in a marriage is important to ACDs, and we will look at three different styles of marital relating: dominant/submissive, competitive, and partnership. Keeping these styles in mind, and using exercises that further communication and enhance intimacy, we will discuss ways of moving a marriage toward a more emotionally satisfying partnership. We will conclude with some thoughts about the transformation of adult children of divorce into adult grown-up children of divorce.

MARRIAGE IN THE NINETIES

Fortunately, the modern notion of a satisfying marriage allows for a range of possibilities. We subscribe less to the shoulds of yesteryear. The reasons people get married have shifted in the last thirty or forty years. Once, security and caretaking were the primary focus of marital relationships; today they share top billing with companionship, love, sex, and togetherness. Marriage partners today play more equal roles in caregiving and in providing financially for the family, because vast numbers of women are actively pursuing careers while raising a family.

As demands on marriages have grown, so have demands on us to realize our full potential as individuals. We are supposed to work, love, and play with equal success. Since we are supposed to have it all, adulthood is seen as a process of working through a long wish list of possibilities.

Given all this, it becomes increasingly difficult to balance aspects of personal growth, aspects that foster changes in personal relationships, with the comfort and predictability of marriage. What do we need to learn to make marriages last? What are the secret ingredients?

Making Marriage Last

A marriage is an entity that is born out of intention, lives on attention, and dies from neglect. Its needs must be heeded just as much as the needs of the love partners. The following ingredients are often said to be essential to marital success:

- high level of mutual trust
- speaking out when you have something on your mind
- sensitivity to each other's needs
- encouragement of growth
- a giving attitude
- the ability to balance intimacy and autonomy
- an unfaltering intention to stay married
- the ability to forgive

These elements play important roles not only in strengthening a marriage, but also in fostering the sheer humanness that makes marriage the relationship of choice for so many people.

Good communication helps marriages survive. Soon after the knot is tied and love is fenced in by marriage, though, communication stoppers begin to emerge. An early communication stopper that unfailingly crops up in ACD marriages is *protectiveness*—a concern that "we have to protect this marriage—even from ourselves." When you feel that you can hurt the marriage with your words, your words become censored, your emotions are guarded, and the spontaneity that ignited love gives way to predictability as two lovers ease into their roles of husband and wife.

For ACDs, another communication stopper is *bad memories*.

When arguments conjure up childhood's divorce and negatively charged memories of arguments, the ACD's own need to talk may fall victim to memories of failure. It is important at the outset to identify those memories and separate them from your own marriage; otherwise you may fall into the trap of avoiding any conflict. Your fear of divorce may stop you from learning to resolve conflict, which, if handled with intelligence, can make your marriage better.

Love Skills

When we speak of love skills, we don't mean techniques of sex. Long before a couple make physical love, they exchange many symbolic acts of love. Studies show that couples who speak affectionately to one another and show their appreciation for one another in everyday activities have the most frequent physical contact, and have the most enduring and satisfying sex life. Love skills help you make love last.

The skills of love are just as important as the emotion of love itself, because without the skills of love, love can easily be misspent—the emotion tangled in misunderstandings. To enhance your love skills, it's helpful to take stock of your marriage from time to time, and ask whether your needs and those of your partner are being met. The longer you wait for your needs to be met, the more vulnerable the relationship becomes. On the other hand, a satisfying marriage that is responsive to the needs of the partners is a great place in which to live, enduring life's buffeting forces.

Maintaining Balance in Marital Love

In Table 10.1 three styles of maintaining balance in marital love are presented:

1. dominant/submissive
2. competitive/competitive
3. partner/partner

The first two styles arise out of the need to control or avoid being controlled. For instance, dominant spouses, usually those who suffered at the hands of a controlling parent or stepparent, fear that if they don't control they will be controlled. It is true that in a dominant/submissive-style family there are but those two positions. However, there are alternatives; people can share the reins of running the home.

TABLE 10.1. STYLES OF MARRIAGE

Dominant/Submissive	Partner/Partner
power over someone	empowering each other
dominating hierarchy	linking
codependency	interdependency
secrecy	openness
brainwashing/indoctrinating	discussing/educating
demanding conformity	allowing creativity
giving orders	asking cooperation
coercing	participating
hurting/sadomasochism	allowing mutual pleasure

Competition between spouses also revolves around the need to be right. For them there can be only one right position, and differing viewpoints must be stamped out. These concerns about power and being right eventually eat into the relationship, because both positions mean that only one voice can be the right voice: thus one must win something; the other loses something. Love eventually takes a backseat to the game of being right or dominating. When one person loses frequently enough, it makes him or her vulnerable to going outside the marriage in order to be a winner again.

When you are in the presence of the competitive couple, you will find messages delivered disparagingly, and people often are not allowed to express their personal preferences. In the dominant/submissive style the contest goes underground, surfacing in games, lies, and manipulations. When you spend an evening in the presence of a competitive couple, you may become fatigued from their competition. When you spend time with a couple with a dominant/submissive style, you feel the tension, but you don't know what the tension is about.

However, when you are in the presence of the partnership style of marriage, you immediately notice that everyone is more relaxed with who he or she is.

In table 10.1 I will contrast only two of the styles of marriage, be-

TABLE 10.2. ASPECTS OF MARRIAGE

Style of Couple	Quality of Love	Style of Relating	Home Atmosphere
Dominant/ Submissive	conditional/ conditional	controlling/ manipulative	fearful, anxious/ angry, anxious
Competitive/ Competitive	conditional	competitive; being one up, putting down, or losing	vigilant, angry, anxious
Partner/ Partner	unconditional	cooperative	relaxed, dynamic

cause the competitive style is easy to recognize; it is more difficult to see the comparisons between the dominant/submissive and partnership styles. In 10.2, however, in which different aspects of marriage are compared, all three are included.

See whether you can identify these styles among your friends. For the next few weeks, sharpen your sensors when you are with couples, and try to identify their different styles. Does Grady demand conformity from his family? Do Sherry and Barry cooperate voluntarily with each other? Do you sense hidden emotional coercion in Terry's home? To help you do this, Table 10.2 shows you a little more about what it feels like to be in the presence of these different styles of marriage.

Tables 10.1 and 10.2 contain merely a few of the many words that describe differences between the dominant way and the partnership way of relating.

Your marriage probably embodies all three styles; most marriages do. At the risk of stereotyping couples, I can suggest that women in most marriages, at least during the time they stay at home to have children and raise them through their years of greatest dependency, center more of their attention on the children and therefore are more dominant in decisions about them. The husband may be more dominant in financial decisions, and they may both participate fairly and equally in deciding where to vacation, what additions to buy for the home, and when and how to celebrate holidays. Each couple, of course, has its own profile arrived at through a series of adjustments; and the profiles change with changes in circumstances.

HEALING JOURNAL EXERCISE: DEFINING YOUR MARITAL STYLE

If your spouse is willing to delve into your marital styles with you, each of you should do the following exercise separately, and then compare notes. Share with your spouse the instructions about journaling in the Introduction.

This is an excellent exercise for taking the pulse of your marriage. Marriages tend to settle into a pattern by default. Most of the time people wait until something cannot be ignored before they analyze their relationship. However, it is a really good idea to do this when the relationship is peaceful. If the discussion stirs up problems, you can rest assured that, were you not dealing with them now, they would emerge in a more intense form eventually.

Write the following list in your healing journal. Next to each item, write *D/C* for areas in which you feel your relationship is dominant/competitive, and *P* where it is a partnership. If there are areas not listed—such as who decides what to watch on TV, which, although it sounds like a small item, may set the mood of the home—then add them to your list. While we are talking of moods, notice whether it is your mood or your husband's mood that more often sets the mood in your home.

- how much money each of you spends and what it is spent on
- how you deal with the children
- how you deal with your extended family
- how you deal with your partner's extended family
- your career plans
- dealings with friends
- future plans
- stepchildren

Then, next to those areas in which the styles work for you, write the word *comfortable*. Share the results with your spouse, and tell him or her about the positives in these areas. For example, if you both enjoy tennis or golf, or if your spouse treats your child from a previous marriage with great consideration, tell him or her about it. "But he or she already knows that!" you might be tempted to say. That may be true, but when something is wrong, we are likely to mention it many times. Why not recognize those things that are right? I'd rather be touched by the velvet glove of approval many times than with the sandpaper glove of complaint even once. And if I get the velvet touch three times, I may not mind the sandpaper once.

Later in this chapter there is a communication exercise. If the two of you find that there is a significant disparity in your respective assessments of your marriage, write these items on a list and plan to communicate about them honestly at a later time.

Linda and Chuck: A Successful Marriage

Linda and Chuck turned their fear of betrayal into trust. Two ACDs who belong to what Albert Schweitzer called "the fellowship of those who bear the mark of pain," Linda and Chuck both know that the aftereffects of their parents' divorces challenge them to make their marriage work. Dedicated to their recovery and to nourishing a lifelong relationship, they also demonstrate that you can consciously participate in each other's recovery and have a good time while doing so. Despite their trepidations, they practice honesty in communication with rigorous discipline.

> Chuck, thirty-three, and Linda, twenty-eight, two sweet, charming people, walked into my office holding hands like honeymooners. They had spoken their wedding vows (quoted at the beginning of this chapter) some four and a half years earlier.
>
> Two devastating catastrophes cut deep ravines through Linda's childhood. When Linda was seven, her father was caught molesting a neighbor girl and was asked to leave home. When she was thirteen, a random act of violence killed her adored twelve-year-old brother, Tim: "After my father and brother left, and my mother's boyfriends came and went, too, I grew up believing that changes take men from your life."
>
> Linda, streetwise early ("My mother always worked"), was fortunate that she was a good kid and lived in a college town, where her influences were the street talk of human rights and politics, not of drugs and sex.
>
> Chuck was nine when his father left: "I felt divorced, needy, and broken in two." Motivated by the loyalty of a nine-year-old for his father, a nine-year-old who felt he had too little to give, he carried nuggets of information about his mom's life to his father, expecting to be praised. Instead, he received his dad's rage. As his father pushed him away, Chuck's mom lavished "too much energy and too much attention" on her son. "She tried to get me to take over as the man of the house, but at the same time, she tried to control me completely," Chuck recalled, "down to what socks I

should wear." Chuck lived for the day that he could leave: "I held my breath from the time I was nine until I blew out of there at seventeen, to go to the farthest college I could."

Chuck arrived at college fearful of people. "Why not?" he asked. "Those closest to me were the most dangerous. My very spirit was endangered by them. I had to dissect and analyze every human gesture, looking for the hidden agenda. What did they want from me? Even a friendly pat on the back might have had a secret meaning." Chuck's first girlfriend tried to show him how twisted his view of people really was and gently guided him into therapy.

By the time Chuck met Linda, he had been through years of therapy. Still, he was wary about romance. Chuck's courage to trust Linda was born of the great love he felt for her. He describes the advent of his love as "very deep and very fast and very honest. Our communication was great; I felt that Linda heard me, and I heard Linda clearly, too."

For Linda, it took more; it took proof, a special moment of understanding: "We were walking across the bridge, holding hands to go home. The closer we got to my house, the more scared I felt. When I feel scared, I get spacey; you know, I go away. To my great amazement, Chuck understood. He said, 'Where are you going? It hurts me that you are not here; I wish you'd come back.' His honesty became contagious, and I blurted out, 'I guess I'm afraid. You have me naked and vulnerable, and I don't know whether I can trust you.' He said, 'You can trust me.' I said, 'You better be sure, because I am going to dive in, right now,'" and she playfully added, "'And you better be nice.' He repeated, 'You can trust me.' I did, and it was the best decision I ever made."

Still, there was much to adjust to: "After I fell in love with Chuck, at first I was in great distress; I could not protect my investment. Chuck owned my heart now, and I couldn't be physically at his side all the time. I still have to work hard to eliminate from my head catastrophic fantasies of dangerous people with knives stalking Chuck."

It is not unusual to have such posttraumatic fantasies after the loss of a family member. Typically they are flashbacks, but they can also be flash-forwards. By rehearsing the dreaded event of losing another member of her family, Linda was processing her pain of loss.

How did two people with enormous fears of loss and of intimacy, and with such distrust, succeed in creating such a well-functioning relationship? Linda and Chuck feel very lucky and marvel at their achievement: "We decided that our marriage is succeeding because we have a similar degree of pain, and we are willing to take care of each other in just the right way," said Chuck. The unspoken other factor was that each of them had worked hard in therapy on old wounds and that this work prepared them to move forward into the emotional challenges of marriage.

In addition, Linda and Chuck recognize other important aspects of their success: love and nurturing bathed in the safety of each other's good intentions. They are not only equally willing to help each other, but also equally understand about each other's recovery.

One of the indicators of a happy marriage is shared goals and interests. Recovery for Linda and Chuck is a top priority, a shared goal of abiding interest. Linda and Chuck talk and listen and make their emotions visible to one another. The ability to know one another deeply, and thereby to provide empathy when needed, makes Linda and Chuck's recovery anything but a grim task; instead, it is a celebration of life.

A mutually supportive environment in which recovery is an accepted way of life is a healing environment. Marriage can be the ultimate in that buddy system in which, ideally, people take turns sponsoring each other's growth. By such active participation, they can avoid fearing changes in one another. After all, those changes and successes are the result of a partnership effort; the success belongs to both spouses.

Because change means discontinuity, and discontinuity to ACDs means painful loss, it is particularly unsettling for them; ACDs generally want to create or control their changes. In their marital vows, Linda and Chuck gave to each other the greatest gift they could give: the right to change without attempting to control.

STAYING THE COURSE

It takes risk to create a relationship, and nourishment to keep it going. The risk of self-disclosure, the same risk that helps sire a relationship, also provides the nourishment couples need to stay on course. Trust thrives on shared understanding derived from mutual honesty. Emotional honesty feels risky once two hearts are officially joined. The inevitable temptation to protect one's vested interest takes over, and we find that protectiveness squeezes out honesty.

Once a couple is married, it feels more risky to be honest with one another. Yet with important exceptions, it's often more risky to side-step honesty than to engage in falsehoods. Omissions and lies poison the well of marital bliss.

When asked what caused their divorce, those couples that don't cite marital infidelity say it was a breakdown of communication. They had stopped talking about their true feelings, and they had stopped listening to their spouse's true feelings as well. Not to reveal emotional truths is risky because they will be communicated nevertheless in some way—if not in words, then in minor sabotages, sexual withholding, and inappropriate targeting of anger. These indirect communications are usually only partially decoded by the other spouse, and misunderstandings are compounded.

The Fear of Losing Love

One of the most common reasons spouses taper off in communication at the outset of a marriage is that each spouse is aware of the idealized notion the other has of him or her, and is afraid to tamper with the splendid picture the spouse fell in love with. Spouses are afraid to show the less attractive dimensions of their personality, which they may not have shown before.

In marriage it is inevitable that these idealized pictures will eventually fade, giving way to disenchantment and disappointment. This phase of disenchantment, unpleasant as it may seem, is a necessary part of the marital transition, which serves to transform the love affair into a productive marital partnership. Many marriages that I call *affairs with papers* end at this time.

In the early stages of marriage, spouses start deciding what they can and cannot talk about, based partly on what conversations are successful between them and what conversations cause problems. Good communication requires not only the willingness to talk, but also the willingness to listen and respond appropriately.

Without the willingness to communicate well, facing conflicts becomes frightening. When one of the spouses attempts to tell the other something that may be out of sync with his or her image, or is for some other reason unwelcome information, this disclosure may meet with resistance, and so the opportunity for that disclosure disappears. But like an iceberg, 90 percent of which hides underwater, the need for communication remains solid. Sharing information about ourselves that may or may not be attractive is not easy. Ideally if the spouses press through the discomfort, the force of the revelation, no matter how strong it seems at the moment, eventually dissipates and merges into the fiber of the marriage. It becomes an everyday part of it—like eating, sleeping, and talking.

HEALING JOURNAL EXERCISE: WILL YOU STILL LOVE ME?

The purpose of this exercise is to bring to consciousness any secrets and omissions that are building walls in your relationship. Once more, you will be compiling a list. The list consists of thoughts, events, emotional responses, and whatever else you do not share with your spouse because you are afraid he or she will lose some love for you.

If nothing comes to mind, ask yourself, What do I hold back because I am afraid of disapproval or other unwelcome consequences? If you look under these fears you will find the fear of loss of love.

Anything can appear on this list, from the insignificant to the most significant. You might want to begin by completing the following sentence: *Would my love partner still love me if he/she knew that* _____? Complete it for each of the following areas:

- money
- family
- sex
- emotions
- prior relationships
- secrets that you tell only to someone of your own sex

Then state the reason you don't level with your partner on these topics.

Here's an example of what I mean: you both have jobs. You are on an austerity program because things have been a little tough. Nevertheless, you need a new suit or an expensive new accessory to bolster your self-esteem for an important meeting. You go out and buy the suit or accessory, and do not tell your husband or wife. The funds come from a small bonus that you received and didn't tell your spouse about. By withholding this bit of information, you act as if you don't trust him or her to understand you, or you don't want to allow yourself to be seen as needy. Or perhaps you don't want to disturb your spouse's image of you. You are sure he or she thinks of you as superconfident.

As a second example, ask yourself whether the following statement applies to you: I don't tell my spouse that I need to have some time alone with my friends. Then state why you don't level with him or her.

You might be taking side trips to the homes of friends without telling your spouse. You could probably tell him or her, except for the guilt you feel. Or perhaps you are starting to feel controlled by your spouse, and instead of tackling that issue head-on, you are creating some space around you without his or her knowing it.

Consider this: if you were to tell your spouse that you needed some space, you would probably accomplish the same thing. Telling him or her about your hemmed-in feelings will, most likely, open up the space you need. You could handle this cooperatively and find a suitable solution that would serve both of you.

Opening yourself up means risk. It is a risk that grows with postponement, because feelings usually become more intense when they are stored; by the time they are addressed, they may cause a bigger upheaval than necessary.

Handling Conflict

ACDs are often left with an immense fear of confrontation and conflict. Handling conflict becomes not only a chore, but a dreaded event. Confrontations are dreaded because of the operating fear that conflict is tantamount to divorce.

Marital problems are often put on the back burner. If the marriage is pleasant, it's easier to escape into denial. "This is a small problem," you may say. "I can live with it." Or "The problem is temporary and it will blow over." Therein lies the source of most marital problems.

The fear of loss is universal among ACDs, its only variation being intensity. If handling conflicts becomes postponed until the marital problems blow up, anger and resentment may refuse to return to their hiding places, and there may be nothing left to lose. Only then do these emotions get the attention they deserve. Unfortunately, by then the healthy parts of the marriage are overshadowed by the torment of the dysfunctional parts, and couples feel the need to escape.

The surest way that an ACD will find himself or herself in the hallways of divorce court is by avoiding appropriate risks in marriage. I do not mean marriage-destructive or self-destructive risks. I refer to risking the honesty of self-disclosure. The following exercise will introduce good habits of communication to the marriage, or enhance your already effective communication. It is going to feel awkward to begin with, but stay with it, because once this system is adopted, communication will flow very naturally. In order to break the cycle of ineffective or bad communication, it is important that the steps be adhered to exactly. This way of communicating openly will re-create or maximize your intimacy.

Is your sex life getting dull? Opening up to more intimacy also has a side benefit. It may be the aphrodisiac you need to enrich your sexuality. It's no secret that sexuality is universally much more exciting before marriage. In marriage, people try to capture sexual excitement, but, like a lion in captivity, it may lose its will to live. The excitement of sexuality lives in uncertainty; it thrives on risk, the zone in which the love bond is created, but not on comfort, where the love bond is secured. "We always enjoy sex much more after we've had a fight," said Liz. "But do we have to have a fight to have good sex?" Couples do not need to fight in order to improve their sex lives.

The way to keep the zest in sexual love is to continue to risk being yourself. That risk will bring with it the touch of uncertainty that allows a couple to recapture the rough-and-tumble days before they melded together.

Most issues can be made safe by taking small bites; you do not have to come to a complete resolution each time. Your discussion may have to be continued. When it is left to be continued, it ought not to be brought back up again until you are in your *safe zone,* which I will describe presently.

The distance that sneaks up on married couples is generally not one that is caused by truth telling; it is the opposite. With each omission or falsehood, a small brick is placed between the spouses. As the withholdings grow, the wall gets taller and taller, and safe topics get more scarce and less personal. Without personal discussions, without talking about true feelings, intimacy suffers and the relationship becomes more and more guarded. The following exercise is designed to reverse the building of walls, enhance your communication skills, improve your marriage, and deepen your intimacy.

HEALING JOURNAL EXERCISE: COMMUNICATION FOR COUPLES

Communication fosters love and sexual desire, and deepens understanding and intimacy. In order to communicate well, the fear of loss of love or of closeness must be overcome. This is particularly true for ACDs. If you are married, your marriage is a valuable asset. Keeping your marriage wholesome and resilient ought to be a top priority in your life. It is much easier to keep a marriage clean and head off problems than it is to fix problems that occur from neglect.

In order to communicate freely, you need to set aside at least half an hour, but preferably one hour, each week. Find a neutral *safe zone:* a place that doesn't ring with yesterday's words, a place that doesn't have you and your partner's personalities imprinted on it. It needs to be a place in which you can talk free of interruption. One of the benefits of talking to one another in such a neutral place is that you can leave everything behind at the end of the appointed time.

In order to assure emotional safety, both spouses must agree that the information exchanged will not be judged, criticized, or used against each other in any way. No one else can criticize you as hurtfully as you can criticize yourself; in order to reveal certain intimate feelings, you need to be safe, even from your own self-reproach. The information revealed needs to be held with respect and tenderness.

The following communication exercise will assist you in improving your marriage. It is for both of you. You will need paper, a timer, and a bell. Prepare for the communication sessions by preparing two lists beforehand. One list will contain communication stoppers: why you are reluctant to discuss certain issues. Add to the list the risks you feel you might be taking in revealing certain thoughts. The second list will contain issues that need attention.

Rules for safe communication. In order to set the stage for safe communication, you need to adopt the agreements that are listed below. Read these rules out loud, and as you finish reading each, tell one another whether you are willing to follow it; if you have concerns about any of the rules, discuss them at the outset.

> You agree to respect the other's right to speak.
> You agree to listen to the other.
> You agree to be open and honest.
> You agree not to use the material revealed during
> the sessions to punish the other.

The following language is acceptable:

> *reporting:* telling what happened; objective statements. You can report about your thoughts and feelings as well as events.
>
> *questioning:* asking questions about what is being said

The following language is not acceptable:

accusing: telling the other what he or she did in an accusatory manner

blaming: telling the other why he or she is at fault for something that happened

judging: evaluating the other's actions as right or wrong

disputing emotions: telling the other that what he or she says he or she feels isn't real

Once you are in your safe zone, each of you reads one item from your list of communication stoppers to the other. The other should repeat *verbatim* what the reader said and acknowledge the communication stopper. Then the reader may ask for needed reassurance.

For example, Shirley and Van are sitting in their safe zone—a small park in their neighborhood—looking at one another.

Shirley: "I am reluctant to speak to you honestly and openly because you think I try to control you and then you get angry."

Van: "You said that [he repeats Shirley's statement]." Then he might say, "I am willing to discuss this without trying to control you or getting angry." Then Van takes one item from his list and reads it to Shirley and the process is repeated.

It may be that the first time you will discuss only communication stoppers. That's fine, because gaining understanding and agreement about that important part of your process is important.

Then each of you selects one item from the list you prepared of issues that need attention. For example, look at one of Van's issues: Shirley and Van want to buy a house. Shirley will have to go back to work, but she wants to stay home with their eighteen-month-old child. If she doesn't add to the family income, they will not be able to afford the house, and Van feels that it is critical they start building financial security.

Give yourselves two minutes to speak. Toss a coin to determine which of you goes first. Set a timer. At the end of the two minutes, the listening spouse will sum up what the speaking spouse has said. The speaking spouse will acknowledge whether or not the summary is accurate. Then the listening spouse will become the speaking spouse. Repeat the procedure. Then take five minutes for unstructured discussion. If it goes well, you need not return to the structured discussion, because apparently you are understanding one another. If the unstructured discussion does not go well, and you think you have reached a good stopping point, set this topic aside and approach it again another day.

If either of the spouses starts to accuse, blame, or judge, the other gets to ring the bell and state what was accusatory, judgmental, or blaming.

Before you abandon the subject, tell each other which parts of the points brought up are negotiable and which parts are not.

At the end of Shirley and Van's discussion, Shirley said her going back to work was negotiable. Although she was not willing to return to work before their child turned two years and three months, she *was* willing to work after that time because then she could use a reliable day-care service she knew about. And she was willing to explore doing part-time work at home.

Later, you might make a record in your healing journal of what happened during the discussion, paying particular attention to the process.

Intimacy: A Double-Edged Sword

Good communication enhances intimacy. Intimacy, however, is a double-edged sword. The deeper the intimacy, the greater the investment, and the more that would be lost if the relationship failed. The reluctance to deepen intimacy shows up in communication. For a man, intimacy with a woman is often threatening because it undermines the separation upon which his male identity has been founded. For a woman, intimacy may be threatening because in adapting to her love partner's needs—which women typically do more willingly than men—she has a greater investment in a man, and the potential loss of that relationship looms larger. For ACDs, as for anyone who has been traumatized by the loss of a significant love relationship, the investment in intimacy is a risk to be approached intelligently. A marriage is an opportunity for deepening intimacy slowly and in increments.

HEALING JOURNAL EXERCISE: INCREASING INTIMACY

The following exercise is a vehicle to help you assess your level of intimacy. It will help you examine your willingness to share your thoughts and feelings, and to explore whether you allow your spouse to share and be close to you. You may find it useful to measure your capacity for intimacy, even if it's only for your own information.

Make two columns in your healing journal, entitling one

Thoughts and Feelings I Share and the other *Thoughts and Feelings I Don't Share*. Organize these lists into topic areas such as work, recreation, children, money, family, friends, and so on. To help prompt your thinking about this, consider the following questions:

- What would you tell about yourself to a good friend that you would not tell your spouse?
- Do you tell your spouse when he or she pleases or hurts you?
- Can you share fantasies or fears of tomorrow with your spouse?
- How long can you sustain an emotionally intimate moment before you have to break the intimacy?
- Can you be physically and emotionally intimate at the same time?
- Do you shut down your emotional intimacy either soon before or soon after making love?
- Can you look at your own body or your partner's body frankly and talk about sexual intimacies?
- Can you ask your spouse for something that you need sexually?

Look over the answers you have given. Evaluate how you feel about them. Perhaps you learned something about your partner. If your level of intimacy suits you, you may grade yourself *suitable*. If it does not suit you, your evaluation might be *needs to improve*.

If there is room to improve, next to the items in the *Don't Share* column place an arrow pointing to the *Share* column. Ask your spouse to work with you and tell him or her your goals. Talk about a list of areas in which you wish to enhance intimacy. Go slowly; if you go too fast, one or both of you may need to retreat.

How to Ask for What You Need

When you prepare to ask for what you need, it is important to be effective. You need to obtain your husband's or wife's cooperation at each step of the way. Ask for cooperation in this way: "Would you be willing to talk to me about something that I need?" Then your spouse has an opportunity to say, "This is/is not a good time." If it's not a good time, set a time that's suitable for both of you. Then say, "I am going to ask for something that I want or need. Is that okay?" Then, if your spouse says yes, you can go ahead. State clearly what you wish from the other person. If you are asking for a new behavior, make your request very specific, so that the other person knows exactly what you want. Statements such as "I want you to make me feel more secure" will leave your partner in a quandary. "I would like for you to tell me when you think I did something well" will give clearer guidelines.

But if you ask for something, you need to be prepared to accept a no as well as a yes. Your spouse has the right to say yes or no, without your judgment. It is also permissible for you to explore with your spouse what that answer means and what stands in the way of his or her granting your request.

You don't have to start on the heaviest item in your pile of needs. It can be something as simple as "I often wish you would not remind me of the five pounds I need to lose." It could also be something about your sexual experiences together: "I would like you to wear a funny costume, be more playful, or want more romance/less fuss."

Then allow your spouse to take a turn. One item exchanged in this fashion will start a process. If it is successful, it will open the door to many more exchanges. The slower of the two of you will set the pace; allow that to be okay.

The trading-card game. You may each write down, on three index cards, three wishes that are within the power of the other to grant. Then try to match them for potential trade-offs. For example, "I would like to sleep in on Sunday and have you get up with the children" might be traded for "I would like you to wear something sexy to bed tonight."

Marriage is a process, and the fun is in the process. What creates a special moment of understanding, such as the one described by Chuck and Linda at the beginning of this chapter, is seeing through your veils into one another's hearts. When you share that kind of a moment, understanding automatically follows, and out of that understanding comes a desire to embrace one another, and one another's needs and goals. Such a moment can bring forth that precious sense of union that marriage is about.

ADULT GROWN-UP CHILDREN OF DIVORCE

Having completed this book thus far, you know that you are not alone either with your feelings or with your adult or your inner-child self. Not only are there many others who feel like you to provide you company, but there are many more who, having read this book, will understand what you have been through. Now that your adult child has a firm voice, the door of opportunity to a joyous adulthood is open.

All of us, regardless of whether we have grown up with divorce or with other problems, have had to work out painful lags in our uneven growth and mediate the different voices within our heads into a blend of consistency.

Adult grown-up children of divorce are special people. They are survivors, and, unlike survivors of a more obvious injury that cannot be ignored, we wish to deny their wounds. But you are an adult now. You can be your own best advocate and you can best acknowledge and respect yourself by knowing that you are getting better and better. You can feel this way having learned that neither the past nor your inner child's neediness has to dictate or sabotage your endeavors.

Adult grown-up children of divorce no longer need to hide from the past because they thought themselves to be "flawed merchandise," as Deborah, one ACD, characterized herself. They no longer have to dwell on it, either. The pain of past burdens can be replaced by the excitement of the discovery of today's bounty.

After completing this book, you may ask, "What if I still feel like a child? Have I failed? And where do I go from here?" Or you might ask, "Will I ever grow up?" or "Should I grow up?" and "If I did, how would that feel?"

Becoming an adult is not an all-at-once occurrence but a journey. "Beam me up to maturity, Scotty" does not work. Do you remember when, as a child, you thought you would feel grown-up at eighteen? And when you became eighteen you thought, "Well, maybe at twenty-one, twenty-five, or later, at thirty." Then, when you reached those magic numbers, you still did not feel like an adult. When would it finally happen?

Be reassured. Each of us has the child inside. The difference between the adult child of divorce and the adult grown-up child of divorce is that in the latter, the child and the grown-up live with mutual acceptance. Once you are the gift as well as the giver, you will feel an explosive delight and a spectacular illumination. It takes both positive and negative energy to make light. It takes an acceptance of your positives and negatives to light the way in your life.

The real question is "Where do I *grow* from here?" There is no adult paradise that, once entered, guarantees happiness forever. Nirvana is in the growth, it is in the joy of realizing *you* and all the different parts of you. Paradise is in the knowledge and in the acceptance of *all of you.*

Celebrate all the ages you have ever been—which still live within you. Like the rings within the trunk of a beautiful oak tree, your life memories are still there. Give due respect to the joyous sense of trust of your three-year-old, the trepidations in facing the world of your five-year-old, the sexual innocence of your eight-year old, and the opposition of your thirteen-year-old. But like a dignified oak that keeps growing as each new ring accumulates around its trunk, you at once expand and hold together the bygones. And you can stand tall and proud in all of who you are.

The test of growth and of victory over the past is in the increased ability to face and integrate life's problems and challenges. The test is in the ability to grow and to move along toward a better tomorrow. The test is in the ability to gain love in your life and to keep loving life.

The test of growth is also in the ability to switch freely between playful emotions and the sexuality of your child when you are playing, and the dignity and competence of the adult when you are working.

The test of adulthood is also in the ability to make appropriate life choices and to continue moving toward these choices as the affirmation of your special, unique vision of yourself.

EPILOGUE: ON BEING A PARENT

R egarding parenting, we are likely to do what comes naturally, and
what comes naturally is what we experienced when we were children ourselves. We have to make a conscious effort to avoid the undesirable behaviors of our beginnings. It is important to bring out of
the automatic, unconscious part of our minds the words and actions
with which we were raised that we felt were harmful to us. If they were
harmful to us, they will be harmful to our children. If we don't remain
alert, we will either repeat the mistakes, or go so far in the other direction that we overshoot our goal.

Toward this end, I have summarized important elements that you
probably wished your life contained as a child, and those elements you
most likely want to honor in bringing a new life into the world. As we
recite marriage vows when we marry, so we can adopt parents' vows as
we create another life. These are vows that parents-to-be may adopt for
themselves.

PARENTS' VOWS

We, the parents, realizing that a strong marriage is important to the
welfare of a child, will renew our marriage vows at the birth of our
child and attempt to keep our marriage strong.

We, the parents, promise that we will work toward greater understanding in our relationship, to keep our home as trouble free as
possible.

We, the parents, realize that changes and adjustments in roles and relationships happen with the birth of an infant, and we will work toward smooth adjustments.

We, the parents, vow to try to keep each and every relationship in the family clean, healthy, and honest.

We, the parents, realize that in order to be good parents, we need to be fulfilled human beings and, therefore, we need to have personal goals and move toward accomplishing them.

We, the parents, vow that if a conflict arises between satisfying personal goals and satisfying our parenting responsibilities, we will place our parenting responsibilities first until our child is grown.

We, the parents, realize that marital problems and conflicts arise even within the best-intentioned marriages, and we vow that we will promptly seek professional help if we ourselves cannot come to satisfactory solutions.

We, the parents, realizing that each of us has conscious or unconscious preconceived notions and expectations of how or who children should be, vow to attempt to see each of our children's individual personalities clearly so that each child is allowed to be his or her own unique self.

We, the parents, vow that we will not place the child in the middle of conflicts, nor will we disparage either parent to the child.

We, the parents, realize that even if our best efforts are employed, we may fail at keeping the marriage intact. Nevertheless we will assist the child in retaining a sense of family through contact with all family members.

We, the parents, vow that if a divorce takes place, we will not engage in a legal battle but will mediate and negotiate conflicts. We also vow to keep our own pain and disappointments from the child and to continue to foster the relationship of the child to each parent, because we realize that this is in the best interest of the child. We vow to keep all lines of communication open and further seek professional help if needed.

BIBLIOGRAPHY

Abbot, Franklin (editor). *New Men, New Minds, Breaking Male Tradition.* Freedom, CA: The Crossing Press, 1987.

Bank, Stephen P. and Michael D. Kahn. *The Sibling Bond: The First Major Account of the Powerful Emotional Connections Among Brothers and Sisters Throughout Life.* New York: Basic Books, 1982.

Bell, Alan P. and Martin S. Weinberg. *Homosexualities; A Study of Diversity Among Men and Women.* An Official Publication of the Institute for Sex Research, founded by Alfred C. Kinsey.

Bettelheim, Bruno. *A Good Enough Parent: A Book on Child-Rearing.* New York: Alfred A. Knopf, 1987.

Biffle, Christopher. *A Journey Through Your Childhood.* Los Angeles: Jeremy P. Tarcher, 1989.

Boszormenyi-Nagy, Ivan and Geraldine Spark. *Invisible Loyalties, Reciprocity in Intergenerational Family Therapy.* Hagerstown, MD: Medical Department of Harper & Row, 1984.

Bowlby, John. *Attachment and Loss.* (Volume II—Separation: Anxiety and Anger.) New York: Basic Books, 1983.

Cherlin, Andrew J. *Marriage, Divorce, Remarriage.* Cambridge, MA: Harvard University Press, 1981.

Duberman, Lucile. *The Reconstituted Family: A Study of Remarried Couples and Their Children.* Chicago: Nelson-Hall, 1975.

Eckler, James D. *Step-by-Stepparenting. A Guide to Successful Living with a Blended Family.* White Hall, VA: Betterway Publications, 1986.

Francke, Linda Bird. *Growing Up Divorced.* New York: Simon & Schuster, 1983.

Friedan, Betty. *Feminine Mystique.* New York: W. W. Norton, 1983.

Geffin, Mary and Carol Felsenthal. *A Cry for Help*. New York: Doubleday, 1983.

Halem, Lynne Carol. *Divorce Reform: Changing Legal and Social Perspectives*. London: The Free Press, 1980.

Munsinger, Harry. *Fundamentals of Child Development*. New York: Holt, Rinehart and Winston, 1975.

Pasley, Kay and Marilyn Ihinger-Tallman (editors). *Remarriage and Stepparenting–Current Research and Theory*. New York: Guilford Press, 1987.

Peck, M. Scott. *The Road Less Traveled*. New York: Simon & Schuster, 1978.

Progoff, Ira. *At a Journal Workshop*. Los Angeles: Jeremy P. Tarcher, 1992.

Rossi, Alice S., Jerome Kagan, and Tamara K. Kareven (editors). *The Family*. New York: W. W. Norton, 1978.

Schwebel, Robert. *Saying No Is Not Enough*. New York: Newmarket Press, 1989.

Sheehy, Gail. *Passages*. New York: Bantam Books, 1976.

Viorst, Judith. *Necessary Losses*. New York: Fawcett, 1986.

Wallerstein, Judith S. and Sandra Blakeslee. *Second Chances*. New York: Ticknor & Fields, 1989.

Woititz, Janet Geringer. *Adult Children of Alcoholics*. Deerfield Beach, FL: Health Communications, 1983.

RESEARCH STUDIES AND ARTICLES

Atkins, Richard N. "Finding One's Father: The Mother's Contribution to Early Father Representation." *Journal of the American Academy of Psychoanalysis*, Vol. 9 No. 4, 1981, 539–559.

Birtchnell, John. "Defining Dependence." *Journal of Medical Psychology*, 1988.

Children of Divorce. U.S. Department of Health and Human Resources, 1989.

Hughes, Della. "Running Away." *USA Today*, September 1989.

Kalter, Neil. "Conjoint Mother-Daughter Treatment: A Beginning Phase of Psychotherapy with Adolescent Daughters of Divorce." *American Journal of Orthopsychiatry* 54(3), July 1984.

Khantzian, E. J. and John E. Mack. "Self-Preservation and the Care of the Self–Ego Instincts Reconsidered." Harvard Medical School at Cambridge Hospital.

Linsky, Arlond S., Murray A. Straus, and John P. Colby, Jr. *Stressful Events, Stressful Conditions and Alcohol Problems in the United States: A Partial Test of Bales' Theory*.

Newman, Philip R. and Barbara M. Newman. "Differences Between Childhood and Adulthood: The Identity Watershed." *Adolescence*, Vol. 23 No. 91, Fall 1988, Libra Publishers.

Remarriage and Step-Parenting. Current Research and Theory, New York: Guilford Press, 1987.

Sexton, Thomas L., Ann G. Hingst, and Kathleen R. Regan. "The Effect of Divorce on the Relationship Between Parental Bond and Sexrole Identification of Adult Males." *Journal of Divorce*, Vol. 9, Fall 1985.

"Step by Step." *Newsweek*, Winter-Spring Vol. 114, 1990.

Tennant, Chris and Elsa Bernardi. *Childhood Loss in Alcoholics and Narcotic Addicts*. Academic Department of Psychiatry, Royal North Shore Hospital, St Leonards NSW 2065 and Chatswood Community Health Centre, NSW 2067 Australia.